Praise for Faith Popcorn

"When they blow the horns and ring in the bells to usher in the new millennium, those of us who have read *Clicking* will have the head start for the future."

—Jerry Della Femina, Chairman,
Jerry & Ketchum

"Clicking. It forces you to rethink your marketing future and reinvent your opportunities."

—Andrew Schindler, President and CEO,
RJ Reynolds Tobacco Company

"The ne plus ultra of trend detectors."

—*Philadelphia Inquirer*

"This clever book shows you how to spot the trends of tomorrow."

—*Mirabella*

"The chief trend blender."

—*New York Times*

"If you're going to succeed in business, you've got to have faith. Faith Popcorn, that is."

—*Innovator* magazine

"Faith Popcorn is America's most highly regarded trend forecaster."

—*Newsday*

"Popcorn has her fingers on America's pulse."

—*Seattle Post-Intelligencer*

"The Nostradamus of marketing."

—*Fortune*

"A supersponge of information."

—Wolfgang Schmitt, CEO,
Rubbermaid

"Because of her on-target predictions, [Popcorn] has become one of the most valuable women in corporate America."

—*Daily News* (New York)

"This is the woman who made 'cocoon' a verb, who foresaw the crash of New Coke, who predicted the rise of the four-wheel drive, the ascent of home delivery, the frenzy for fresh food, and the retreat from the corporate rat race to home-based businesses."

—*Washington Post*

"[Faith Popcorn] has a reputation as one of the United States's most successful and high-profile trend-spotters. . . . She says simply, 'I believe in people.'"

—*Toronto Star*

CLICKING

ALSO BY FAITH POPCORN

The Popcorn Report

CLICKING

17 TRENDS THAT DRIVE YOUR BUSINESS—AND YOUR LIFE

FAITH POPCORN
and
LYS MARIGOLD

HarperBusiness
A Division of HarperCollins*Publishers*

HarperCollins books may be purchased for educational, business, or sales promotional use. For information please write: Special Markets Department, HarperCollins Publishers, Inc., 10 East 53rd Street, New York, NY 10022.

FIRST EDITION

Library of Congress Cataloging-in-Publication Data

Popcorn, Faith.
    Clicking : 17 trends that drive your business—and your life /
  by Faith Popcorn and Lys Marigold.
        p.   cm.
    "Revised and updated."
    Includes bibliographical references and index.
    ISBN 0-88730-857-0
    1. Success in business.   2. Success.   I. Marigold, Lys.
  II. Title.
  HF5386.P754   1998
  650.1—dc21   97-40278

98 99 00 01 02 ❖/RRD 10 9 8 7 6 5 4 3 2 1

For my sister, Mechele Plotkin Flaum,
who has been the constant click of my life.
Always fair, always there, with love.

. . . FAITH

For the two generations so cherished
and central in my life—
my mother, Virginia Davis Ackerman,
and my warrior-baby daughter, Skye Qi

. . . LYS

CONTENTS

CONTENTS

ACKNOWLEDGMENTS

Dear Reader:

Before we go on to recognize the many who helped us with this book: a moment for my co-author, and best friend, Lys Marigold. Her uncanny genius lies in her ability to search out the "right" stories, reveal the emerging trends, follow the bread crumbs of new directions, express them eloquently and support them logically. Even after all these years it's always startling. Her gift is extraordinary; to weave, to wander, to invent, to shape, to create with humor and irony, and then paint a big, broad, and brilliant societal vision. A trillion thanks, Lys.

Love, Faith

Thanks to the BrainReserve family, who, as well as running a full time consultancy, helped support the creation of this book. It's a credit to our shared passion for brailling the culture and their brilliant ability to be an ensemble. They are the best people-to-have-around-you people every day.

Ash DeLorenzo, who made sure that our concepts were supported, relevant and current. His endless reading and commenting on this manuscript was done without complaint. Michele Rodriguez-Cruz, who kept us financially (and rationally) balanced. Carmen Colon-Medina who cheerily greeted us each morning, saying her mantra, "It's going to get done." David Hardcastle, our talented Creative Designer whose visual sense added something special. Our wonderful TrendView Director, Suki Diamond, who is going on to create our Clicking seminar. Janet Siroto, our Creative Director, whose thoughtful contributions are in many chapters. To Jenny Noonan, our upbeat, tenacious Project Director who kept us moving forward. Carrie Macpherson, who gave us the British sense of humor, the dry, the wry, to get this bloody thing done. And to Mechele Flaum, who took care of us: encouraging, creating, and again watching the store, while we watched the book. Extra, extra special thanks to Mary Kay Adams Moment, whose loving loyalty got us through. Her calm wisdom, her patience, her instincts, her insights, her ability to anticipate, helped make every page perfect.

To all the publishing pros whose support and advice helped achieve our dream: Jack McKeown, Seer and

Prince of Patience; Binky Urban, universal negotiator, friend; Gladys Carr, superlative playful editor; Joseph Montebello, creative curator; Lisa Berkowitz, public-relations spark; Cynthia Barrett, diligent overseer; Linda Dingler, diva of design; Alma Orenstein, book architect extraordinaire; Ruth Lee, perfect picture placer; Joel Avirom, cover sorcerer; Jason Snyder, the sorcerer's support source. And on the softcover update, special thanks to Joëlle Delbourgo and big thank yous to Caryn Murphy, Christina Braun, Donna Sammons Carpenter, Ellen Mary Carr, Maurice Coyle, Martha Lawler, Helen Rees, Sebastian Stuart, Saul Wisnia, and all the staff at Wordworks, Inc.

Gratitude to Ayse Manyas Kenmore, the brightest light: her intelligence, her humor, her good spirits, her constant comments were a source of strength.

And significantly, to Gerti Bierenbroodspot, whose support to Lys and this project never wavered. She gave the spark of her boundless energy, her creative genius, her unparalleled imagination.

A special and separate thanks to Dr. Ethel Person for her ongoing and beautiful belief in this book and in me; and for bringing her analytic powers to bear.

To my good friend Adam Hanft, for his "thereness," his ideas, logic, cultural comments, insight, and foresight.

Lastly, but importantly, to Kate Newlin, who spent many of her weeknights and weekends contributing her clear, keen mind, marketing prowess, astounding strategic thinking, and her heart. The center held.

We also want to thank all of the people whose insights, memories, and wisdom permeate this book. Whether they're directly quoted or not, their stories are here. They shared their time, their ideas, their childhood dreams: Their stories are emblematic of our society . . .

A lot of books are written from an internal voice, but a book like this can only be written by listening to the cultural voice, the real experiences of real people.

Patricia Allen, M.D.

Ted Athanassiades, Vice Chairman of the Board, MetLife

Margaret J. Barrett, President, Consumer Direct, GE Capital

Lynn Beasley, Senior Vice President, R.J. Reynolds Tobacco Company

Jeffrey Berg, Chairman & CEO, International Creative Management

Michael Braverman, Sothebys International Real Estate

Dennis Carey, Co-Managing Director, SpencerStuart

Tom Chappel, President, Tom's of Maine

Laurel Cutler, Vice Chairman, FCB/Leber Katz Partnership

Susan Davis, Executive Director, WEDO

Jerry Della Femina, Chairman, Jerry & Ketchum

ACKNOWLEDGMENTS

Robert F. DiRomualdo, President & CEO, Borders-Walden Group

Jeremy Dorosin

Kevin J. Doyle, President, Wassall USA, Inc.

Thomas M. Fallon, Vice President, Advertising & Publicity, The Carlisle Collection

Richard D. Fairbank, CEO, Capital One Financial Corporation

David Fink, Esq.

James A. Firestone, General Manager, Consumer Division, IBM

Peter Flatow, President, CoKnowledge

Sander A. Flaum, President/CEO, Robert A. Becker, Inc., EURO/RSCG

Frederick Frank, Senior Managing Director, Lehman Brothers

Marcia & Gene Garlanda

Vikki & Gary Gralla

H. John Greeniaus, President & CEO, Nabisco, Inc.

Amy Gross, Editor in Chief, *Mirabella*, Editorial Director, *Elle*

Flora Hanft

Mike Harper, Chairman, RJR/Nabisco, Inc.

J. Tomilson Hill, Senior Managing Director, The Blackstone Group

Isabelle Hupperts, Conseiller du Groupe Suez pour le Japon, Compagnie de Suez

ACKNOWLEDGMENTS

Robert E. Ingalls, Jr., Vice President, Consumer Marketing, Bell Atlantic

Carole Isenberg, Writer/Producer

Jerry Isenberg, Professor/Executive Director Electronic Reading, USC School of Cinema-Television

James W. Johnston, Chairman & CEO, R.J. Reynolds Tobacco Company

Robert H. Kenmore, President, Equivest Partners, Inc.

Rick Kundrat, Vice President & General Manager, Thomas J. Lipton Co.

Linda Lanz, Director of Research, Ameritech

Carl Levine, Carl Levine Consulting & Licensing

Gayle Martz, Sherpa's Pet Trading Company

Colleen May, Chairman, Intervine Incorporated

Marnie McBryde, Senior Director, SpencerStuart

James Morgan, President & CEO, Philip Morris U.S.A.

Fran Myers, Senior Director, Integrated Marketing, Nabisco Biscuit Company

Jerry Noonan, Senior Vice President of Marketing, Nabisco Biscuit Company

Jessye Norman

Richard C. Notebaert, Chairman & CEO, Ameritech

Paul F. Rickenbach, Jr., Mayor of East Hampton

Leonard Riggio, CEO, Barnes & Noble Inc.

Diane Sawyer

ACKNOWLEDGMENTS

Andrew J. Schindler, President & COO, R.J. Reynolds
Tobacco Company

Toni Schmitt

Wolf Schmitt, Chairman of the Board & CEO, Rubbermaid Incorporated

Jeffrey Schwager, Sales Manager, Mevisto

Marsha Scott, White House Deputy Assistant to the
President

John Sculley, CEO, Live Picture

Vivian Shapiro, Vice President, David Geller & Associates

Patti Walton Silver

Jacqueline Albert-Simon, Associate Editor, U.S.
Bureau Chief, "Politique Internationale;" Sr. Resident
Scholar, Inst. of French Studies, New York University

Pierre F. Simon

Bill Smail, General Manager, The Smail Family
Dealerships

Ray Smith, Chairman of the Board & CEO, Bell
Atlantic

Liz Smith

Gloria Steinem

Mary Tanner, Managing Director, Lehman Brothers

Susan Thomases, Partner, Willkie Farr & Gallagher

Tony Van Hook

Leslie Wexner, CEO, The Limited

INTRODUCTION

The idea and inspiration for *Clicking* grew out of the enormous outpouring of interest in my first book, *The Popcorn Report*. The last line was an open invitation; it read "Call me, fax me, write me, beam me up," and readers responded. Looking back, letters, faxes, phone calls, and E-mail came pouring in. I was delighted (and proud) that the 10 trends described in the book inspired many budding entrepreneurs who were agonizing over "should I or should I not take the plunge?"

One letter came from Donald Gammon of Andover, Massachusetts, who took his lead from my S.O.S. (Save Our Society) trend. "Here are the results of you as a catalyst," he wrote. "After a series of 'Aha!' reactions in me, I'm making all-natural, personal care products, called Nautilus Naturals, for the hotel industry. They're based on water hyacinths from Florida, and I'm donating some of the profits back to protect the environment."

One reader specifically was motivated by the chapter "Ask Not What Your Consumer Can Do for You, But What You Can Do for Your Consumer" in which I talked about how important it is to go beyond packaging, beyond style, beyond hype, to build a business. This imperative especially applies to those store owners whose traffic has slipped because many consumers are staying at home (the Cocooning trend) and mail-ordering by phone or computer. An appliance store mail-buddy wrote that he was trying specific "Cocoon Penetration Systems," such as cross-marketing with other local stores (delivering homemade bread with every toaster oven or a basket of laundry products with every washer); and personalizing his service by offering routine at-home tune-ups to get past the Cocoon's radar and earn customer loyalty.

A clever man named Jonathan Lewis recounted how he and his two partners had leveraged Fantasy Adventure (the "safe thrills" trend) into three successful restaurants, basing their concept on the premise of offering "an experience beyond dining." Jonathan created Cafe Tu Tu Tango, which serves tantalizing *tapas* and is decorated with Latin American props—a far cry from a traditional dining experience. With its crazy rhythms and witty fun, going to Tu Tu Tango is like dropping in on a private party you can count on every single night.

INTRODUCTION

O. Alex Mandossian, chief operating officer of Rodell Research, Inc., sent us samples of his whitening toothpaste and mouthwash called Supersmile. The products are very on-trend: Being Alive (the wellness trend) and 99 Lives (the busy-dictates-convenience trend). The products are made with Calprox, a noninvasive whitener, baking soda, and fluoride; they contain no alcohol or sugar and the mouthwash comes in a packet that actually opens up into a cup (perfect for travel). His gracious note said, "Thank you for teaching me simple ways to eliminate many frustrations and uncertainties in my business and personal life. I'm grateful for your work."

Brock Green took the time to describe in detail his trend-based concept, Designs for Education. "It's a marriage of capitalism and activism. We allow teenagers to design the clothes they wear and, at the same time, raise money to support the art programs in American schools." Sixty-five schools participated and entered 6,000 designs. The final selections were made into unusual, stylized T-shirts and sweats, and sold through major department stores like Dayton-Hudson and Macy's. One dollar for each item sold was contributed back to the art/design programs in those schools. Trends? Fantasy Adventure, S.O.S., and Egonomics (the personal statement trend).

Marsha Wagner from Minneapolis was inspired by a

specific idea in *The Popcorn Report* that described a new profession called dream architects. She now has a personal- and career-consulting company called Castle-Visions (Making Dreams Come True), which does everything to help its customers Click, from résumé writing to creatively helping them identify, clarify, and implement a change in their lives. A full and integrated life Click.

Chip Conley, owner of the Nob Hill Lambourne Hotel in San Francisco, used Being Alive and Small Indulgences to add a new dimension to his concept of comfort and service. Guests are now offered some unusual amenities: a health bar in every room, aromatherapy, yoga, and reflexology (foot massage).

Pamela Serure and Nancy Sorkow tapped into Being Alive when they started a small organic-juice company in Bridgehampton, New York, with a great name, Get Juiced. They quickly branched out from a delivery system of expensive fresh juices to a three-pronged operation: opening a chain of retail stores with juice/elixir bars; selling their blends of organic juices wholesale; and, the one with biggest potential, marketing a body-detox-cleansing program, a three-day $99 "Juice Fast" kit that anyone, anywhere can use (rumor has it that Donna Karan, Barbra Streisand, and Christy Brinkley are regular "Juice Fast" customers!).

As diverse as these individuals are, they are linked

by common threads: They are determined to jump over any personal obstacles and brush aside any fears. They are dedicated to seizing new opportunities and anticipating the future. One word seems to sum up what all these ambitious and intuitive men and women are seeking to do: They want to *click*.

CLICKING WITH THE FUTURE

Design your best tomorrow

lick. The very word, the very sound—think of fingers snapping—wakes people up, shakes people up. A light goes on, the puzzle pieces tumble into place, and suddenly you're newly aware and alert to the chance for a brave new future.

The dictionary defines "click" as "to fit together, to become suddenly clear or intelligible." The colloquial definition is "to succeed, make a hit," such as when former Boston Celtics player Robert Parish recalled the days he and teammate Larry Bird "played absolutely effortlessly and clicked on the court." At the computer, clicking makes you all-powerful: single clicks, double clicks, sending commands, moving icons. Click and you're on the Internet and linked to the world. Click and an image flares to life. Click again, and you can trash it—gone forever.

Some have described their personal clicking experience as a thunderbolt, a surge. There's a wonderful seismic word, *tsunami,* meaning a gigantic ocean wave caused by an earthquake or volcano. That's a terrific way of capturing the feeling of a real click—a powerful wave that's capable of changing your world, your life.

CLICK = C-L-I-C-K

C = Courage
L = Letting Go
I = Insight
C = Commitment
K = Know-how

Too many of us spend our lives feeling slightly off-kilter, slightly out of step and out of synch with our expectations. Something isn't clicking: a job, an idea, a product, a place, the sum total of what we're doing and where we're going. We fumble around trying to find the right combination to break into a new life. And, then, *click*—control, focus, clarity, success.

My coauthor, Lys Marigold, had taken the law boards, loved the detective aspect of legal research, but at the last moment, opted for a life in New York as a magazine writer (courage). Except for one year driving a little blue humpbacked Volvo around Europe, she pounded the typewriter keys as a copy chief for many of the major women's magazines. Reasonably happy, until one fateful day at *Ladies' Home Journal* when a workman came by to brick up the window in her office, explaining that a new high-rise building was being built flush against it. That wall suddenly seemed to symbolize her job—too closed in, too confined to writing about food, fashion, beauty, and decorating.

Letting go meant joining BrainReserve as its creative director, expanding into the world of business, learning a new marketing lingo, developing the trends. Twelve years later, after a move to Europe, but tethered to BrainReserve by the eternal search (insight) for new products, Lys came back as the writer of our first book, *The Popcorn Report* (she knew the case histories, the biography of BrainReserve better than anyone else).

Lys's heart click came when she went to live with the Bedouins in the ancient red-rock city of Petra in Jordan. She found and photographed the writing of its early inhabitants, the Nabateans, carved in the deep ravines. And on high cliffs, she discovered little carved indentations, in rows, and realized that these were gaming boards from 1 B.C. to A.D. 2. She deduced that the wealthy caravan tax collectors must have had lookout stations and that those sentries, when bored, played games. Next on her agenda, Lys is investigating the development of similar games for CD-ROMs (good for children worldwide—no language skills needed) or creating virtual reality adventure treks through the caves and temples of Petra's archaeological wonders. Her business experience (know-how) will continue to prove invaluable. And she might even write the libretto of an opera on Queen Zenobia of the Desert. A global click.

But how? For a handful of people, clicking comes easily, intuitively. Those are the fortunate among us, those who can honestly say, "From the time I was four, I knew I would be a painter," or "I love running this bakery. Always did, always will." This book isn't for that blessed group (although I hope they will learn something, too). Nor is it for the lucky few who have just won the lottery. (We all hope we will hit the jackpot, but, let's face it, the odds are 12,913,583 to 1, and even learning to click can't change those odds.) Clicking is for the 99.999 percent of us who require soul-searching and a real commitment, who need an extra push to give them the courage to recognize when insight and enlightenment smile upon them.

My goal, my hope, is to help you find your own best future. And—as the pages that follow will show you—that future is just a click away!

The BrainReserve TrendBank

Trends are the long-lived forces that are shaping our society and will shape our future. At BrainReserve, we scan today's culture for signs of that future. The seeds are everywhere: in restaurants, bars, and clubs; in the mall and on Main Street; in the music we listen to; in the games we play; on the Internet; in the books and magazines we read; in the television programs we watch. In the programs we don't watch and the products we don't buy.

At BrainReserve, we pay attention to what business is selling us and what government is telling us. At Brain-Reserve, we pay attention to e-v-e-r-y-t-h-i-n-g.

All this looking, listening, and studying goes into our BrainReserve *TrendBank*. Our TrendBank provides a bird's-eye view of the consumer landscape, bringing into focus a panoramic vision of today and tomorrow. The TrendBank serves as an early predictor of consumer moods and attitudes, of our psychological yearnings, of our fears and desires. Understanding these trends enables you to predict what new products and services will be most sought after (as well as which ones

5

Nitty-Gritty

At BrainReserve, the main thrust of our daily business isn't the fun of predictions. It's the nitty-gritty work of coming up with substantive, long-range strategic visions for our clients. Besides consulting our TrendBank, we regularly (and globally) interview about 4,000 consumers a year on 20 different product categories; read about 350 publications in several languages monthly; go to movies, the theater, and concerts; listen to the top-10 music hits; keep up with best-seller lists; and BrainJam (brainstorm) new ideas with our staff, our clients, and our TalentBank of thousands worldwide. We also go on TrendTreks around the planet, looking for new stores, new formats, new product ideas wherever we go.

Every time we meet someone with an interesting job or slant on life, we ask him or her to become, in an informal way, part of BrainReserve by joining our TalentBank. So far, more than 5,000 people have filled out brief questionnaires, or "bios," that are entered into our main computer so that we can readily tap into their unique perspectives.

These activities help us identify and decode trends and have become the basis for what Brain-Reserve is all about: getting our clients and our readers ready for the future.

will be rejected), and where any market gaps are located. The trends also shed invaluable light on the best careers and business opportunities of the future.

Here's a quick overview of the 17 trends in our TrendBank:

- Cocooning: Consumers are shielding themselves from the harsh, unpredictable realities of the outside world and retreating into safe, cozy "homelike" environments.
- Clanning: Consumers seek the comfort and reinforcement of those who share their values and beliefs—or even their interests.
- Fantasy Adventure: As an escape from stress and boredom, consumers crave excitement and stimulation in essentially risk-free adventures.
- Pleasure Revenge: Tired of being told what's good for them, rebellious consumers are indifferent to rules and regulations. They're cutting loose and publicly savoring forbidden fruits.

- Small Indulgences: Busy, stressed-out consumers, seeking quick-hit gratification, are rewarding themselves with affordable luxuries.
- Anchoring: Reaching back to their spiritual roots, consumers look for what was comforting, valuable, and spiritually grounded in the past, in order to be secure in the future.
- Egonomics: Feeling unconnected in the depersonalized Information Age, consumers are drawn to customized, individualized products and services.
- FemaleThink: The way women think and behave is impacting business, causing a marketing shift away from a hierarchical model toward a relational one.
- Mancipation: Rejecting their traditional roles, men are embracing newfound freedom to be whatever they want to be.
- 99 Lives: Consumers are forced to assume multiple roles to cope with the time pressures produced by ever busier lives.
- Cashing Out: Stressed and spent out, consumers are searching for fulfillment in a simpler way of living.
- Being Alive: Recognizing the importance of wellness, consumers embrace not only the concept of a longer life but a better overall quality of life.

- Down-Aging: Nostalgic for the carefree days of childhood, consumers seek symbols of youth to counterbalance the intensity of their adult lives.
- Vigilante Consumer: Frustrated, often angry consumers are manipulating the marketplace through pressure, protest, and politics. They cannot be taken for granted.
- Icon Toppling: Skeptical consumers are ready to bring down the long-accepted monuments of business, government, celebrity, and society.
- Save Our Society (S.O.S.): Concerned with the fate of the planet, consumers respond to marketers who exhibit a social conscience attuned to ethics, environment, and education.
- AtmosFear: Polluted air, contaminated water, and tainted food stir up a storm of consumer doubt and uncertainty. How safe is anything?

We Told You So

At BrainReserve, we have a large file that we've labeled "We Told You So." We're not blowing our own horn, but it's important to remember that what may sound futuristic in the chapters that follow is actually just around the corner.

For example, way back in 1981 we saw Cocooning

on the horizon. Although it was the era of sex, drugs, and rock and roll, we foresaw that the future consumer would be drawn inward. We recognized that Cocooning could mean everything from ordering food and products in instead of going out to a new emphasis on starting a family, to even starting a business at home. Many laughed. The few who listened immediately took action to prepare their businesses for future Cocooners. Some smart folks reconfigured their fancy restaurants into family-style cafés/pubs, and the even smarter ones began offering home delivery of dinners. Other insightful people moved into the home theater business, offering turnkey installations of larger-screen televisions and state-of-the-art surround sound. Some put out a shingle for home-office design; or got interested in upstart personal-computer companies and began investigating the possibilities of shopping on-line.

Egonomics was another area in which we saw further, faster. We said, "Imagine the possibilities of applying the Egonomics trend quite literally to fashion. You go to a mall, pick the components you want for a pair of jeans . . . the compu-tailor measures your body . . . and for the first time in your life, you have a pair of jeans that are made exactly how you want them, in design and in body-fit." Today, our "wild-eyed" prediction has become commonplace—Levi Strauss, the world's largest manufacturer of jeans, is selling computer-customized

Trend or Fad?

We're often asked about the difference between a trend and a fad.

A fad is a flash in the pan, a quick trick you can turn to make your money and run. Fads are about products. Pogs were a fad. The milk-bottle tops made for a fun game, but kids collected them, played with them, and tired of them all too quickly. Too many were produced for them to become collectibles. Stores that stocked up are still sitting on mountains of the colorful disks.

While fads are about products, trends are about what drives consumers to *buy* products. Trends are big and broad. Although they start as small seedlings (we call them drifts) scattered here and there, they have a way of gathering strength until they make up a whole forest. This may sound simplistic, but it's the best way to describe trends. When you're in the midst of these towering trend trees, and if you were there early, you can say smugly, "Of course, I saw them growing." Conversely, if you arrived late, you will probably say, as many critics do, "How obvious." Timing makes the difference between reading the trends for pleasure—or for profit.

If you study trends and drifts (as we at Brain-Reserve do), you get good at spotting early indicators, subtle signals of change. All that is required is to click with them. True, it's possible for a crisis such as an energy shortage, a natural disaster, or a war to make slight alterations or shifts in the trends. But even those unforeseen occurrences don't make sweeping changes in a trend. Trends are rock-steady. They last an average of 10 years or more (certainly long enough to base a business plan on them). You can rely on the integrity of the trends to read the climate now and project into the decade beyond.

One question reporters often ask is, "Can you personally start a trend?" The answer: "You can't create a trend; you can only observe it. And you can't change a trend. You can only change people's minds about believing in it."

"Personal Pair" jeans for women. Next? Customized blazers, bras, and shoes.

We also made another high-tech prediction: "The biggest technological achievement of the 99-Lives era will be a way to *edit down* all the information that assaults us daily. Maybe a computer that scans selected publications and edits out information we want or need to know, based on intimate knowledge of our lives, our tastes, our inclinations." But who knew it would happen so fast? The latest development on the Internet is called push technology. Companies like the innovative Point-Cast scan hundreds of news items searching for the stories and subjects you've requested. The news stories are then automatically "delivered" to your computer—either as a series of messages on your screen saver or directly onto your hard drive. That's why it's called push—it comes to you, you don't have to go to it.

One suggestion we made as part of the Small Indulgences trend is now coming true. We wrote, "And thinking trend-smart can inspire Big Indulgence–makers to rethink, scale down, make their luxury accessible to a whole new 'deserver.' How about, for example, the new Maserati mountain bike?" When we were recently in Copenhagen on a business trip, we saw an unbelievable leather-covered Hermès bicycle. And a sharp reader from Down Under, M. J. (Mike) Martin of Perth, Western Australia, sent this fax: "When I read my *Sunday Times* of London (a thoughtful yearly subscription from my mother-in-law), lo and behold, there was a mountain bike—not a Maserati, but a genuine James Bond Aston Martin Mountain Bike." Are you listening, L.L. Bean and Orvis?

It was in 1992 when we first identified the entrepreneurial trend of Cashing Out and what it would mean to the traditional business universe. "Even if a new company can't handle a four-day schedule or flex time, the new trend will be to let the staff relax on Fridays. Wear jeans and tees, bring in the kids. Giving the office a mom-and-pop feeling helps to break down hierarchies and makes everyone feel that someone cares." If you followed the trends and had a retail clothing store or were a manufacturer, this would have been advance warning to lighten up on the navy-suit-and-tie look.

In January 1995, the *New York Times* published a story on specialty retailer Eddie Bauer's move into a new line of indoor casual clothing. "The chain hopes to cash in on what it sees as a consumer trend toward the wearing of more casual clothing on the job." Before anyone fully saw what was coming we dubbed this upscale outdoorsy look "Log Cabin Chic." Now a decade later, Banana Republic calls its Friday-to-the-office line "Cabinwear."

We also wrote: "Imagine the possibilities for a Virtual Reality Supermarket—a super-high-tech, shop-at-home-for-home-delivery system. . . . This means putting capital spending into warehousing and delivery systems . . . to build a strong, believable foundation for the Virtual Reality supermarket . . . in the future."

It seems like Dick Notebaert, chairman and chief executive officer of Ameritech, agreed. Recently, his regional Bell company went shopping for an on-line gro-

FoodClicks

Who will be the first to create a bag of chips or crackers with healthy additions, targeted to specific age groups and their needs, from toddlers to elders? This would be the first step in answering one of our eternal marketing questions: Why, if a great many people like salty tastes as well as sweet, do so many things come in dessert flavors? Why are all frozen pops sweet? Instead of marshmallow fudge or cherry coconut, why not icy gazpacho on a stick? Why are most yogurts fruit-based with sweet globs of jam? Why not copy the Mediterranean taste of cool cucumber/mint or crunchy vegetable yogurts for lunch or a snack? And those diet shakes that are a substitute for meals—why should dieters have to drink a sweet chocolate, vanilla, or strawberry dinner? Why not tomato-basil, herbed chicken, or wild mushroom, all closer to regular soup flavors? We're still waiting for some trend-savvy company to click on these ideas.

Anyone?

cery service that delivers food, liquor, medicines, and just about anything you need to more than 10,000 homes. Ameritech now has a significant investment position in Peapod, a groundbreaking service where, as we predicted, shoppers can stroll up and down virtual aisles, via their PCs, seeking out the best buys or foods designed for a special diet (low-fat, low-salt) or hard-to-find specialty products. If you live in the test regions of Chicago, San Francisco, or Boston, you can have your order delivered to your kitchen door in around three hours.

Clicking with the Trends

When you understand the trends that are driving the consumer world, it's possible to gauge whether something will click—or merely clunk. Using the trends as a screen (and as a screen *test*) can eliminate false starts, misguided attempts, or outright failures in whatever venture you have in mind. If you study each of the trends carefully, you will be able to zero in on the rich texture and relevant details that make up the larger picture of business and society. This will enable you to not just benchmark your idea against the trends but to plan for a refinement or expansion of your plans.

To test if you're on-trend—that is, if a business idea is right for the future—our rule of thumb is that the concept needs four or more trends supporting it to click. Otherwise, you might be reaching a too-small segment of the marketplace or your idea may be a fad. For example, let's test the concept of growing *herbs* as a business against the trends.

To start with, we are talking parsley, not peanuts. *Gardening* has gone far beyond retirees and the flowered-hat clubs to become a baby boomers' obsession, big time. The National Gardening Association estimates that more than 75 million people are involved in mulching and mucking the soil, many in the highly marketable, college-educated, 30-to-49 age group. Literally hundreds of new businesses have been started around the concept of home gardening—selling greenhouses, tools, clothing, composters, birdhouses, grape arbors, follies, and so on.

But let's focus on the business of raising herbs. Fresh, green herbs are now sold year-round in most supermarkets. Some catalogs, such as *Gardeners Eden,* offer edible wreaths and kitchen bouquets of herbs to dry on your door, display on your walls, or hang from the beams of your house. There's also the other route of dried culinary herbs, whole or crumbled. But herbs are even more than culinary accompaniments; they form the basis of the growing field of alternative, holistic medicine.

The trends that support a business venture in herbs are Cocooning (people cooking at home, weekend chefs); Fantasy Adventure (herbs an exotic, culinary diversion); Cashing Out (they embody a retreat from urban sophistication to the simple pleasures of country life and its profound realness); Being Alive (herbs are healthy); Egonomics (herbs allow you to prepare foods to your taste); FemaleThink (women have always used them for cooking, perfuming, and curing ills); Small Indulgences (they add something nice for only pennies); and, finally, S.O.S.(herbs are environmentally correct).

With just that amount of trend analysis, it's clear that a herb business could click. You could sell flats of herbs in season and fresh bunches to restaurants, general stores, and convenience stores; or sell them by mail directly to individual customers; or freeze-dry them for yearlong sales; or design and make herbal papers, books, and assorted paraphernalia. We have seen beautiful chintz-covered pillows called Sweet Dreams by Harvey & Strait, which contain "a sleep-inducing mixture of herbs and spices to ward off insomnia and cheer the soul."

To push the herb idea even further, set up a brainstorming session to come up with new uses for traditional herbs or whole new directions to explore for a unique business.

What we're trying to do is force you to think differently, find new patterns, question the obvious. Clicking is about breaking clichés, ripping apart what we call refrigerator-door philosophy (those comforting "words to live by" that don't necessarily hold true anymore). If you click with the trends, you will click with the future.

CLICK
OF FAITH

As founder and head of BrainReserve, I get to work on diverse and challenging projects for clients, all based on a mixture of ideas, societal trends, and a vision of the future. Then I have the fun of airing my views and predictions on television and in the press and of giving my seminar, TrendView, to thousands of people all over the world. I have finally moved from my studio apartment to a town house where I live and work. On weekends, I retreat to a tiny rose-covered cottage on a serene swan pond in East Hampton, New York.

But it hasn't been a uniformly smooth trip.

I'm often asked about my history and the history of BrainReserve. Actually, it's the same question.

The first full-color memory I have of my childhood is seeing my maternal grandparents, Rose and Isaac (whom I adored), standing on a Manhattan pier and waving farewell to my mother and me. We were headed for Shanghai, China, on the *Queen Mary* to join my father, who had been stationed there as a captain in the Army and was now lawyering for the Criminal Investigation Division (forerunner of the Central Intelligence Agency). My mother, also a working lawyer, wasn't thrilled that she was being uprooted. And me? I wasn't overjoyed either.

China wasn't heaven for a Jewish American girl. (Even today, it's not a culture that reveres women: Witness the 400,000 Chinese baby girls abandoned at orphanages each year.) The only safe school (less chance of kidnapping) was at the Convent of the Sacred Heart, where I was, to put it mildly, "nun" too familiar with the daily litany and where I quickly became a displaced person.

This feeling of displacement didn't disappear, even when we returned to New York several years later. My travels made me different from my classmates at P.S. 63, and the strict but excellent education I had received in Shanghai left me bored with schooling in the United

States. I had also developed a habit at Sacred Heart of crossing myself and genuflecting in front of every church I passed. This so horrified my Orthodox Jewish grandparents that my grandmother immediately enrolled me in a five-day-a-week Hebrew school. Now, instead of being with the other neighborhood kids, I was ordered to go to "horrible Hebrew." I went, but, in rebellion, I refused to learn.

The only time I was really happy as a child was when I was sitting around with my grandparents and talking shop. "Shop" was the small haberdashery they owned at Fifth Street and Second Avenue. They lived in the apartment above, and I spent endless hours there, discussing whether the windows were set up to maximize the attention of passersby (my first "positioning" lesson), how to improve sales, how to make sure customers were satisfied, and how to earn their loyalty for life. Shoptalk isn't usually what turns on your average 12-year-old, but it thrilled me. (My first click.) It's not surprising that I, like my grandparents, have chosen to live "above the shop," debating the very same kinds of questions, combining home and work and life.

By the time I reached my early teens, I had turned into a beatnik, the 1960s version of today's nonconformist computer nerd. I was suddenly cool, hanging around the fountain in Greenwich Village's Washington Square Park, playing bongo drums. I had perfected a serious and dramatic look, dressing from head to toe in black, lining my eyes with kohl (an eyeliner from exotic Arabia), and pulling my hair back into a long, tight braid. Lest anyone question my existential credentials, I didn't let a soul catch me smiling for five years.

It was the perfect attitude for my next incarnation: actor. At age 13, I decided to apply to the High School of Performing Arts, well known for its drama department. I didn't make it into the coveted drama courses, but I was admitted into the newly formed playwriting department. There, I learned voice and diction (getting rid of any New York accent). Later, those skills paid off when I started giving my trend seminars.

When it came time to leaf through college catalogs, I dreamed about heading far from home to a place with ivy-covered towers and small-town movie theaters. Unfortunately, my middling-to-minus C average landed me at New York University (NYU)—my parents' alma mater and exactly four blocks from home. Both my mother and my father had gone to law school at NYU, and they hoped I would follow in their footsteps. But whatever vague plans I had about studying law were about to be changed by tragedy.

When I was 19, my father was killed in an automobile accident on New York's Taconic Parkway. I lost my mentor and best friend. Gone forever were our endless discussions and debates. He had been a criminal lawyer, well known for his pro bono work, and we often spent hours discussing how to engineer the perfect crime. Without his influence, I lost interest in academics.

Instead of staying on in school for some advanced degree, I took a detour. My steady boyfriend was Alan Kupchick (I encouraged another last name for him: Kelwyn), who had just started out as an art director at Grey Advertising (he is now president of the Los Angeles office). In my quest to be his perfect mate, I decided to learn about his profession and signed up for a School of Visual Arts course in advertising concepts. My teacher was one of the best copywriters around, Frankie Cadwell. Almost immediately afterward, she guided me to my first job: copy chief of a New York agency, Salit & Garlanda.

This small step became a leap for me. My boss, Gene (Gino Constantino) Garlanda, had a profound influence on my life. He showed me how to write advertising copy—strong, sharp, riveting prose—and recognize good design. In a serendipitous moment, Gene gave me the nickname Popcorn. He decided it was more playful than Plotkin and a lot easier on his Italian tongue.

Click! Suddenly, I had a name that fit me: Fun. Funny. Funky. Alive. Weird. Liberating. Unforgettable. What more could I have asked for? Although a few naysayers tried to convince me that it was too kooky, I didn't listen.

My position at Salit & Garlanda was the first of four advertising jobs. I was fired from the next one (for writing poetry instead of copy) and the one after that (for wearing a rabbit-fur micro-miniskirt to a maxi-client meeting). My fourth, at Smith/Greenland, was an unqualified success. In retrospect, it seems perfectly logical that promotions came swiftly and that I was given the title of creative director at the age of 26. I loved my bosses, and my clients loved me. I won creative-directing awards, and I had lots of support from my creative partner, Stuart Pittman. I thought I had clicked at last.

But one day, after an executive roller-coaster ride (would I be promoted to president?), I burned out on agency life. It was too compartmentalized, too departmentalized. I craved my own shop. It was 1974, and Stuart and I opened BrainReserve, even though we didn't have a clue what a "BrainReserve" was or could be or would be. What we knew was that clients needed trend-supported, long-term strategies rather than a series of quick-fix commercials. We also knew it was far better to solve tough problems by brainstorming with the smartest creative people (thus the name, BrainReserve) than to go it alone. So we set out to sell our brainpower.

Looking back now, I see that we were a case study in how *not* to start a business. Although we were smart,

enthusiastic, and willing to make sacrifices, we didn't
have a business plan . . . and we didn't have any business.
We could not get a marketing assignment because we
had no track record in marketing. And we couldn't
afford to staff up until we were at least a little established.

Determined to succeed, our three-person company
(Stuart and I were joined by Ginny Danner, who kept us
organized) decided to think big and act bigger. Sometimes you simply have to project yourself into your own
future. When one senior vice president of marketing
from a large company asked to check out our staff and
tour our offices before he assigned us a project, we
immediately created the world's first virtual office. Our
real offices were located in a ground-floor professional
suite, but we often rented the impressive wood-paneled
library in the Lotos Club next door when we needed a
conference room.

This time, we rented the whole top floor of rooms;
we brought in desks, typewriters, drawing tables, telephones connected to nowhere (we crossed our fingers
that the client wouldn't ask to make a call); and we pep-
pered the place with freelancers and friends. Even
though we didn't get that assignment, it proved a useful
exercise.

If the vision is there, the means will follow. That was the
valuable lesson I learned from that makeshift episode.
And I began to understand that if BrainReserve was

going to click, I was going to have to market myself. I needed a vision of the future, and I needed to base my business on it.

What happened next could fall under the category of a lucky break, but it actually came from the tenacity I inherited from my mother. About six years after we set up shop, BrainReserve was getting some recognition, and people had begun to spread the good word. Then Isadore Barmash, the summer replacement for advertising columnist Phil Dougherty of the *New York Times*, called to say that he was intrigued by the names Popcorn and BrainReserve and wanted to set up an interview. Pandemonium and panic set in. What should we do? What should we say?

I rang up my friends and family, casting about for the way to make the most of this tremendous opportunity. My thoughts ran like this: "If we could get a favorable mention in that column, we'd be made." (Today, I would phrase it differently: "We'd click.") But there were no major success stories to brag about, nothing concrete that we could point to and say, "Here's a product we've launched, a campaign we've developed." Since I couldn't impress Barmash by spinning tales of recent triumphs, I decided to describe what we talk about every day . . . predictions of *what* we thought was going to happen in the world and *why*. It was as simple as that: a big, beautiful click.

Here are some of those predictions (remember, it was 1980).

- Consumers will be cutting back on salt for health reasons, so they will be looking for alternatives—say, fresh herbs and spicier foods.
- Flashy U.S.-made cars will come back and replace the bland, boxy look.
- With an aging population, gray will be more than okay. Beyond that, middle age and older will be viewed as sexy.
- Fidelity will be popular again.
- There will be a renewed interest in the family.

Instead of writing me off as a flake, Barmash wrote it right. Furthermore, the article served as a benchmark, proof positive that our predictions were on the money.

BrainReserve was recognized as a futurist marketing (or a marketing futurist) company, and I was its fearless leader. We had clicked, and I felt as if *I* had finally clicked. After so many scared, friendless, uncomfortable, hard years, I had figured out what I could do that was unique: turn problems into solutions through a future vision.

The next giant step forward came out of a new-products assignment from Campbell's. Such assignments can be sheer pleasure. We build on projections of what consumers will be buying and eating three to five years down the road. We came up with an astounding 100 new product concepts. But instead of just handing over an alphabetized list to Campbell's executives, we hit on a way to link each new product to a specific societal trend that we believed would continue to grow over the next 10 years—in other words, we clicked with the trends.

The people at Campbell's gave us high marks. They said that it was the first time any marketing company had ever presented new products from the perspective of tomorrow's consumer. At that presentation, BrainReserve's TrendBank was born.

As BrainReserve has evolved, so has our definition of who and what we are. We're constantly BrainJamming to reposition ourselves. Over the years, we've gone from being a "think tank" to a "marketing consultancy" to a "small, caring clinic for future thinking." At the BrainReserve of today, we describe ourselves with the motto "Cool, Hot, Visionary, Fearless." That's what it takes to stay on top of the trends and keep clicking.

CLICKING WITH COCOONING

Consumers are shielding themselves from the harsh, unpredictable realities of the outside world and retreating into safe, cozy "homelike" environments.

W hen we first identified the Cocooning trend, we talked a lot about hunkering down, ordering in, and watching our favorite television shows. Cocooning conjured up cuddly images of hanging out, nesting, enjoying ourselves in our own homes, clicking with those we love. Home Sweet Home meant Home Cozy Home.

But while we have been weeding our gardens and channel-surfing in our home-entertainment centers, anxiety and dread have crept in. Where we once

Cocooned because it was fun, we now Cocoon out of fear.

We're looking for Home Safe Home.

To get a handle on how this trend has evolved, picture a turtle tentatively peering out from under its shell. Instead of looking eagerly at the world, the turtle is wary, scared. At the first sign of trouble, it shrinks back inside its protective cover. We are those turtles. They're you and me and many of our friends. As much as we want to venture out, learn more, try new things, even the bravest of us are intimidated—or at least worried that unexpected havoc could strike at any moment. And it isn't just the threat of specific violence that has us staying close to the calm comfort of home. Strange new diseases, pollution, traffic, crowds all add up to create a vague and ill-defined—but nonetheless very real—sense of foreboding.

Like the turtle, when we venture out, we venture out carefully. Places where we once felt secure are threatened. Churches are being torched; post offices laid siege; hospitals make you sicker; movie theaters are installing metal detectors.

A recent survey showed that 33 percent of consumers have changed their shopping habits because of fear of crime. Of these, 43 percent no longer shop after dark.

An increased awareness of stalkers and the potential danger of obsessive love has made even the most starry-eyed among us wary. A 1996 antistalker law has made it easier to prosecute those with "fatal attractions." Real-life cop shows and courtroom TV programs proliferate, adding to a general sense of uneasiness and insecurity. We're frightened by what we see but, somehow, we can't look away. All we can do is develop new ways to guard against a world gone mad by burrowing deeper into our protective shells and safe little Cocoons.

One in four junior high students claims to have seen a gun on school property. The airwaves are filled with tales of serial killers and random, senseless drive-by murders. In a recent case, "road rage" led one motorist to cut off another, causing the second motorist to slam into a truck. The result: permanent disability. We've abandoned patience. We're fed up and we want control, even if it means going to extremes. Violence has been called "the high of the '90s."

Talk about distress overload!

Nothing surprises us anymore: Cannibalism. Dismemberment. Office bombings. A sniper on the observation deck of the Empire State building. The JonBenet Ramsey case. Kids who kill their parents.

Inner-city crime has made some urban dwellers desperate. And in an effort to "take back" neighborhoods, their solutions go far beyond the Neighborhood Watch

Fingertip Shopping

Part of our precious home time is spent poring over the deluge of catalogs we receive in the mail every day. Mail-order companies are clicking in a big way, publishing and mailing out *billions* of catalogs to loyal customers or "Current Residents." It's mind-boggling. And the saturation point is nowhere in sight. If it can find the right niche and market to the right audience, a catalog will click. And why not? Mail order offers a perfect fit with Cocooning—a way to build that soft and cozy nest while safely snuggled within the arms of your favorite easy chair.

Both computers and television are feeding into Cocoon-based shopping. We're just starting to comparison-shop on-line or with CD-ROMs, electronically paging through catalogs and clicking on an order. At BrainReserve, we once made daily treks to the nearest bookstore. Now, we log onto Amazon.com, type in a title, subject, or author, and receive an on-screen display of pertinent information. With a credit card we can order as many books as we want. That's it: no walking, no waiting, no phoning, no leaving the Cocoon.

We're also abandoning the mall for the convenience of ordering from infomercials, the Home Shopping Network, and QVC. In 1996, QVC's phones rang 55 million times, and the company sold over $1.2 billion in merchandise in this country alone. Stay tuned for totally interactive television shopping.

idea. There's a movement afoot to cordon off whole neighborhoods to maintain order and protect homeowners. There is a growing number of private companies that upgrade deteriorated services—security, sanitation, tree care, holiday lights, to name a few. A section of New York's Upper East Side has devised a plan to hire between 350 and 500 private security guards to patrol the streets.

In *Elect Mr. Robinson for a New World,* novelist Donald Antrim depicts a United States where seemingly reasonable people build moats around their homes and commit barbaric acts of torture in the name of civic responsibility. It's not such a far reach from moats to gated communities. Five Oaks, Ohio, has, according to the *New York Times,* installed metal gates "designed to rebuff prostitution and drug dealing and the automotive traffic that often supports them." The barriers have created a safer inner community, all part of a plan called Crime

Security Systems

One in three new homes is built with an in-house alarm system. Home and car security is now a $1.5-billion per year industry and growing. Mace sales are soaring. Exercise buffs are snapping up canisters of Jogger Fogger Counter Assault Red Pepper Spray. Or for pricier peace of mind, they spring for the handheld Air Taser, which shoots barbed probes up to 15 feet, knocking aggressors off their feet. It works via electrical signals that block neuromuscular control. Police can also track the perps, if they do still manage to run off, by homing in on the microdotted barbs.

Our quest for safety has made bodyguards, armed with the latest beepers and 007 tricks, the "techno-butlers" of the '90s. The National Institute of Justice estimates that by the year 2000 we will be spending $104 billion annually on private security.

One of the most effective ideas for using a traditional weapon—in this case, guard dogs—in a new way comes from Shelley Reecher, a woman who was once brutally attacked. Shelley chan-neled her pain into creating Project Safe Run, now a 45-station network that provides ferocious-looking dogs to accompany women and the elderly on shopping trips, walks, and runs around the park. The program currently boasts over 42,000 excursions without an attack.

For those who want to order protective products from inside their Cocoons, the catalog *Safety Zone* sells items such as motion sensors that bark like a don't-tangle-with-me dog.

Perfectly Safe, another mail-order catalog geared especially for parents, sells a reassuring Baby Watch Video Monitor for $299.95. Nervous parents can implant "nannycam" video-recording devices into their kids' teddy bears to spy on baby-sitters.

Prevention Through Environmental Design, or CPTED. Nearly 4 million Americans now live in gated communities—with ever taller, thicker, higher walls being built each week.

Kids pose a special problem for Cocooning parents. Everyone knows that children need the benefits of socializing with their peers. But many parents these days are wary of just letting the kids go out and play. One answer: for-profit indoor playgrounds. Parents' fears are quieted at these urban and suburban play centers. The little darlings can't wander off, no strangers can

Phone Tips

The phone, and all its innovative add-ons, is helping us feel safer, smarter, and more protected—in a word, Cocooned. Many people think of their in-car cell phones as a safety feature, not a convenience.

The baby Bells have clicked with Cocooning by offering a full menu of what they term "protective" basics. There's Caller ID, a feature that lets you see the incoming caller's telephone number. And to keep the person you're calling from knowing that it's you, you can block the display of your number using Call Restrict (*67). Unlisted phone numbers, an old standby, have grown in popularity—almost one in seven households nationally employ them. For even more control, Call Trace can be enlisted to fight obscene callers. The date, time, and phone number of the last caller will be forwarded to the phone company's Annoyance Call Bureau. Too bad there isn't Call Revenge, to give those nuisance callers a mild electric shock.

approach, no drugs can be sold. WonderCamp, an indoor playspace chain, has mazes, electronic delights, and a cool clubhouse, all in cheery primary colors. Across the country, almost 30 million kids have played at the more fitness-oriented Discovery Zones (315 locations and growing), as well as the start-up, Ali Oop Play Environments.

When Cocooners do leave their homes, they take the Cocoon with them. Even the more modest makes of cars are turned into rolling playpens. Loaded with a six-disc player and a stack of CDs, a fax, a phone, bad-back Shiatsu cushions, and football-team vanity license plates, cars have become mobile Cocoons. Coffee-cup holders are now a given. Will future clicks include mini-microwave ovens, refrigerators, and fold-down trays?

Protecting these rolling Cocoons has become another major click. Go down any street in any city and look at the steering wheels on parked cars. Many will be securely locked with an easy-to-spot red gizmo. Last year, even though car thefts declined by 4 percent, sales of The Club (or look-alikes) continued to climb. If you want to catch the criminal in the act, there are products such as the Smoke Defense Dragon, a device that fills a car with smoke when someone tries to break in. But if all else fails and your car makes a detour to the chop shop, let's just hope you've had the foresight to have a tracking device installed, such as the Lojack Recovery System.

Even the most devoted Cocooners often have to face the inconvenience of earning a living, which more often than not requires going to an office. The solution: as with cars, take the Cocoon with you. One of Brain-

You Know You're Cocooning When

You know you're Cocooning when you forgo honking at someone for cutting you off on the freeway (the other driver may have a semiautomatic!). You know you're Cocooning when you smile and try to pacify, rather than argue with, an aggravated postal worker, a scowling salesperson, or a short-tempered waiter. You know you're Cocooning when you stop going to rock concerts or basketball games because you're convinced that large crowds of overstimulated people could turn into roiling, rioting mobs at the drop of a hat. You know you're Cocooning when your idea of a dream vacation is staying home and playing house.

Reserve's clients, the telecommunications company Ameritech, has made a Cocooning-based change in its workplace. When you enter the sleek steel-and-glass headquarters of the company's Consumer Services Division in Hoffman Estates, Illinois, you can hear the soothing sounds of Gregorian chants or the staccato ruckus of a rap lyric. The space looks curiously residential. In fact, it looks like a cozy family room with overstuffed furniture, a small dining room, a work-at-home area, and a home-entertainment center. There's not a fluorescent light in sight.

According to Linda Lanz, director of research at Ameritech's Consumer Business Unit, the idea behind all this homey comfort is that the latest communications products should be tested in a environment that mimics a consumer's home, not a sterile lab. Actual customers are sometimes asked to come in to the homelike environment and try out Ameritech's state-of-the-art wireless and switching technology. Company employees can use the corporate Cocoon for relaxing, checking out the latest best-sellers or magazines, surfing the Internet, listening to music, or watching the large-screen TV. It's also a popular place for holding meetings. Business presentations take on a different tone when co-workers are stretched out on sofas or have their feet up on the plush ottomans.

For Microsoft founder Bill Gates, home is where the microprocessor is. One reads with fascination the snippets about his $35 million lakefront house, where display screens are hooked up to a central database holding untold thousands of works of art. A guest spending the night can request an O'Keefe in the bathroom or a Renoir beside the bed. How long until mere millionaires will be clamoring for these same options?

The heart of every home's Cocoon is the bedroom and the bath. We want virtual minispas, places where we

Smart Houses

Already, there are about a thousand so-called smart houses in the United States that are preprogrammed to make our lives easier—for about $20,000. From your car phone, you can give verbal commands to open doors, turn on the lights, deactivate the security system, switch on an appliance such as your washer, dryer, or VCR, and even run a bath.

In the future we'll see:

- Ovens that can be programmed from outside the home.
- Appliances that talk back and update you on the status of dinner or call repair services when needed.
- Refrigerators with built-in video screens complete with a CD-ROM recipe drive.
- Pantries that scan and self-monitor their internal food supplies. You'll be reminded—and your store alerted—when you need more chunky peanut butter or black bean soup, or when milk needs to be pumped into the cold storage tanks.
- Video screens on which you can view your baby and baby-sitter on your car monitor, or even better, on your wrist.

- Cookware with built-in testers to evaluate the safety and purity of food. No more guess-work on whether all the bacteria have been neutralized in the pork or chicken.
- Countertops with hand-scanning technology to take your daily temperature, prescribe drugs or vitamins, and tell each member of the family what nutrients they'll need for energy.
- Home water-distillation systems. After all, who wants to tote those heavy bottles home from the store?

can de-stress and recharge. The bed-and-bath business has grown to over $16 billion a year. We're four-postering and four-pillowing our beds with Italian linen sheets, cashmere throws, and pleated silk dust ruffles. And we're changing our utilitarian bathrooms into luxurious retreats by installing whirlpools, saunas, Rain-Storm shower heads that spray 127 separate streams of water, automatic hand dryers, and heated towel racks for our monogrammed towel sets.

Many designers are exploring (and clicking with) *fēng shui* (pronounced fung shway), the ancient Chinese art of placement—the conscious effort to maximize the qualities of light and harmony by rearranging the items in our environments. *Fêng shui* is a major click in Hong Kong and Singapore—and, increasingly, in the United States. In fact, Donald Trump—hardly known for his spiritual qualities—made a *fêng shui* ritual part of the dedication ceremony at his newly completed luxury condominium and hotel tower, Trump International.

Fêng shui consultants help design your space to work with the building's *qi,* or life force, minimizing conflict and encouraging spiritual growth. Mirrors are used strategically to channel energy flow. According to the practice, you have to be properly situated in the universe to prosper. An architect we know hired an expert in *fêng shui* to design and balance his office in a way that would foster creative thinking.

Fêng shui enthusiasts believe that where a desk is placed in relation to a chair sets up an aura of harmony and orderliness. We believe it's a major click.

Gardening is the perfect pastime for Cocooners—a way to burrow in and feel healthy, wealthy, and wise, not to mention creative. We're spending small fortunes (more than $25 billion annually) on gingerbread gazebos, wisteria arbors, kits for digging your own pond for lily pads and koi, underground sprinkler systems for ever greener grass, and other gardening paraphernalia. Cocooners are putting their (gloved) hands in the muck and their feet in calf-high imported wellies as they turn

over compost, plant topiary and weeping spiral ever-
greens, and build multitiered birdhouses. The circulation of magazines such as *Martha Stewart Living, Garden
Design, Horticulture,* and *Organic Gardening* is growing
faster than a honeysuckle vine on a hot summer's day.

Serious gardeners are even braving the world outside their Cocoons, jetting over to English gardening
shows to hear lectures about mossy stones, spotty
mildew, and the palest Victorian roses. One such enthu-
siast, Marjorie G. Rosen, returned with the idea of
designing strong, simple, wrought-iron hanging baskets
after scouting Europe for them in vain. Result: Georgica
Baskets made by old-world craftsmen at La Forge
Française in Southampton, New York, costing about
$200 each.

House and Garden Television (HGTV) reaches
about 10 million viewers with hands-on features on gardening, home repairs, pets, decorating, and crafts. The
network has become a big-time click with Cocooners
coast to coast.

Sewing is another Cocoon click. Antique fabrics—
which remind us of a cozier past—have soared in value.
Old buttons, too, are becoming expensive collectibles.
Tender Buttons in New York is a treasure trove of
unique oldies. In Paris, the Marché Saint Pierre, a
wholesale fabric market, is jammed with both foreign
and French home-and-hobby seamsters and seam-

stresses. Sewing is heading into cyberspace. Compu-Serve has a section called Go Crafts, where you can log on to a quilting bee at 10 P.M. ET on Tuesdays.

Whether we're laying low from being scared or stressed, or just baby boomers slowing down and seeking the comforts of home, Cocooning has established itself as a driving force in American culture and society. Our homes and gardens feel like the last places where we can control our lives, can create a personal Shangri-la, can obtain a deep sense of satisfaction. Home is definitely where the click is.

CLICKING WITH CLANNING

Consumers seek the comfort and reinforcement
of those who share their values and beliefs—
or even their interests.

A t BrainReserve we wear small enameled pins
depicting a planet, complete with glittery stars
and Saturnesque rings. Often, visitors will ask
where they can buy one. "Sorry," we tell them, "you can't.
They're just for those in the BrainReserve constellation."

The pins resemble the image on the cover of *The
Popcorn Report,* and we have them made up every year in
a different color for our team, clients, and colleagues.
Wearing them is a gesture of unity and group pride. It's
a perfect example of Clanning.

Clanning links us up with others who share our interests, ideas, and aspirations. "I'm part of a group, and proud of it. I *belong*." It's not a surprising trend, given the way Cocooning has swept—and continues to sweep—the globe. All that huddling in the safety of our homes has left us, at times, feeling isolated. We humans need and crave social contact. The world still scares us, and so we reach out to people who pose little threat: those who share our interests and passions. The more fragmented our identities and fractured our days, the more we yearn to connect. Allying with like-minded souls, networking with those of the same interests and needs, is both comforting and stimulating.

Even the isolated writer can venture forth to exchange ideas with fellow scribblers in a writing group or at an artists' colony such as the legendary Yaddo in Saratoga Springs, New York. A common interest gives Clan members an immediate rapport. Maybe it's the Diving Dentists Society (DDS), or the Moles—not CIA operatives or animal lovers but a group of tunnel and subway workers. In Baltimore, there's the Johns Hopkins Hospital Bone Marrow Transplant Reunion, where survivors of this harrowing medical procedure gather to give thanks and trade war stories. In Los Angeles, we find LADIES (Life After Divorce Is Eventually Sane), a Clan of ex-wives of Hollywood stars and executives who find strength in rehashing custody battles, betrayals, and alimony settlements. Imitating the popular movie *The First Wives' Club,* groups of divorced women are uniting all around the country to process their experiences.

Our growing concern with status feeds into the Clanning trend. Private clubs are reporting an upsurge in membership—from the Princeton Club in Manhattan to the Boise Bridge Club. Waiting lists and exorbitant initiation fees do little to deter wanna-bes. Some Clanners actually hire membership consultants to advise them on admissions. There's a smugness, an aura of safety when you belong to a bastion of sameness— whether it's based on a shared interest in golf or tennis, on having attended the same college, or on simply keeping the rest of the world out. No wonder then that Clanning appeals to Cocooners.

Examples of the Clanning trend range from the sublime to the ridiculous and can be found in all strata of society. Clans can be political, economic, communal, spiritual, or virtual in nature. They can have 20 members or 20,000. Some are rigidly structured with an undisputed leader and a flock of followers. Others are models of equality.

Young adults are responding to the call of the Clan: Fraternity and sorority membership has found renewed popularity on college campuses. We have noticed, too, that the Grateful Dead—now disbanded after the death of Jerry Garcia—isn't the only rock band capable of commanding a fanatic Clan. These days, roving groups of "Phish-heads" troop after the band for months on end. And those who made it through the mud of Woodstock II will forever be members of a Clan, just as the generation before them formed immutable bonds at Woodstock and Altamont.

Another kind of Clan revolves around call-in radio shows. They fill a niche, a simpatico haven for the lonely and the verbose, a kind of virtual neighborhood. In the long middle-of-the-night hours, the voices in the dark provide a safe haven for the lost and dispossessed—and all too often the angry vigilante cries of the extreme right wing.

Ever hear of the Society for Creative Anachronism? These fanciers of medieval culture gather in flowing velvet robes to mine the pleasures of 11th-century verse, music, and culture. For fanciers of a different kind of fantasy world, some Clans sit around the TV. On Monday nights, from Spokane to St. Petersburg, *Melrose Place* fanatics gather to watch the show, placing bets and predicting which characters will sleep together, how a date will turn out, or who will get into a fight. And there was the phenomenon of Ellen DeGeneres coming out as a lesbian on *Ellen,* an event which spurred thousands of cheering house parties at gay and lesbian households across the United States.

Healing Clans

The National Institute of Mental Health has estimated that more than 500,000 different kinds of support groups are meeting in communities across the country. Just open the phone book or call your local community center. Under the letter "A" alone, besides Alcoholics Anonymous you will find Alien Abduction Victims, Airplane Phobics, Artificial Limb Patients, and Asthma Sufferers. It's hardly an exaggeration to say that for every problem, there is a healing Clan. And for every healing Clan, there are probably a dozen or more chat rooms and bulletin boards on the Internet. Whatever your vice, from overeating to nail-biting to gambling to compulsive sex, others with the same problem want to talk to you.

Even junior and senior high schools are organizing their own therapeutic groups by age. If you're a student at Austin High in Texas, you can choose to attend Alcoholics Anonymous, Narcotics Anonymous, Cocaine Anonymous, or Survivors of Incest—all during the school day. Austin High also recently started a program for girls who have been battered by their boyfriends, and another for the boyfriends who have done the battering.

In the best of all possible worlds, healing Clans are a place to come to grips with problems, unburden yourself of secrets, and find a commonality with others. The meeting rooms for these Clans are where people share their struggles and joys. They are a place to talk and listen, to participate in a healing dialogue. For millions of Americans, these Clans represent the equivalent of a sacred space—a "family" that's more caring, sharing, and supportive than the one into which they were born.

Alcoholics Anonymous has become one of the largest Clans in the country. People who travel frequently can call for a detailed listing of meetings in the cities they are visiting and can use the program as a way of connecting with people facing similar challenges. We know one New York woman who practically makes a beeline from the Los Angeles airport to the Malibu women's AA meeting as an efficient way of announcing "I'm here" to her West Coast friends. She then opens her Filofax and makes appointments for lunches and dinners (but not drinks).

Remember how we all fell in love with that cozy little bar known as "Cheers." Some Clans are based at neighborhood taverns, diners, cafés, or gyms—in short, a place that's as friendly and as protected as your own Cocoon, but one that offers a change of scene, a bit more stimulation, and that needed fix of human contact.

In Manhattan's East Village, the Résumé Cafe posts job listings, helping its bohemian customers find work, as well as serving them pizza and *gelati*. In Beverly Hills, a clan of cigar aficionados has emerged at Havana, a nightspot where people get together to light up stogies and share the not-so-politically-correct pleasures of a good smoke. On Christmas Eve, Jewish Americans who feel left out of the Santa loop can attend one of nine "Matzo Balls" across the country. Started in Boston, the dance party/event has spread to Washington, D.C., San Francisco, and Boca Raton, Florida.

Suppose when you looked out your living-room window, all your neighbors were people you'd handpicked. Sound like science fiction or maybe the Stepford Suburb? Actually it's the ultimate in Clanning—and cohousing is making it a reality. A community living concept pioneered in Denmark, Sweden, and the Netherlands about 20 years ago, cohousing is clicking with Clans in the United States. Popping up from Rhode Island to Bainbridge Island, Washington, it is based on cluster housing and averages about 30 units. In most cases, residents—a mix of young professional families and some older singles—have separate living quarters but enjoy communal facilities, such as play areas, gardens, laundry rooms, and often a dining room. These communities seek a return to small-town life, where you know and help out all your neighbors. Plenty of baby-sitters, someone to get your kid off to school if you have the flu, only one lawn mower to buy (and fix)—that's what it's all about.

What attracts people to cohousing? The reasons vary. Sometimes, it's simply a case of like-minded souls with a homesteading spirit. Generally, they are ecologically aware, but instead of tackling the global concept of "changing the world," they focus on the narrower goal of "changing *my* world." Other times, cohousing participants are united by their demographics or life circumstances. For people who don't have a mate or are empty-nesters, *cohousing* can offer a way to connect with others. One small tribal village in northern California was formed by a group of long-term friends—four married couples and three single women, all in their 50s and 60s—who ardently believe that they live longer, more active lives if they stick together. They fish, make wine, pool computers, and stay busy running successful cottage industries, such as a local bookstore/bakery. And they're happy.

Communes were big in the '60s, based on the pot-smoking, free-love, search-for-utopia mind-set so popular in those days. But the more middle-of-the-road aspects of communes—togetherness, sharing of chores and resources, a sense of responsibility—strike a chord in many hearts. (I once sat around with our Burton's client, Stuart Rose, and bandied about the idea of purchasing a few hundred acres somewhere, like Montana, selling off 10-acre plots to friends, sharing a central library and community house, and living in peace and quiet.)

In a larger sense, all of the communal Clanners are engaging in a form of social secession, much like the Pilgrims who came to Massachusetts to escape oppression and build a better life. A member of one collaborative community put it like this: "The way we have been living doesn't work. Families are small and scattered, so our kids have no chance to experience the joys of a big support system. They rarely see their grandparents and most of the elderly are treated like pariahs. The whole notion of borrowing a neighbor's ladder, or even a cup of sugar, has all but disappeared. We're craving some deep, meaningful contact."

A Clannish feeling is being recaptured at both mega-bookstores and strong independents. They have become communal hangouts for those who want to identify themselves as book lovers and sensitive individuals. Owner Joyce Meskis describes The Tattered Cover bookstores in Denver as a "living room," one she's been working at creating since 1974. Overstuffed sofas, wing

The Dark Side of the Clan

Unfortunately, Clans can become breeding grounds for intolerance and violence. Lawless gangs and dangerous cult Clans are on the rise. Roving "crews" or "posses" spray-paint graffiti signatures ("tags") or rush stores to shoplift en masse. Such groups are not confined to the inner cities: Suburban "yuppie" gangs around Denver, San Antonio, Omaha, Phoenix, and White Plains, New York, are mimicking L.A.'s notorious Crips and Bloods. Uglier still are the hate groups, white supremacists, and skinheads who threaten racial holy wars, using the Internet to spread their venom—and instructions for building homemade bombs.

The Oklahoma City bombing has focused a harsh spotlight on the scores of antigovernment Clans that are tucked into hidden corners of the United States. Mainly right-wing survivalists residing in so-called covenant communities, they're against paying taxes, and basically want to be left alone to live "off the grid." It can be fairly easy to disappear (dropping off the federal tax rolls) down a long, dusty road in sparsely inhabited Idaho or Montana. A new twist is that the fringe movement is spreading into the more populated parts of the world. A 1995 article in New York City's trendy weekly newspaper, the *Observer*, talked about the emerging concept of "sovereign citizens." A woman named Sharon Biggs teaches a "three-phase, 40-week course . . . on how to successfully remove oneself from the system." The sovereign path begins by banishing Social Security cards, driver's licenses, marriage contracts, voter registrations, insurance policies, credit cards, and bank accounts.

As discontent with the established government grows, and as the United States loses some of its muscle as the world's superpower, we can expect more acting out of the frontier fantasy by individuals who feel powerless and put-upon, burdened and betrayed. Starting over, being totally self-reliant, circling the wagons to protect yourself and your neighbors—such actions can portend trouble in the wrong milieu.

chairs, wood shelving, and wall-to-wall carpeting provide a warm and welcoming space where patrons can enjoy poetry readings while sipping hot coffee and nibbling on pastries.

In these Clannish bookstores, the pleasant atmosphere makes people feel secure enough to talk to one another, whether it's about the occult, Oceanus, or the ocarina. It feels like a safe haven because you can be nearly certain that everyone is reasonably literate, intelligent, and shares a love for books and browsing. The Barnes & Noble megastore on Manhattan's Upper West Side has become a popular place to meet suitable dates—many people would rather begin a relationship with a quiet chat than the tipsy blather common in singles bars.

In the past few years, sewing circles, bridge clubs, and roving poker games have begun attracting a new, nostalgic generation of enthusiasts, giving Clanning a decidedly retro twist. Says a 20-ish designer in Indiana who joined a quilting group: "It's creative, calming, and a great excuse to get together with some friends and gossip." Artichoke Joe's in San Bruno, California, is a 24-hour poker parlor that attracts up to 300 people at once—everyone from college professors to burger flippers.

The Internet, of course, is spawning a whole new generation of CyberClans. When a 40-year-old cyberspace aficionado died, his friends held an on-line wake. Although they had never met him face-to-face, his virtual family mourned him for weeks on the networks where he was a regular. Many people visit virtual lounges by clicking away at the keys of a laptop rigged up at their favorite

What's Clicking Next?

Cohousing counselors, akin to certified social workers, will match up would-be neighbors or housemates. Cohousing clearinghouses on the Internet (or 900-number phone lines) will allow people to post openings in these communities and screen applicants.

More businesses will click with healing Clans—cruises devoted to spiritual and physical well-being, specialty bookstores, recordings, videos, resorts, retreats, even dating services.

Here's an idea from our Ameritech client, Jim Firestone (now at IBM): "In the not-too-distant future, we'll all have a 'window' in our kitchens, a flat-screened television monitor which will mostly show a pleasing picture. However, on Sunday mornings, from 8:00 to 10:00, it's just 'on.' It's also 'on' in my mom's kitchen, my sister's kitchen, my brother's kitchen, and so on, at the same time. If you walk by, you say 'hi.' It's real time, like leaning out of a window or talking over the fence in the old days. You could do the same with any sort of community of interest."

coffee bar. The CyberSmith Cafe in Cambridge, Massachusetts, is one of a growing number of cafés around the country that are clicking with CyberClanners.

What is it like to join a Clan on-line? CyberClanners say it is the ultimate experience. Their reasoning: In an age rife with prejudice and hate, on-line communication is a nobler, purer expression. It's not what you look like, how you dress, or where you're from. It's what you say and how you say it.

It's no surprise that romances—known as "net-love"—flourish. We read about a virtual marriage where the bride, who lived in Washington, and the groom, who was in the Amazon rain forest, met electronically and fell in love over discussions of international ecology. They have floppy disks documenting their entire courtship. Forgetting romance, we all know about good old-fashioned cybersex by now. The on-line services themselves admit it's driving a healthy percentage of their growth.

Clans are everywhere and new ones are being formed every day. They help to shape our culture and define our lives. They provide both individuals and businesses with almost limitless opportunities. The possibilities to click with Clanning are endless.

CLICKING WITH FANTASY ADVENTURE

As an escape from stress and boredom
consumers crave excitement and stimulation
in essentially risk-free adventures.

"When you're safe at home, you wish you were having an adventure; when you're having an adventure, you wish you were safe at home." That's the Thornton Wilder quote that introduces the Fantasy Adventure trend, which relies more on flights of the imagination than on flights on a B-52 fighter jet, to our Clicking seminar audiences.

Fantasy Adventure is about seeking thrills and chills in small doses. It's about veering off the beaten path without getting too close to the edge. We want adventure and excitement—as long as we can still get to bed by 11 P.M. Even daring pilot Amelia Earhart wistfully said, "Someday, I would like to write a piece about the fun of voyaging with maps . . . without ever leaving home."

We all like to feel courageous, open to new experiences, partaking of life's banquet. But the fact is that most of us live fairly routine lives: job, family, home. And those routine jobs carry with them their share of stress, tension, anxiety. We crave that fleeting thrill that lifts us from the mundane to the magical—and then deposits us safely back on terra firma. This trend can be about a delve into the exotic (ordering Indonesian *lumpias* instead of the usual Chinese egg rolls), dipping into the strange (checking out a vampire bar—fangs optional—instead of dancing at your usual nightclub), or flirting with the forbidden (flashing a temporary tattoo on your biceps or thigh).

Fantasy Adventure is about being an armchair explorer, sporting the accoutrements of true risk-takers: a Breitling chronograph that was made to track a pilot's cruising speed or a rugged Tag Heuer watch that ticks to a depth of 200 meters. Most of us will probably never fly a jet or search for a sunken treasure galleon, but having the same equipment as those who do gives us a contact kick, feeds our fantasy life, stokes our imaginations, gives us vicarious victories.

For many of us, food is the road to instant Fantasy Adventure gratification—it's fast, easy, and affordable. Take something as simple as salsa, for instance. Introduced nationwide only in the past decade, today this versatile condiment outsells ketchup. Once our taste buds had been inflamed by jalapeños, we craved the whole Fantasy Adventure enchilada of south-of-the-border cuisine. Today, Mexican restaurants have become almost as commonplace as hamburger joints.

Cruised your local supermarket lately? The selection of exotic foods has exploded—food purveyors have gotten the Fantasy Adventure message loud and spicy. Fusion foods, which combine multiple ethnic cuisines to create unique taste sensations, are hot right now. By melding Mexican and Italian, Señor Felix's Gourmet Mexican Foods has come up with a southwestern lasagna, featuring melted ricotta and mozzarella cheeses, tomato sauce, and salsa between layers of tortillas. Other adventurous blends are pizza burritos, nacho-flavored bagels, smoked-salmon-and-cream-cheese pizzas, Tex-Mex egg rolls, and Thai salsa.

On the subject of zippier taste: For the first time ever, the spicier, zingier Dr Pepper has edged out Diet Pepsi as the fourth-ranked soft drink in the United States after Coke Classic, Pepsi, and Diet Coke. And recently, a ginseng-flavored vodka has been introduced, going way beyond citron and currant. It's not only the

Theme Restaurants

Theme restaurants are flourishing here and abroad, appealing to the fantasies we all have of being rock and rollers (Hard Rock Cafe), movie stars (Planet Hollywood), bikers (Harley-Davidson), models (the Fashion Cafe), or just hormone-rich good ol' boys (Hooters). Watch for a Broadway-theme chain of restaurants. The first will be in Los Angeles, proving that even the denizens of the movie capital fantasize about being on the Great White Way.

stranger, stronger tastes that are in demand now. Startling packaging can click, too. Arizona Iced Teas virtually built their business with oversized cans and interpretive graphics. The Saratoga Springs beverage Toga wraps itself up in racy comic-strip labels that have a plot change every six weeks (a panel of 18- to 25-year-olds helps create the story line).

Globally, Fantasy Adventure spells opportunity—a savvy way to exploit national differences. Iced tea took 100 years to catch on here, but it's still practically unknown—i.e., still an adventure—in most other parts of the world. Many times, what's humdrum in one place has an electric novelty elsewhere. When McDonald's opened in Moscow,

Havana

BrainReserve was asked by Estée Lauder's Aramis division to come up with a positioning for men's fragrances of the future. A key theme that emerged from our research was escapism. The men we interviewed wanted to put on a fragrance and feel transported to another place, another identity. One of the favorite fantasies was Latin elegance in all its seductive permutations: fla-menco guitar, the running of the bulls at Pam-plona, the machismo of Antonio Banderas, the pleasures of a thick cigar, the sensuality of tropical heat. As a result, Aramis developed Havana cologne with its sexy air of danger.

India, and Beijing it created near riots of eager customers. Look at America's recent love affair with the southwestern "wraps." These soft tortillalike shells enrobe a myriad of fun fillings and give us the fantasy of "eating on the range"—no fork, no spills, no problem.

A natural path to Fantasy Adventure is through out-door activities. Witness the in-line skating craze. When you're blading down a sloping country lane or a crowded city sidewalk, you feel like a test pilot pushing the envelope. This trend also accounts for over 9 million mountain bikes sold in the U.S. over the past five years. (Hippest model: BMW's folding bikes. Beautifully engineered, they're sturdy, speedy, and easy to transport.)

From the BrainJams we've been having with 18- to 24-year-olds, we've learned that their Fantasy Adventures revolve around "realness": a longing to be immersed in a totally genuine state of existence. Look at the success of MTV's *Real World* pseudo-cinema-verité series. There's nary a rock god or teen queen to be found. Instead, seven regular folks (okay, seven very attractive regular folks) are tossed together in a house with a camera rolling. And whether you are watching Beach *Real World* out of Venice, California, or London *Real World,* you can expect a fair share of untarnished reality. Entry-level job blues. Battles over refrigerator shelf space. Fumbling attempts at romance. High drama, it's not. Fantasy Adventure, it is.

There's a flip side to this generation—a sizable minority that has no interest in playing it safe. They're buying into the taboo-rock fantasy of Marilyn Manson; the nihilism of Trent Reznor from Nine Inch Nails, who rages, "I'd rather die than give you control"; or superstar-of-the-moment Beck's "Loser," in which the singer sociopathically (if somewhat satirically) snarls, "I'm a loser, baby, so why don't you kill me?"

This generation is also sparking to Fantasy Adventure with on-the-edge cosmetics like Urban Decay. This

Mountainview, California, company is hitting it big with streetwise nail polish colors like Uzi, Gash, Bruise, and Acid Rain.

What's new about angry musicians and kids who click with them? Attitude. There's a raging and defiant cult of self-destruction going on. Heavy drugs are getting heavy play. Ecstasy is the drug of choice for the rave scene, often followed by a snort of Special K (originally a cat tranquilizer). Crystal meth. Mushrooms. Even heroin (aptly coded "poison" or "body bag") has suddenly become chic, glamorized in the pages of hip magazines like *Details*. Is it fear of a frighteningly complex world that's driving too many of our kids into the clutches of drugs? Tragically, for those who continue to abuse drugs, Fantasy Adventure soon becomes reality death.

"Goth" (short for Gothic) culture and music have gained a strong foothold in the college crowd. Goth devotees—influenced in part by Anne Rice's vampire books—dress in flowing capes and silver jewelry, experiment with androgyny and sadomasochism, and live in a fantasy realm that manages to be both futuristic and 19th century at the same time.

But enough about the sliver of the population that worships "sex, Satan, and rock 'n' roll." The vast majority eschews the real edge and opts for less threatening incarnations of Fantasy Adventure.

America's fantasy adventure extends to its obsession with celebrity—it's one of the strongest traits in our national character. This fascination seems to be reaching new levels of intensity. Is there no limit to our curiosity about the private lives of our movie stars, pop singers, and politicians? We love our celebs—and we love to know all the sordid details of their clay feet. Show me anyone who can resist scanning the tabloid headlines while in line at the supermarket! Even though on some level we know that they're only human, we fantasize their lives as being infinitely glamorous, exciting, filled with champagne, romance, and adulation.

It's no wonder we desperately want to own a piece of our homegrown gods. Look at the prices fetched at the auction of Jacqueline Onassis's possessions, or the Pamela Harriman auction, the never-ending mania for Elvis collector plates, the frenzy over Princess Diana's gowns, the $7,000 paid at auction for the metallic bra Madonna wore on her Girly Tour. Just recently, a New York publisher announced it was issuing Jacqueline Onassis's will in book form—what could be more intimate and personal than that? Who among us hasn't dreamed, at least fleetingly, of being a movie star? It's as American as apple pie and Seinfeld.

The lure of personal transformation—the dream of becoming, if only for a little while, someone more beautiful, more glamorous, more exciting—is an important component of this trend. Makeovers are a staple on television talk shows and in women's magazines. Fantasy photo shoots which promise pictures that make even the plainest Paula look like Cindy Crawford are doing a booming business. In Japan, large numbers of women are signing up for a try-a-new-you tour called Dress Up Tokyo. The Hato Bus Company whisks participants to a posh hotel where everyone is given a whole new look— wardrobe, makeup, hair, even tips on etiquette and how to sit and walk gracefully. The women choose extravagant evening gowns or frothy white wedding dresses and are photographed in flattering poses. Another Japanese escape is called the Transform-Into-Maiko (or apprentice geisha) Package. A few thousand women per year leave their routine lives and playact the provocative and sensual geisha role.

Remember when kids wanted to go to sleep-away camp to learn to swim, sail, and make lariats? Now the summer vacation of choice for the junior high set is the real, and really trend-savvy, Space Camp in Huntsville, Alabama. There, junior astronauts experience weightlessness and learn what it would be like to fly and land the Space Shuttle. What's more, adult Fantasy Adventurer astronauts can now join up, too. And baseball, basketball, and football camps for adults are a big hit. For a hefty fee, aging sports fans can live out their fantasy and actually take the field against their heroes.

Dream Duds

Browse the J. Peterman Company's *Owners Manual*. Its owner, John Peterman, started out with one product—a long, canvas horseman's duster coat, advertised in magazines like *The New Yorker*. Put it on and—presto!—you were a cowboy out on the range, primal and alive, not a stockbroker stuck in a stuffy office. Subsequent offerings that clicked: a hat modeled after Hemingway's, a tugboat captain's sweater, a David Niven blazer, a Gatsby shirt, a Bacall blouse, even Garbo pants. The founder's philosophy is: "People want things that are hard to find. Things that have romance, but a factual romance about them. Clearly, people want things that make their lives the way they wish they were." J. Peterman has hit such a trend nerve that its founder, the eponymous J. Peterman, is a character (Elaine's boss) on *Seinfeld*.

Outer space occupies a place dear to Fantasy Adventurers' hearts. *Star Trek—The Motion Picture* has had so many sequels that the *Enterprise* crew is beginning to stagger around, paunchy and wizened. Futuristic films such as *Men in Black, Independence Day,* and *The Fifth Element* draw huge crowds—we love seeing mother earth defend herself against alien invaders. The Sci-Fi Channel has replugged all those vintage Buck Rogers shows, the ones that have Buck sitting stiffly in a studio, looking down on a cardboard mock-up of a "Future Metropolis." It's been announced in 1998 there will be a 24-hour Future Channel on cable covering the new developments in product advancements and scientific inventions, kind of like "The Future in Review," one of our favorite names for a TV special about BrainReserve. The rerelease of George Lucas's *Star Wars* trilogy had moviegoers lined up for blocks in major cities around the country and introduced this all-time moneymaker to a new generation. And the award-winning television show *The X-Files* became a Fantasy Adventure classic its first season on the air.

Fantasy Adventurers are tuning in to the Discovery Channel to delve into more serious stuff—galaxies, black holes, and whether dinosaurs were exterminated by an errant meteor or rogue virus. There's something undeniably spine tingling about realizing how fragile our planet is, how it could be obliterated in an instant by a hurtling meteor.

Somewhere between heaven and earth is cyberspace. One of the strongest Fantasy Adventure clicks is embedded in the intricate circuitry of the mighty microchip. Drifting through cyberspace, Fantasy Adventurers can stretch their horizons as never before. There are home pages for every hobby, obsession, and fetish that exists.

Cybertravelers can talk live to their favorite celebrities, write movie and album reviews, or enter an erotic chat room posing as Marilyn Monroe or John F. Kennedy Jr. Wild Dog's web site offers horse riding in Mongolia and crossing the Himalayas on a vintage motorcycle. There are 500 more to choose from at www.Wild-Dog.com. In the electronic, immediate anonymity of cyberspace our deepest fantasies are only a keystroke away.

Another wildly popular computer game that has clicked with Fantasy Adventurers is *Doom* and its follow-ups, *Doom II* and *Doom Gunn*—and the more recent releases *Riven* and *Quake*. Next click: *Doom* movies, books, virtual arcades. A lighter cyberclick is the consciously nonviolent CD-ROM game *Myst*. Or consider companions of Xanth, the game based on books by fantasy adventure writer Piers Anthony, or Death Gate, set in the fantastic surroundings of Margaret Weis's and Tracy Hickman's best-selling novels. For international, intergalactic fantasizing of "Let the games begin" we hear the popular Japanese computer game Megami Tensei is headed for U.S. shores.

Superstores are getting savvy to Fantasy Adventure, too. At Travelfest, a vacation wonderland in Austin, Texas, adventurers can fulfill every travel need from luggage to maps to inflatable pillows. Best click: Customers can cyber-visit exotic (and not-so-exotic) locations to check out hotels and attractions. They can also

Suburban Safari

Fantasy Adventure is behind the Range Rover's incredible success in the U.S. market. These tough four-wheel-drive vehicles, originally made to climb the sand dunes of the Sahara and ford muddy mountain streams, now cruise the asphalt of city streets in vast numbers. In a Range Rover, a driver towers over the road, able to meet any challenge and roll right over it. Ice, snow, mud, water, and wilderness? No problem. Never mind that most of us don't venture beyond the stop-and-go traffic of our commuting routes. At the controls of our four-wheel-drive fantasy machines, we're big-game hunters and all-terrain terrors.

With sales of four-wheel-drives soaring, don't you ever wonder how much bigger, longer, more cumbersome our vehicles can get? We predict that, in a flip, we'll soon be driving smaller utility vehicles, easier to maneuver and park, less expensive to fuel and maintain, with a softer, cushioned ride. At this writing, BMW and Swatch are planning to introduce a new car concept. A two-passenger, tiny 8-foot-long, 60-miles-to-the-gallon car-cart. It's aimed for 1998 market introduction at $10,000. Its name—self-explanatory—

Smart. We'll also see return-to-elegance cars, similar to the new BMW convertible.

But why, we ask, can't there be modular cars? Completely adaptable, hardtop or convertible, ready to fulfill any fantasy. Adding extra trunks for trips, a clear top for touring, a hydraulic lift to see over traffic. Maybe even a feature like the accordion-pleated center that some of the long, snaky buses have—with different "tails" to add, depending on your current fantasy.

comparison-shop for hotel rates and airline fares, even buy tickets and get boarding passes, right on the spot.

Virgin Group Ltd. scored a superstore click when it opened the world's largest music and entertainment store in New York City's resurgent Times Square. The 70,000-square-foot megastore carries 150,000 CDs and tapes and features a café with live performances, a four-screen movie theater, and a sports restaurant called the Official All-Star Cafe. The joint is a Fantasy Adventure wonderland.

At Bass Pro in Springfield, Missouri, customers are taught to tie flies, and can test their prowess at an indoor trout pond. There are also pistol and crossbow ranges on-site, plus a resident taxidermist.

Amusement parks—which have been providing Americans with Fantasy Adventures for over 100 years— are booming again. The granddaddy of all rides, the roller coaster, has become a national icon, a nostalgic thrill that has earned a cherished place in our country's collective consciousness. But the coaster is hardly mired in the past; new and more terrifying ones are being built all over the country. Elitch Gardens in Denver has Twister II, a twisting, turning wooden coaster that will make your hair stand on end. And in Las Vegas, the Stratosphere Tower Hotel has two roller coasters on its roof. Riders swoop around stomach-churning turns at up to 1,100 feet above the gaudy glamour of the strip.

Each year new rides appear to dazzle, delight, and terrify. Houston has the Mayan Mindbender, an indoor thriller ride encased in a huge pyramid, on which you creep and zoom in the dimmest light past scary things that glow in the dark (yikes!).

In addition to their famous rides, Disneyland and Disney World offer a low-tech, high-romance Fantasy Adventure: fairy-tale weddings. The bride wears a gown copied from Belle, Snow White, or Cinderella and arrives not in a limousine but a horse-drawn carriage. How about chocolate slippers for dessert and less-than-comely stepsisters (actually Disney employees)?

Fantasy Adventurers can ride the waves at the world's largest indoor beach at SeaGaia, Japan. Or windsurf across a choppy indoor lake at a park outside Paris. Or rock climb at one of the mountain-wall sports parks opening up across the United States—all the thrill of scaling the heights with none of the danger of rock slides and serious falls. Japan even has a synthetic slope, created within a shopping mall, where the snow is always perfect. In the UK, the Tamworth Snowdome boasts a 9,155-meter run of real snow. Fantasy Adventure is also part of the lure of Mall of America, which is built around a full-scale amusement park.

BrainReserve has identified a drift within Fantasy Adventure that we call Wildering. It's about men and women pitting their civilized selves against the wilds of mother nature. Wildering is the reason why 275,000 people per year raft down the headwaters of the Arkansas River in Colorado. Or why sea kayaking has become one of the hot sports of the late '90s. Why trekking in Nepal has become the status trip of the decade. And why wealthy (and too often ill-prepared) climbers tackle mountains like Mt. Everest—sometimes with tragic consequences, as Jon Krakauer writes about in his best-seller *Into Thin Air.*

And for those tourists who are ho-hum about yet another five-star hotel, there's the increasingly popular category of "tough luxe." Many travelers are spending thousands of dollars to hike in New Guinea with local tribesmen, walk with the elephants in India, trek to an

---

What's Clicking Next?

Dior cosmetics just launched Mascara Flash, an instant hair color process, that lets you add a streak of color to your hair with a flash of mascara wand.

Computer-savvy Sony is testing the concept of advanced cyberparks offering thrilling virtual-reality rides. If the first prototype—set to open in late 1997 in San Francisco—scores, Sony plans a national rollout geared to urban adults.

---

outback bush camp in Australia, spend their honeymoons in tents on the African veldt. Blue-lipped tourists in northernmost Jukkasjarvi, Norway, pay top dollar to stay at the spectacular Ice Hotel, a vast, elaborately designed—and annually redesigned—igloo. Chairs, tables, even beds are made of ice, then draped with thick reindeer skin for comfort. Rough? Definitely. But, ultimately, safe. In the extreme, Wildering is about testing your mettle, pushing your level of endurance, but having a warm shower (or a cold vodka) waiting at the end of the day.

For quieter Wildering, there's the growing sport of orienteering (called the thinking sport by its devotees). Participants are dropped off in the forest with only a map and a compass. This can be a solitary challenge or a competition—a race among peers to see who can navigate his or her way out the fastest. There's a five-day meet in Sweden, the O-Ringen, that attracts about 25,000 orienteers.

Another increasingly popular way to respond to the call of Wildering is a sport called tracking. Participants get close to nature by spending up to a week in unknown terrain, fending for themselves, finding their way in the wilderness. It's a high-concept version of being an Indian scout: keen of eye, light of foot.

Fantasy Adventure feeds a basic human need for stimulation and excitement. Danger is seductive, and when our hearts race the adrenaline rush makes us feel alive, vital, connected to our animal selves. With most of us trapped in sedentary and often mundane jobs, even vicarious thrills can bring a refreshing jolt of exhilaration into our lives.

To click with Fantasy Adventure, focus on the everyday and the humdrum, then add a whiff of danger, a hint of excitement. Stir in a suggestion of uncertainty and risk—while assuring the purchaser of safety. At Brain-Reserve, we see Fantasy Adventure playing a key role in future marketing. The message to the consumer is: You can be a hero, an explorer, a hunter, an idol, a legend—in your own mind or in your own time, often in the space of a minute.

CLICKING WITH PLEASURE REVENGE

Tired of being told what's good for them, rebellious consumers are indifferent to rules and regulations. They're cutting loose and publicly savoring forbidden fruits.

No more Goody Two-shoes. Good-bye, Rebecca of Sunnybrook Farm! Adios, Mary Poppins. The emerging trend of Pleasure Revenge means we're fed up with self-deprivation for the sake of being healthy, polite, or politically correct. As consumers, we're ready, willing, and able to pursue pleasure. Not sweet and pure, sunny and perky enjoyment, but the hidden, forbidden delights of full-blown indulgence and instant gratification. We're hauling out our ids and satisfying their demands. Pleasure . . . with a vengeance.

We're smoking defiantly, drinking harder, slathering butter on our steaks, flaunting our furs, gorging on goodies, and tossing out the oat bran in the bargain.

Why the semidestructive change? Because we tried being model citizens and paragons of virtue and life still threw us curves. We got laid off; our kids rebelled; cancer rates continued to rise; cars crashed and planes fell from the sky. In spite of our following all the "right" advice, we were still afflicted with heart attacks, ulcers, and angst. Now we're mad as hell and we're striking back, hanging up our halos, and pulling out all the stops.

A case in point: The Harvard School of Public Health reported that, contrary to earlier findings, most margarines are no better for you than butter. After all those years of shunning better-tasting butter, consumers rebelled. Sales of some margarines—Unilever's Promise, to name one—dropped by as much as 32 percent in a matter of weeks. It seems like hardly a week goes by that the medical establishment doesn't reverse itself on one issue or another—from margarine to mammograms, beta carotene to coffee. The net result: We've started to tune them out, become skeptical and cynical about their findings. Add to that consumers' widespread dissatisfaction with profit-driven, treatment-depriving managed-care companies and you have a sizable population that's going to make its own rules when it comes to its own health.

We're on an I-deserve-it spree. And when we make a decision to be bad, we do it consciously. We know the consequences, but sometimes we just feel like ordering a martini and topping off our thick, juicy steak with a cigarette or four.

We're sick of "perfect people." The number of Americans who say they're trying to avoid fats has plummeted to around 50 percent. We're tired of tofu, bored with bran. Food is one of life's great pleasures and we're not going to deprive ourselves any longer. Sales of hot dogs are up and the best-selling pizzas are enormous concoctions with thick, three-cheese-stuffed crusts and layers of pepperoni heaped on top. In restaurants, heart-smart broiled seafood sales are sluggish, while fat-and-calorie-packed deep-fried clam and calamari platters are all the rage. Dig in, America!

Farmer-sized breakfasts of bacon and eggs are back. Even the American Heart Association has upped its suggested consumption of whole eggs to four or more a week (there's less cholesterol in yolks than originally thought—there they go reversing themselves again). Cheese courses—wedged between robust entrées and delectable desserts—are making a comeback in top-notch restaurants on both coasts.

Our willpower is weakening by the moment—and

we don't really care. Wow, do we have a national sweet tooth! (But you knew that already.) Sugar-coated cereals are being spooned up by adults as well as children. We're buying cookies by the bagful and ice cream by the gallon. Sales of Ben & Jerry's fatted ice creams have trebled over the last six years. For total revenge, premium ice cream makers somehow stuff every forbidden delight—from marshmallows to nuts to cookie dough to peanut butter to fudge—into ever more fanciful flavors. While yogurts may still have an aura of health, super-premium frozen yogurts resemble their ice cream counterparts in richness and caloric content. In other words, we like nonfat vanilla yogurt, but we like it better when it's loaded with enough add-ons to sink a diet in two bites.

And take a look at your supermarket shelves—chips, chips everywhere. Americans spend almost $20 billion a year on snack foods. Doritos are still among America's favorite crunch, followed by every possible variation of potato, corn, rice, bean, and vegetable chip.

We're even splashing down calorie-laden liquids. Quite surprisingly, sugar-sweetened, caffeine-pumped sodas are enjoying new popularity, while sales of diet sodas have stagnated.

In the fast-food arena, KFC's Skin-Free Crispy didn't fly, while its newer Popcorn Chicken, dipped in batter and deep-fried, is a big winner. McDonald's (the

What's Clicking Next?

Our love affair with luscious indulgence shows no sign of waning—the trick is to come with something original and incredibly yummy, something that screams: "Yes, it's worth the calories and fat grams!"

What about a franchise of shops, simply called Baba's, serving variations of the fatty French treat, *baba au rhum*?

Consider a strudel shop that sells buttery strudel logs stuffed with everything from raisins and nuts to seafood. Or Danish-style pastry places, specializing in prune, poppy seed, and those spread-out, flaky bear claws. And how about topping everything with thick Devon cream or its Turkish equivalent, creamy-dreamy *kaymuk*?

What about an upscale pancake chain? Who could resist fluffy buttermilk pancakes with creamery butter and real maple syrup?

A streetwise reader could imitate the Dutch/Belgian pushcarts that sell crisp, crunchy, delicious French fries. They're cut medium thick, well salted, and sold in paper cornucopias. Why not go all the way with Pleasure Revenge and offer lemony mayonnaise for dipping, as the

Dutch do? Add a touch of exotica with a variety of spicy ketchups and relishes.

Sticking with the greasy stuff, what about pork-and-cheese tamales served in cornhusks, a sidewalk treat from Latin America?

Couldn't some astute tobacco company click into Pleasure Revenge and the social-smoker market with herbal (no, not that kind of herb) cigarettes, wrapped in beautifully designed papers? Or cigarettes that slowly release a pale tinted smoke? Wouldn't it be interesting to incorporate some kind of aromatherapy element—imagine cigarettes that could change your mood, curb your appetite, even energize you?

largest food supplier in the world) tried hedging its bets by offering a lower-fat burger called a McLean Deluxe, as well as a hefty half-pounder with cheese sauce christened the Mega Mac. Guess which one did better in this just-say-yes world? Even in ultra-health-conscious Los Angeles—where everyone seems to exist on alfalfa sprouts and aerobics—the sales tally was 60-to-1 Mega Macs over McLeans. Mickey D recently deleted McLeans from its menu. Wendy's, too, has entered the heavyweight competition with its Big

Bacon Classic, a virtual orgy of beef, bacon, cheese, and mayo.

The rate at which we're biting burgers is almost frightening. The all-American staple is ordered in restaurants more often than any other food: Some 5.2 *billion* are eaten in the nation's restaurants every year. And that's not counting all those patties frying on backyard barbecues.

We born-again carnivores are hardly satiated by puny patties. We want the thickest, most tender, most heavily marbled (read "fattiest") cuts of prime sirloin, porterhouse, and filet mignon. On their way in are authentic Brazilian rotisserie restaurants, called *rodizios*, in which waiters make their way around the tables carrying spit-roasted meats on huge skewers. Diners beckon the waiter, who carves off thick slabs of beef, pork, lamb, and more beef until signaled to stop.

One crucial caveat to this button-busting trend: Pleasure Revenge is not a way of life. We may be going for the sizzling steak, but we're only going once a week (oh, all right, maybe twice). One group, calling themselves the Red Meat Club (a Pleasure Revenge Clan), meets to gorge themselves once a month; members convene, order a quarter-steer, blood-rare, and have a jolly fine time carving and consuming. That's all well and good for the hard-core, but there are many others who are squeamish about admitting to a weakness for

---

Scale Smashing

The May 5th Coalition (no, it's not a Mexican rev-olutionary group) is behind International No Diet Day, which the group describes as "a day to renounce the tyranny of thinness, proclaim our freedom from the demands of the diet and fash-ion industries, and celebrate the many shapes and sizes of the people in our world." Miriam Berg, the Coalition's coordinator, urges all of us to listen to our bodies and feed them if they want to be fed. Every May 5, you're supposed to wear a light-blue lapel ribbon, smash your bath-room scale, and pig out!

---

red meat. We know one New Yorker who proclaimed herself a vegetarian but couldn't resist sneaking off to her neighborhood steak house to furtively gnaw on a plateful of greasy beef ribs. Now that's Pleasure Revenge!

Food is hardly the only outlet for Pleasure Revenge. Like drinkers during Prohibition, today's smoke rebels are huddling together to light up their cigarettes. Evi-dence indicates that the 25-year decline in cigarette smoking may be eroding. This lends support to an aggressive new attitude, a kind of self-righteous swagger. Diehard smokers are tired of being social pariahs; they're inching in from the back doors, the loading docks, and the stoops. They're sick of the nico-fascists who deny them their basic right to light up.

Smoking has become cool, celebrated in movies chronicling the life of young urban retro-hipsters. Surprisingly, college-educated adults earning over $35,000 a year are also pushing up cigarette sales. Claiming to be "social smokers," they are thoroughly enjoying less than a pack a week.

This moderate approach to smoking seems to be clicking. I was once a two-pack-a-day smoker. More than a decade ago, I gave it up completely. But for the last few years, I've had a "planned smoke" every once in a while to stave off a feeling of deprivation. And it goes no further than that. Knowing the taboos of smoking, but being able to keep it under control, makes it thrilling. It's a feeling of being bad—of reveling in an illicit delight. Perfect Pleasure Revenge.

Cocktails are clicking with Pleasure Revenge. Especially the martini. Not just the traditional jigger of gin with a dropper of vermouth in a V-shaped glass, but new '90s variations. Catering to the palate of a younger generation, these martinis are sweeter rather than drier. The Four Seasons Hotel in Manhattan has devised a martini-only menu. In the mood for a peachy Bellini martini, a strawberry Metropolis martini, or a crème de

Stogie Chic

Cuban cigars have been banned in America since 1962, but a thriving cigar underground has been clever about locating Montecristo A's, which cost $36 each and take a hundred days to blend, dry, and hand-roll. While lighting up, cigar smokers can sit back and leaf through *Cigar Aficionado,* a magazine click of genius from publisher Marvin Shanken. Recent cover models have run the gamut from portly Rush Limbaugh to mega-celebs Arnold Schwarzenegger and Demi Moore. Cigar sales in 1996 were estimated at $3 billion.

Manhattan's Monkey Bar recently held an all-female "smoker," and about 150 women paid $95 to attend the dinner. They puffed vanilla-flavored cocktail cigars with their champagne, and larger ones (requiring expertise with a cigar cutter) over coffee. Cigar lounges with heavy leather chairs and oversized ashtrays are popping up all over the country. Stogie enthusiasts flock to them to smoke their odoriferous treats and trade opinions on brands and blends of tobacco. Even Godiva Chocolates has gotten into the act featuring individual chocolate cigars as sweet smokes. (Pleasure Revenge meets Clanning.) And the patrons are not the stereotypical fat-cat men but college students and young execs of both sexes.

menthe Candy Cane martini? Belly up to the bar—smokers welcome.

Lounge music—led by the revival of Esquivel and currently hot bands like Combustible Edison and Squirrel Nut Zipper—is making a big splash in record stores and nightclubs across the country. Laid back and just a little bit tacky, it sets the perfect tone for Pleasure Revenge—slipping into a dimly lit booth, sipping a martini, and lighting up a cigarette.

Marijuana, often estimated to be America's biggest cash crop, is stronger than ever (both more popular and packing more punch). In 1996, California voters approved—by an overwhelming majority—a binding referendum to make marijuana legal for medicinal purposes. With a doctor's prescription in hand, pot smokers no longer have to fear arrest. The law is, many believe, the first step toward eventual legalization. More surprising still is that voters in conservative-leaning Arizona approved an even more liberal law.

Pot appeals to the Pleasure Revenge impulse

because it's naughty and forbidden, but rarely viewed as having the serious consequences of heavier drugs. And the smell and paraphernalia associated with the drug hark back to the hedonistic, happy-hippie '60s.

We're not exercising quite as fanatically as we once were. "No pain, no gain" is a passé refrain. Talking about health and fitness from the comfort of a BarcaLounger is the latest exercise craze. A full 60 percent of American adults admit that they aren't sweating to the oldies or the newies—in fact, they just plain aren't sweating. The number one excuse: no time. But even among those who do have the time, there are a sizable number who simply don't enjoy working out. People who hate to exercise are ignoring the shame game played by the fanatically fit. Their refrain: "It's my body and I'll lie (in bed) if I want to!"

Even the word exercise has recently been replaced in the governmental lexicon: The President's Council on Physical Fitness now refers to workouts as the more benign and ambiguous "physical activity." In pure Pleasure Revenge terms, "exercise" connotes leg lifts and bench presses, while a nice long walk (perhaps stopping along the way for a cappuccino and cannoli) could qualify as duty-fulfilling "physical activity." In the long run, the walk might be better for our overactive digestive systems—and overstressed psyches.

Every day, it seems, a new ab exerciser (physical

activity facilitator) or aerobic conditioning contraption is introduced on one of the home shopping networks. Somehow each one manages to be easier to use and less strenuous than the last. Inevitably, we're heading toward "passive exercise" machines that do the work for us while we recline in front of the megascreen TV.

Which brings us to the subject of liposuction. This procedure, in which fat is literally sucked out of the body, is by far the most common plastic surgery in the country. These days, it's relatively safe and affordable and there's little stigma attached to having it done. Pleasure Revengers are saying: "To hell with the sweating and grunting. Just knock me out and turn on the vacuum."

Another indulgence that's clicking with Pleasure Revenge is fur, that consummate symbol of luxe. Sales are up as fur aficionados defy People for the Ethical Treatment of Animals (PETA). As Wall Street and the economy boom, people want to flaunt their success and their moxie. What better way than stepping out wearing fur accessorized with the "no one can tell me what to do" attitude emblematic of Pleasure Revengers.

Tanning salons are more popular than ever. A fit and handsome fellow named Chuck Holmes in San Francisco has a deluxe tanning pod right in his home. When asked, "Isn't that dangerous?" he drawled, "Hell, living is dangerous." That refrain seems to sum up much of the Pleasure Revenge philosophy.

The very real dangers of AIDS and other sexually transmitted diseases, as well as a backlash against indiscriminate promiscuity, did much to dampen the sexual revolution of the 1960s. But today, the erotic is back with a blast—fueled by the safety promised by cyber connections. *Penthouse* magazine logged over 800,000 visits on its first day on the Internet. And on the World Wide Web, *Playboy* is not only zinging out stories *and* pictures of its playmates, it has also put out a call requesting that women age 18 and over E-mail their exact measurements and a photo of themselves, wearing a bikini—or less. Adult movie rentals account for a large portion of video profits. Because chains such as Blockbuster refuse to carry X-rated films, many mom-and-pop video shops have found a niche in adult rentals. In some cases, porn rentals make up more than 50 percent of their business. The porn industry itself—while hardly a model of ethical business practices—has found a kind of acceptance in mainstream culture. *The New Yorker, Esquire,* and *Details* have all run lengthy profiles of porn stars and directors.

In embracing the erotic, Pleasure Revengers are also reacting to the sanctimonious moralizing of the religious right. The sexual and financial shenanigans of Pat Robertson, Jimmy Swaggart, and Jim Bakker—among others—have unmasked the hypocrisy of these self-appointed cultural arbiters. Americans just plain

don't like anyone telling them how to live their lives—
and when someone does, the rebellious streak that
guided our founding fathers and still runs through our
national character rears its proud head and Pleasure
Revenge kicks in.

The key to clicking with Pleasure Revenge is to fur-
nish consumers an occasional, but unapologetic,
splurge and overindulgence. Be the provider of no-
holds-barred, throw-caution-to-the-wind, go-all-the-way
excess. As artist Paul Gauguin reasoned, "Life being
what it is, one seeks revenge."

CLICKING WITH SMALL INDULGENCES

Busy, stressed-out consumers, seeking quick-hit
gratification, are rewarding themselves
with affordable luxuries.

I f we go for the gusto in Pleasure Revenge—believing that "living well is the best revenge"—how do we Small Indulge? Isn't a steak, a glass of wine, a cigar, or a rich dessert a small indulgence? Technically, yes. But in Pleasure Revenge, there's an edge of anger, a decision to go ahead and be naughty, a who-cares-what-anyone-else-thinks attitude. A vengefulness. Small Indulgences is a sweeter, softer trend; it's more about treating yourself well—and not busting the bank in the process.

The American psyche is undergoing a transformation. The recent rash of corporate downsizings coupled with the global economy have made us question our invincibility and our status as the world's undisputed economic powerhouse. We grew up imagining that quality of life inevitably improved from generation to generation. We would have material advantages and luxuries our parents never had; isn't that what they were working for? Then, without warning, the rules changed and the promise was broken, smashed, tossed onto the garbage heap.

Most of us don't have as much job security or make as much money as our folks; we can't be certain that our skills will stay marketable; that Social Security will stay solvent; that we'll be able to send our kids to college; that we'll ever scrape together the cash for a down payment on our dream house. In fact, there's not a whole lot we *can* be certain of. We're working harder and enjoying it less.

To reduce our stress and lower our anxiety levels, we're turning to mini luxuries and minor indulgences. They don't solve anything, but they make us feel pampered and a little bit rich for a brief, but refreshing, moment.

Can you blame us for jumping into Small Indulgences head-first? It's an age-old method of getting an emotional fix (when the going gets tough, the frazzled go shopping). We're sad and we're mad and we feel entitled to some sensory gratification. Something to delight the nose, smooth the skin, and most important of all, dazzle our taste buds. One of the easiest ways to indulge is with our mouths open.

What we look for in edible Small Indulgences is high quality: You can't indulge on everyday eats. Nor can you get much of a psychic soul-lift on junk food. By nature, certain treats are so irresistible and special we're willing to overpay for them. In fact, we *want* to overpay for them, just to feel a tiny bit spoiled. More . . . well, indulgent. We choose two perfect, platter-sized Portobello mushrooms instead of a bagful of ordinary small white toadstools. We forgo the Mazola and take home a little bottle of basil-infused olive oil to drizzle over our spaghetti.

When you think Small Indulgences, think about a pitcher of fresh-squeezed orange juice, a basket of plump purple figs, a bowl of tart kumquats, a plate of thick white asparagus (the kind Belgians serve with blackened butter), a smear of artichoke paste (how many barbed leaves had to be scraped, how many hearts had to be broken, for one jar?), and bags of chocolate-dipped Tuscan biscotti. How about porridge? McCann's award-winning whole grain Irish oatmeal, packaged in an attractive and serious-looking tin, is unbelievably good and selling (for $7.50) unbelievably well.

Upper Crust

All over the country, enterprising bakers are opening shops that specialize in fresh, crusty breads. At
New York's incredibly earthy Ecce Panis, it's hard to
choose between warm, crusty focaccias, topped
with sun-dried tomatoes; chewy bread braids,
interlaced with onions, anchovies, and olives; and
rustic round peasant breads. The prices would
make the Sunbeam girl faint, but bread lovers line
up for the elegant loaves.

Sometimes when we're feeling at wit's end and in
need of a little babying, a minivacation can be just the
Small Indulgence the therapist ordered. A weekend at a
nearby bed-and-breakfast. An afternoon at an urban
minispa that includes a sauna, aromatherapy, and a
facial. Or something as luxurious and simple as a back
rub. Bill Zanker's Great American Backrub Shops feature "BackRub Plus, a 10 minute luxury for $16.95."
Bill's concept? McRub. A night in a less-than-glamorous
motel to ignite some erotic sparks. Even a midafternoon
trip to a local museum or balcony seats at the opera can
feel like a renewing, indulgent getaway.

Yet there are moments when high-status items click:
You may not be able to walk into one of the Bulgari

Gold Rush

The 20-something crowd has gone wild for gold—a Swiss liqueur called Goldschlager Cinnamon Schnapps, that is. The bottle is like a snow globe. But in this case, the "snow" is real: edible gold flakes, swirling in the schnapps.

---

shops around the world to acquire a signature gold watch (around $14,000). But you might splurge on one of their limited-edition black-face models for $320 (that is, if you can possibly locate one; they all sold out in a week).

Fortune magazine labeled this "decadent utility," explaining that "status now resides in enduring value and utility." The writer of the article called BrainReserve to get our slant on the subject. Among my answers was this very Small Indulgence–oriented view: "People want real quality products with a history and an ethical heritage."

The Small Indulgences trend shows no signs of abating. It's like a protective net beneath the high wire of our worries. A balm for our psyches. It's a very soothing click.

Pens are perfect Small Indulgences. Fountain pens costing in excess of $50 are the fastest growing segment of the writing instrument market. Over $300 million of top-of-the-line Mont Blancs, Dunhills, and Cartiers are sold each year. Mont Blanc has even opened its own boutique to sell its limited-edition pens, some named after literary luminaries such as Ernest Hemingway and Agatha Christie. The whole category of upper-crust pens is not just for graduation and "today I am a man" presents. They are Small Indulgences, purchased to bring out the poet in us and last (at least) a lifetime.

The soothing ritual of a warm cup of tea is a delightful Small Indulgence, one that comes without the guilt of calories or bank-account depletion. Celestial Seasonings pioneered the market for specialty teas. Now we're Indulging in Cranberry Orange, Passion Fruit, Moroccan Mint, and the more exotic blends Macadamia Nut and Coconut Rum Creme.

New York's Takashimaya department store is one of the most original in making tea a Small Indulgence. Besides elegant rice paper tea bags, it offers polished wooden tea scoops and sugarcane swizzle-stick stirrers. In a Swedish market, we saw shelves lined with long cylinders containing different varieties of tea leaves, so customers could blend their own brews. One of the market's teas, called Tropical Beach, featured little chunks of dried pineapple, mango, papaya, orange rind, hibiscus, and coriander. Delicious. And made to order for an I-deserve-it moment.

Astute entrepreneurs are opening up tearooms. Tea Luxe, in Boston and Cambridge, Massachusetts, serves as many as 120 varieties of teas in a relaxed atmosphere inspired by low-key British tearooms. A sense of order and control—a whiff of a world long gone—only adds to the Small Indulgence experience.

Small Indulgence hotels are finally coming to American cities and rising to the standards of the Draycott in London or L'Hotel in Paris. Once scarce in New York City, there's a growing choice of town house charmers or human-scaled boutique-hotels, such as the Inn at Irving Place, the Franklin, Morgans, the Shoreham, the Wales (by designer John Barman), and the Mansfield. San Francisco has the Sherman House and the Nob Hill Lambourne (where, instead of a goodnight chocolate bonbon, guests get some healthy antioxidant tablets, along with an enigmatic saying, such as "No pillow is as soft as a clear conscience"). These small hotels add a rarefied aura to Small Indulgences, making us feel special—if only for an all-too-fleeting night. Let the herds stay at the 1,000-room megahotel down the block.

The instant gratification offered by bath and beauty products is high on any Small Indulgences list. Demeter's Atmosphere offers scents in lavender, cedar, orange, or geranium, that you can spritz anywhere—on your pulse points, your musty beach towel, your odorific tennis sneakers, or just into the air as a bathroom or car freshener. Inhaling an intoxicating scent, one that lifts us out of our lives and transports us to a Gauguin pastoral or a Monet garden, may be the ultimate sensual balm.

Consider the success of Anita Roddick's Body Shop and Estée Lauder's Origins shops. For under $25, you can satisfy your desire to smell fresh, clean, smooth, and soothed. The stores offer a delighting array of aromatherapy items—infusers, inhalers, oil burners, scented pillows, fragrant eye masks—all Small Indulgences that deliver that longed-for quick-fix lift. How heavenly to retreat to the tub for a long, luscious soak in fragrant, soothing water! Aaahhh.

In our hectic city or suburban lives, nature herself becomes a Small Indulgence. In fair weather, office workers crowd nearby parks, drinking in that ultimate refresher—our glorious planet. We know many people who drop everything when they're having a terrible day, hop in their cars, and drive to nearby bird sanctuaries or nature preserves. A short walk in the fresh air is a delightful, renewing Small Indulgence.

And, in her infinite wisdom, Mother Nature has given us our original Small Indulgence: flowers. Whether it's one long-stemmed red rose on your desk or a Calyx & Corolla bouquet sent to your mom, fresh flowers have gone from an occasion item to a Small Indul-

What's Clicking Next?

Being trend-savvy can mean giving an old tune a new twist. One way is to downscale, rethink, or rework big-ticket items into Small Indulgences. We've been dreaming of:

- Golden Door Spa-at-your-door vans.
- Range Rover night-vision binoculars.
- A mahogany Chris-Craft canoe.
- Sleek Porsche or BMW flatware.
- A perfectly pitched Steinway clock radio.

gence. You can order mums, miniature rosebushes, birds of paradise, and bonsai trees by phone or computer 24 hours a day. The flower business represents a major click that is in full bloom, spreading a lot of green around the industry. 1-800-FLOWERS, for example, reported a 35 percent increase in revenues in 1996, to $300 million.

Millions of Americans—city dwellers, empty-nesters, the happily single—have become doting (often to the point of obsession) pet owners. If we can't provide ourselves or our children with all the material plenty we would like to, there's always Fluffy and Fido to Small Indulge. Perhaps your declawed kitty would like a taste of the wild? *Super Kitty Video,* featuring one hour of chirping birds, scurrying mice, and scrambling squirrels, should get her in touch with her basic instincts—and keep her amused while you're at the office. The back pages of *Cat Fancy* and *Dog Fancy* magazines offer pet raincoats, pet papooses, doggie beds, kitty carriers, perfume, mouthwash, and a wide array of dazzling designer outfits for doggie. There's even a home page on the Internet for people who custom-design clothes for different canine breeds.

Pet superstores, giant emporiums of 10,000 square feet or more, are catering to the $15-billion-a-year pet business. A big click. These pet stops are following the same concept as Home Depot—stocking everything you could possibly need to Small Indulge your pet, from aquarium gravel to gerbil feed to Santa suits to tartar-control toothpaste. These chains have mastered the art of turning shopping into entertainment. There are contests, puppies to coo over, amazing iguanas, photo ops for you and your Snookums. Customers are encouraged to shop with their pets, making it a breeding ground for "getting to know you" conversation stops and long-leash playtimes. Some even have doggie "salad bars." Instead of lettuce and bacon bits, you'll find rawhide chews, fancy kibble, and beef jerky strips.

Small Indulgences is actually a big and lasting trend. No matter what our circumstances, we all yearn to feel pampered and privileged. Those who can afford big indulgences take off to Canyon Ranch for a week. The rest of us buy a little piece of the American Dream and revel in it. Savvy companies should aim their products squarely at this vast market—one that eagerly reaches for its pocketbook when it finds an irresistible, instantly gratifying Small Indulgence.

Have you partaken of a Small Indulgence today? If not, what are you waiting for? You deserve it.

CLICKING WITH ANCHORING

Reaching back to their spiritual roots,
consumers look for what was comforting,
valuable, and spiritually grounded in the past
in order to be secure in the future.

The bad news: Our society is adrift. The good news: It's still afloat.

Even though we've been tossed about on the sea of life—our values, morals, and ideals battered and bashed—we're renewing our spirits by grabbing on to a hope-line, a connection that anchors us to our spiritual core. After several decades of materialism and meanness, we're looking for simpler answers. "Yes," we're saying, "you can take away outer layers—my job, my wallet, my car—but you can't squash my inner spirit." There's an old Italian motto: *L'ultima che si perde è la speranza,* "The last thing we lose is hope." Fortunately, we haven't arrived there yet. And we have faith we never will—the human animal is resilient, caring, and infinitely resourceful.

It's not surprising that we're turning inward to keep hope alive. Years ago in *The Popcorn Report,* we predicted: "This decade will see a full turn from fast-track living to a return to home and self-protection. We'll experience a new morality, new religions."

But to many, established religions seemed to be part of the problem. Their familiar homilies sounded stale, rigid, didn't speak to the realities of life in the late 20th century. People began looking elsewhere for their spiritual sustenance. At BrainReserve, we labeled the pioneers of this movement the Mystical Tribe. Stores in Manhattan such as Enchantments and Star Magic do a brisk business in goddess candles, harmony balls, wave machines, old-fashioned kaleidoscopes, and astrology decoders. Many small towns have shops specializing in crystals, geodes, and mystic ambers. Top jewelry designers have taken a mystical bent, from Byzantine and Maltese crosses to Robert Lee Morris's talisman necklaces.

Several polls have confirmed the appeal of mysticism. A *Self* magazine study reported that 84 percent of respondents said they believed that "a higher power listens to and answers prayers," 76 percent believed in miracles, 63 percent in life after death, 55 percent in ESP, 51 percent in Satan, 46 percent in out-of-body experiences, and 39 percent reported they had "personally experienced or witnessed a miracle."

There can be little doubt that in the shifting quicksands of modern life, there is a profound yearning—a *need*—to build a sturdy inner foundation. This is the core of Anchoring. In seeking the answers to the big questions in life, we're taking a backward glance at what was safe, secure, and comforting in the past. We're digging deep into our collective memory searching for some leap of faith to help us cut through the daily chaos and lead us into a new century.

Even though change rarely occurs in fell swoops—a major problem on December 31 at 11:59 P.M. will certainly remain a major problem at 12:00 A.M. on January 1—we tread carefully and superstitiously around the turning points. Contemplating the year 2000 is triply awesome. All those fat round zeroes. This is no ordinary New Year's Eve. It's the coming of the third millennium. In the last one 50 generations ago, in the year 1001, time moved at the speed of an oxcart. Now, we're hurtling into the unknown at the speed of light. What *will* tomorrow look like? Will there be more natural disasters? Is the recent rash of typhoons, tornadoes, floods, earthquakes, and volcanic eruptions a warning from God of impending doom? Will the New Age fulfill its promise of universal love? Will another Messiah show his face, *her* face?

The spiritual quest at the heart of Anchoring is a focused search. We're looking for that intangible *something* that once gave meaning and order to our lives. We want to feel part of an eternal, nurturing whole—rather than insignificant cogs in a runaway wheel. We want to feel connected to our work, our play, our planet, *ourselves*. We scan the stars and hope to find solace in the belief that a higher power is holding everything in this vast universe in its place. As the poet Tennyson penned, "Cast all your cares on God; that anchor holds."

The search for life's Anchor can't be dismissed as weird, wacky, or cultish anymore. It's moved from California fringe to national mainstream. Condé Nast, the magazine group that publishes *Vogue, Glamour, GQ, Gourmet,* and *Vanity Fair,* offers its employees a midday *t'ai chi* break. Talk about inspiring collective kinship and radiating energy. Who of us couldn't benefit from a daily meditation break? Even "shock jock" Howard Stern—dedicated to all things offensive and outrageous—proclaims the virtues of his twice-daily meditation practice.

For those who can't find a quiet place to meditate (and these days who can, with some modern machine either ringing, singing, whining, belching, or buzzing in the background?), there are many serene hideouts around the country. In California, there's the Soto Zen Buddhist monastery, Tassajara; the tough ashram, Marin County's Spirit Rock Meditation Center; and the 160-acre Zen Mountain Center in the San Jacinto Mountains. And in upstate New York there's Zen Mountain Monastery. All are places where you can meditate to your mind's content.

One of the biggest draws of these centers is total silence. At the Insight Meditation Society in Barre, Massachusetts, you can go for three-day, ten-day, or three-month silent retreats: no talking, no distractions, just living every present moment to the fullest. After such a stretch of outer and inner peacefulness, your breathing improves, your mind is more focused and alert. The experience restores your body and cures its ills: Chronic pain is reduced; insomnia fades away; fertility is enhanced. You can keep this bliss going by saying a mantra (a simple word, phrase, or sound) once or twice a day for ten minutes or so. Keep it different from the anxiety-ridden yuppie mantra: Get ahead, get ahead, get ahead.

These havens are not necessarily all Zen-based. There are the more traditional cloisters such as the Abbey of Gethsemane, near Louisville, Kentucky, and Wainwright House in Rye, New York, which cater to midlife transitions. Visitors can go to "feel the wisdom" of their future selves. At Wisdom House in Litchfield,

Connecticut, set up as a religious sanctuary with an emphasis on feminism and the arts, you can retreat to deepen your faith. In Darien, Connecticut, the Catholic Sisters of Saint Brigitta have set up the Vikingsborg Guest House as a "B&B" for the world-weary. Even in London, you'll have a chance to unwind in the ultrahip Life Centre, housed in an old church building, which has a staff of holistic therapists offering Shiatsu, non-allergenic foods, and yoga.

In Jungian thinking, the sea holds the collective memory (and future) of all mankind. It's not only that the waves of the ocean soothe us but that the water itself is symbolic of everything spiritual. Wasn't the sea, after all, our first home? Do we all carry molecular memories of our species' ancient past? Is it surprising that we so often turn to the sea in our journey toward wholeness? We drive to the beach and instinctively sit on the sand or perch on a rock, gazing out at the endless expanse of water. (For those who are landlocked, there's a 60-minute video called *Ocean Waves*.) This hypnotic gazing, according to Jung, takes us back to the flood, birthing, and baptisms—and to those months of innocence floating in our mothers' wombs. It Anchors us in our spiritual past.

Jung also had a way-out theory that the piercing songs of whales and dolphins might be some kind of laser beams that hold up the sky (wow). In Japan,

Buddha Rising

According to Helen Tworkov, editor of *Tricycle,* a trendy Buddhist review with up to 150,000 readers, America is on the verge of a breakthrough in Buddha-dharma, a flowering of the wisdom that has enlightened untold billions of souls around the world. This quarterly reports on everything from Virtual Reality to "Awakening with Prozac." It even profiles such regular guys as Phil Jackson, coach of the Chicago Bulls, who has been meshing Zen principles with his work life. And thanks to celebrity meditators such as Richard Gere, Oliver Stone, Ellen Burstyn, and Tina Turner, the remote purity of the Dalai Lama's teachings is now known to America's millions of celebrity watchers. Not druggy or flaky, many of the American Buddhist set, including a few Rockefellers, are powerful and connected.

there's a "dolphin therapy" video for stress reduction. A priest from the Kyoto Temple's Dolphin Ki Healing Center guides you as you view the videotape of dolphins swimming and talking. Couple this with the truly awesome recording *Songs of the Humpbacked Whales* and you may well find spiritual nourishment. To take this communion with our evolutionary roots further, we should make it an earthly priority to stop polluting our waters. For are we not, in effect, polluting ourselves?

Whatever a person's specific spiritual click, one thing is evident: We're all at the start of a great awakening, a time of spiritual and religious revival. What's different about this awakening is that there's very little agreement on who or what God is, what constitutes worship, and what this outpouring means for the future of our civilization. After the greed-driven, soulless '80s, we're trying to put passion and meaning back into our everyday lives, to get in touch with the old values— faith, hope, and charity. President Clinton's recent summit on volunteerism brought together a nonpartisan constellation of America's best and brightest in a common plea for community and commitment. We're a nation looking to regain its lost (or at least tarnished) soul.

One way people have of finding that essence is through a relationship with the divine, the ultimate expression of Anchoring. What else could explain the 400,000 teenagers who came to hear the pope in Colorado? Or that, as an author, John Paul II would have not one, but *two* global best-sellers? Or that years after American Catholics had successfully banished Latin from their services, they'd be snapping up a double CD of the pope reciting the rosary in that ancient language?

Or that the pope would be a major marketer, so much so that for his 1995 visit to the East Coast, 23 official papal products were blessed and hawked?

Besides performing the still-sacred ceremony of marriage, clerics have a new responsibility performing the latest in trendiness: divorce rituals. Couples, presumably the ones still speaking to each other, join together in front of a minister or rabbi to remember the good times in the relationship and to forgive each other for the hurt.

The need to Anchor has found expression in all of the world's religions whether they celebrate the Old and New Testament God, Buddha, Allah, Brahma, unnamed higher powers, or self-discovery. Those expressions can be found in any number of clicks that consumers of every stripe are making.

The original "soul" music is a popular way to click into Anchoring. CD sales at religious bookstores are included in *Billboard*'s Top 10 List tracking system. Warner Bros. and Sony have launched substantial Christian music divisions. And what MTV did for rock, the Z music channel will do for Christian devotional singing. There's also a small but devoted audience for the CDs that Lys collects of the legendary cantors. They have been made from historic recordings that managed to survive World War II, giving us a chance to hear the lulling and lyrical tenor voices of the "Caruso of Can-

Church-tainment

Church attendance is soaring. More people attend church than all sporting events combined. Megachurches sometimes have to rent the nearest stadium to hold the thousands of faithful who come for Easter Sunday service. Some have large-screen TVs to show the follow-the-bouncing-ball lyrics to the new "pop" versions of the hymns. Often the services include rock bands and skilled dancers and skits. To attract even more parishioners, many ministers have been hiring professional stand-up comedians to crack up the audience with cleaned-up jokes. And sermons have loosened up; often they're filled with more practical and political advice than Scripture. Critics of these nontraditional ways may fear that this is the McDonald's-izing of religion, but isn't it closer to the communality of the early churches, when the populace craved the spectacle as much as the spiritual?

tors," Josef Rosenblatt, and of Gershon Sirota, who perished in the Warsaw Ghetto.

Isn't it astounding that in this rap 'n' roll era, *Chant,* a collection of Gregorian hymns (again, in Latin) sung by the cloistered Benedictine monks of Santo Domingo de Silos, could have topped the music charts? In a mere nine months, almost 3 million copies were sold. Its follow-up, *Chant Noel,* turned into a Christmas classic. The fad started in Europe and quickly caught on here. There are a slew of me-toos: *Chill to the Chant, Beyond Chant, Quietude,* and *Old Roman Chant.* Their ethereal harmonies and hypnotic repetitions create an Anchor to deep meditative thinking.

We seek out people—even those of dubious credentials—who can guide us into our spiritual selves. Astrology is experiencing its biggest boom in 400 years according to a *Life* cover story, "Astrology Rising." Forty-eight percent of Americans say astrology is valid according to a recent poll, and the annual market for astrology books is $20 million as we approach the millennium. An ancient Indian astrology called Jyotish imparts practical as well as mystical insight. Psychics and palm readers are no longer considered "corny." In certain restaurants, it's possible to get a reading over your arugula. And for those who prefer to get their fix at home, there's always Dionne Warwick's Psychic Friends Network and its numerous imitators. At $3.95 a minute, you can phone in your questions and receive "psychic insight" into your problems. (One warning: A former employee blew the ethics whistle, claiming that phone callers were strung out on the line for 22 minutes, so that an average call cost over $80. Put on your kitchen timer.) While these Ma Bell mystics are often no more than out-of-work actors and single moms trying to make a buck, there can be no doubt that their popularity is a strong Anchoring indicator.

If you're still doubtful about the surge of Anchoring, just listen to the flutter of wings as angels descend to earth in record numbers. Earth angels, teen angels, dream angels, sheltering angels, lusty angels, trusty angels, even fallen angels. *Time* magazine's cover story, "The New Age of Angels," cited a poll indicating that 69 percent of Americans believe angels exist and 46 percent believe they each have their own personal guardian angel. Some 20 million viewers tuned in to the NBC special *Angels: The Mysterious Messengers.* These downy-winged creatures have supposedly been given the power to bring us sacred little handwritten notes from God. And they can wrap us in the glow of unconditional love and protection.

CBS is in heaven over *Touched by an Angel,* a weekly show about an angel's earthly visits. The program is a surprise smash hit that routinely makes the Nielsen list of top-10-rated shows. On the more serious side, the Broadway hit *Angels in America, Parts I and II,* featured a winged actress who swooped down from the rafters to offer heartfelt but cryptic advice on the salvation of the world. The play has won every major prize including the

Tony Award and the Pulitzer Prize and is on its way to becoming an American classic.

Today's angels are guides who gently awaken our better selves, leading us toward the righteous path. They're spiritual nannies. Theologians have suggested that these angels offer people who've been disenchanted with traditional religion a safe new bridge to God.

Getting in touch with our ancestral roots is another form of Anchoring. The American Genealogical Society reports that record numbers of people are trying to trace their lineage. In fact, genealogy is listed as the third most popular hobby in America. More than preparing a pedigree, it Anchors you in your family history. Computer software makes the backtracking easier: Family Ties for Windows or DOS and the superduper Family Tree Maker Deluxe CD-ROM.

Family ties matter. Since everything from liberal voting patterns to adultery is now thought to be genetic, you can create your own "genogram"—or behavior tree—that will reveal multigenerational characteristics. Books such as *How Healthy Is Your Family Tree?* and *Voices in Your Blood: Discovering Identity through Family History* guide you through this illuminating (and sometimes disturbing) process.

Many people have been inspired to make pilgrimages to find their ancestors' graves. Will the practice of

Nourishing Roots

For black Americans, reclaiming some version of African culture—through African names, religious practices, music, clothing, and food—is a way of establishing an Anchor in the heritage erased by the overwhelming tragedy of slavery. Although most African Americans can never hope to trace their actual genealogy—slave traders hunted people like animals and refused to recognize human connections such as family and bloodlines—the communal celebration of African culture offers a strong sense of belonging and history.

To create a spiritual holiday celebration that African Americans can truly call their own, Kwanza was developed almost 25 years ago. Coming around the same time as the hustle and bustle of Christmas and Chanukah, Kwanza is a family festival lasting seven days, during which loved ones gather to feast and light candles dedicated to guiding principles. One principle is "Uja-ama," a Swahili word for cooperative economics. In a small-business expo held in New York, over 300 participants came to show off Kwanza holiday products, African sculpture and fabrics, and depictions of Nia Umoja, the counterpart to Santa Claus.

making tombstone rubbings become more popular? Descendants of the six million people who perished in the Holocaust make emotional returns to family villages, searching for the scattered remains of old family possessions and whatever birth and death records remain. Elie Wiesel, author, Nobel Prize winner, and concentration camp survivor, tells us over and over, "Never forget." The U.S. Holocaust Memorial Museum in Washington, D.C., also Anchors that unspeakable epoch and hopes that its reminders will keep the past present, so the horrors will never be allowed to happen again. In 1996, attendance reached almost two million. We walk through in tears, gasping for air in the museum's actual boxcar, stunned by the photographs, sick in our hearts from its recorded testimonies. Coming face-to-face with the very depths of man's inhumanity is a powerful Anchoring experience, one that drives us deep into ourselves in a search for explanations and meaning, in a dedication to living moral and enlightened lives.

Remembering and honoring the dead appears in other guises, from the finely chiseled Vietnam Memorial to the sad, storytelling patches that are sewn together in the AIDS Quilt.

This is certainly a new age, one in which God's messengers use modern technology to spread the gospel. Televised religion has established an intimate connection with the public. Televangelists are burning up the cable channels. The Faith & Values Channel runs 24 hours a day, reaching at least 20 million households. Charlton Heston stars in a series of Bible videos, filmed in the Holy Land. We've witnessed thousands of Hasidic Jews outside a New York hospital, waiting for their 92-year-old rebbe to give them a sign that he was the Messiah. A major difference from the days of Christ: These Lubavitcher Jews wore beepers, all the quicker to signal the Word to one another. (Update: Now that the rebbe has passed on, his gravesite is covered with thousands of messages *and* faxes.) Why should people in 1997 have to worship in the same fashion as people did 50 years ago?

We wish we had a dollar for every time we've heard someone piously say, "By the way, I've just finished *The Celestine Prophecy,* and it changed my life." This book is one of many spiritual uplifters that are continuing their strong hold on the best-seller list. The prophecy hearkens back to an ancient Peruvian manuscript that reveals nine key insights into life itself. Its mission is to move us along from the material world to a spiritual one. James Redfield, the author, paints a picture of a Utopian future in which we will be paid for brain-work instead of brawn-work. His most delightful foresight: If you can heighten your spiritual energy enough, you can become invisible. Will we all be able to float past one other, creating mischief, undetected?

Another big hit, selling in the millions, is Betty J. Eadie's *Embraced by the Light,* a tale about her 1975 experience of "passing on" while having an operation and returning five hours later with the secrets of Jesus. Similarly, there's *Saved by the Light,* by Dannion Brinkley, who tells his dramatic story of being struck by lightning, shown a "cathedral of knowledge" of future events, then revived in a morgue. That the *Light* books are reportedly true and current makes them less cosmic and crystal-y than *The Celestine Prophecy.* To an aging baby boomer population coming to grips with mortality, near-death experiences are compelling because they give us a reassuring peek into the bright light-at-the-end-of-the-tunnel.

Originally self-published, Marlo Morgan's *Mutant Message Down Under,* about a spiritual trek with the aborigines in Australia, sold over 350,000 copies before HarperCollins picked it up. Similar story for the minibible of homespun wisdom, *Meditations for Women Who Do Too Much.* This volume sold around a million copies in its original desktop-published incarnation, before being picked up by a publishing house.

Yoga is a major '90s click. Meaning "unity" in Sanskrit, yoga has the same root as the English word "yoke," which carries the double connotation of "to unite" as well as "to place under discipline." This 4,000-year-old "discipline" of mind and body health is knocking the athletic socks off

What's Clicking Next?

Satan Redux. If angels are everywhere, can devils be far behind? Fiery red Satan, the Prince of Darkness, and his horned tribe have long captivated our imaginations—our halos have been known to slip. Connecting to the dark side, trying to find some solace in understanding—although not following the teachings of—fallen angels may well be a big click in the future. We can stay fascinated with "good" things for just so long. Haven't Americans always glorified the devilish outlaw (Jesse James), the ruthless gangster (*The Godfather*), the fiendish vigilante (Bernard Goetz)? Imprisoned killer Charles Manson has released an album, *Commemoration,* on White Devil Records. The paintings of John Wayne Gacy sell for high prices at auction. "Dr. Death" Jack Kevorkian has the whole country debating whether he is a savior or a ghoul who takes too much pleasure in death.

aerobics. Frantic exercising seems too close to real life. With yoga, you get to leave the everyday world and focus inward. Its quiet intensity increases your flexibility, improves your concentration (great for golf games), and strengthens unused muscle groups. Just in one Manhattan neighborhood alone, there is a wide selection of yoga centers: Yoga Zone, Urban Yoga Workout, Iyengar Yoga, Astanga Power Yoga, and Sivenanda Yoga Vedanta Center. Watch for yoga centers to spread across the country as fast as coffee bars. There's already an 800 number to find a class in your area (800-359-YOGA).

If you can't find a practitioner, you can always join in a TV yoga class on Lifetime or PBS or buy one of a myriad of yoga videos, such as *Jane Fonda's Yoga Exercise Workout* or the magnetic *Buns of Steel Yoga. Yoga Journal* is just one of several monthly publications with a rapidly growing circulation. And celebrity yogis such as Raquel Welch, Woody Harrelson, and Sting are making the practice hipper and more popular than ever.

There's a whole yoga market out there. Yoga fans need outfits with plenty of give so the pants don't stretch out at the knees and the belts and cuffs don't bind. There are meditation pillows and collapsible benches for all-day sittings, sticky rubber mats for non-skid, high-energy PowerYoga workouts (some sell for more than $30), incense to put you in the mood, and all kinds of straps, bands, pillows, and poles to help your align your spine and stretch your muscles.

For specific help in business, you can read *Jesus CEO: Using Ancient Wisdom for Visionary Leadership,* by Laurie Beth Jones, based on the motivational skills used by Christ in his relationships. A high standard to live

Heavenly Bodies

Fashion can click into Anchoring. A very tuned-in design team from Arnhem in the Netherlands captivates customers with the sheer magic and erotic joy expressed in their clothes. Geert de Rooij and Hans Demoed named their company The People of the Labyrinths. The two men produce only as much as they can handprint in their workshop. The gossamer silks and soft leathers covered with poetic messages look like opulent 16th-century creations and are in demand worldwide.

Every six months they change their theme—from Lava to Angels to Reverie to their favorite, Taurus. When the whim hits, they may accept a commission to custom design. Recently, Hans related the story about a pregnant woman who requested a special bedcovering on which she could birth her child. They concocted one with "symbolism capturing strong things in life: eagles, lions, hands, crowns, old references such as Ice Age and meditation and new references such as DNA." Prices are high, but each piece is a work of art.

up to. There's also *Sphericles—The Business Oracle: Your Intuitive Guide to Enlightened Business Behavior,* by Joanne Black and Christine Roess. Sphericles are numbered marbles; the kit comes with a guidebook explaining what each number means. To tap into your creative powers, you reach into a velvet pouch, pull out three marbles, then read what the book says about your choices. It supposedly works, "not because there is magic in them, but because there is magic in *you.*" And even if you don't locate the perfect business solution, dipping into the bag during a meeting can spark lively, creative dialogue. The advertising agency Bates Worldwide apparently agrees: They ordered 1,000 kits as gifts.

Some of the more open-minded CEOs we know are consulting with spiritual guides to help them understand their businesses. They hire people like Charles Nunn, who discovered over the course of his business career that he had "intuitive gifts" and that he could "read" people and situations in remarkably accurate ways. Now he's hired to go to board meetings, introduced simply as a "consultant," and then, afterward, fills in the chairman on what he "senses" is really going on. He's a witch doctor and a business strategist rolled into one.

If "intuitive consulting" isn't your thing, maybe "archetypal analysis" is. This involves a myth expert who analyzes the management styles and personalities of your executive team. You can actually find out what archetypes (magicians, warriors, discoverers, travelers, etc.) are active in your company and what journeys these people are on. Why does it matter? Well, a senior management team with a lot of warriors may do well against the competition; the downside is that these same warriors may engage in constant internal squabbling. A deskbound traveler may chafe at his restrictions. A preponderance of discoverers could mean a shortage of people to perform workaday details.

All across the spectrum of the Anchoring trend—from church to boardroom to mysticism—there is a common thread. We are all searching for meaning that transcends the corporeal, the material, the temporary. We long to find a touchstone, something that connects us to the past, to the future, to eternity. We want to do right in our lives and sometimes, being human, we're not sure of the best way to go about achieving that honorable goal. And so we reach out for an Anchor. While we may not always find it, or it may occasionally slip from our grasp, the reaching is in itself a fulfilling and enriching act of spiritual growth.

CLICKING WITH EGONOMICS

Feeling unconnected in the depersonalized Information Age, consumers are drawn to customized, individualized products and services.

Me, *Myself,* and *I* are the driving forces behind Egonomics. "Me" wants customization; "Myself" wants to be a person with a name, not a faceless consumer with a number; and "I" demands individual attention and personal service.

The human potential movement has, in the past generation, become a tenet of American culture. In endless self-realization books, in magazines and on television, at retreats and seminars, we are told that each and every one of us is a unique human being with a basic right to happiness and fulfillment. We have become confident and assertive—a nation of individuals who demand the best for ourselves.

Egonomics is in evidence *everywhere*. Customers want to be in the driver's seat—in many cases, quite literally. The driver's seat in Faith's Mustang can be programmed to perfectly fit three different people. That's Egonomics—thinking about an individual customer's comfort.

Faith's Mustang is just the beginning of auto Egonomics. A print ad for the Lincoln Continental slyly states, "It Knows Your Voice, Height, Even Your Weight. (But Don't Worry. It Also Knows How to Stay Quiet.)" The rest of the copy details how the Continental offers voice-activated phone dialing (just sing out a name) and how the suspension adjusts to your weight and load (luggage, groceries, etc.) so the car stays level and the ride stays smooth. A Lexus ad succinctly sums up the Egonomics message: "For centuries man has adapted to his environment. What about vice versa?"

Egonomics means that business must become more personal—striving to meet often idiosyncratic consumer needs. As the old 9-to-5 schedule fast becomes a quaint anachronism, Egonomic businesses are rushing to adapt. All-night diners and convenience stores were early Egonomics clicks. But now we have Kinko's, the chain of 24-hour copy shops, to run off multiples of reports at 3:00 A.M. We have major supermarket and discount drugstore chains staying open around the clock. Many catalogs will take your toll-free call any time of the night or day. And let's not forget casinos that never close and Las Vegas chapels that are ready to marry you off whenever the urge strikes.

For daily newspapers, Egonomics is truly a matter of survival. Since 50 percent of 18- to 24-year-olds in one poll said they never pick up a paper, the obvious answer is to go on-line. This allows a newspaper to organize itself by topic, so that readers can ignore all the features that don't interest them. Those who don't want to wade through business news or world affairs (and get their fingers inky in the process) can scan and search for the information that matters to them.

In 1989, only 42 newspapers had ventured on-line; today close to 3,000 are taking that route. The *New York Times,* for example, is published on-line every day. The "front page" is a screen of graphical icons (business, sports, entertainment). Readers click (in more way than one) into their passions. One of the pluses of on-line news is finding out what's "behind the story." For real news buffs, it's possible to click and access in-depth information such as court records, press conference transcripts, maps, and photo files. The on-line newspaper becomes a veritable treasure trove of customized information.

Blockbuster Video and IBM are working together to develop a machine that allows consumers to custom-design their own CDs from hundreds of thousands of songs and artists. Time Warner was the first to release an interactive movie; each member of the audience is given a handheld device and votes to decide which choices the characters will make and what the outcome will be. Girl gets boy? Push "A." Kill the villain? Push "B." Interactive movies will click in the future with a generation brought up on video and computer games and used to directing the action of their on-screen entertainment.

Airlines have also leapt on the Egonomics band-wagon, and not a moment too soon. A United Airlines ad tells first-class passengers to "design your own flight experience." You can choose a major meal or a light snack, set the pace of dining, pick times to nap. It used to be that if you didn't eat at the moment the cart rolled through, the food would vanish into thin air. Swissair woos first-classers with a pledge that "every minute you spend with us is your time. To be spent precisely according to your wishes." That includes a concierge at Zurich or Geneva to whisk you through check-in, priority baggage handling, early boarding, and luggage delivery to your home or hotel. On night flights, there's a heavenly

Express Yourself

Nowhere is individuality and personal point of view more important than in art. What better path to self-expression than through music, painting, writing, or performing? What better way to click with customers? Restaurants, cafés, bookstores, even some hair salons are using their empty walls as "gallery" space.

Pernod Liquors has paired up with Liquidtex to sponsor painting parties at New York City restaurants. You can get that licorice-y drink, some paints, and a prestretched canvas with the instructions "Express Yourself."

Malibu Comics, the country's sixth largest comic book outfit, sees the commercial potential in encouraging home artists. They recently ran a "Create Your Own Hero" competition and invited comic book fans to draw and describe a new superhero.

Dream Time Service that supplies a duvet, sheets, and pillows. Wide awake? Watch your own personal video monitor with a choice of more than 30 movies. Another airline has computer games on the backs of seats, even in coach.

Passport to the Future

To speed up the logjam at customs, the U.S. Immigration and Naturalization Service has launched a pilot program called INSPass. This biometrics system records your handprint on an ATM-like card. Preselected travelers get to skip the lines at JFK or Newark airports by inserting the card in a machine and then placing their hands on a scanner. If this becomes accepted worldwide, you'll never need a passport to cross a border again.

Virgin Atlantic Airways, founded by a creative British entrepreneur Richard Branson, offers a unique hands-on approach. On select flights, massage therapists can be booked to knead the kinks out of your neck and shoulders, work the pressure points on your feet, or soothe you with fragrant aromatherapy oils. It's even possible to get a manicure (although not a change of polish—flammables are prohibited). On the ground, first- and business-class passengers can get a free cut, facial, manicure, and pedicure at the clubhouse in Heathrow. With gambling legal above international waters, the airline is trying to set up in-flight video gambling games. Sound farfetched? Not for Virgin. This iconoclastic airline already has a croupier at

Heathrow airport, where passengers can gamble at a blackjack table for frequent-flier miles. Other savvy airports, too, are trying to make layovers more Egonomically attractive.

Egonomics drives The Body Shop when it takes your order for your favorite peppermint foot lotion and refills it through the mail, according to a timetable that you personally set. Ditto for Starbucks's "Encore" coffee delivery, which allows you to write your own delivery schedule—and then change it as many times as you like.

Another Egonomics trick (click?) is venturing off the beaten path to tantalize a new audience. The 18- to 35-year-old market has been avoiding malls and department stores in recent years. What to do? Bring the mountain to them. For instance, Calvin Klein introduced his hit unisex fragrance, CK One, in Tower Record stores throughout the country. Why not low-fat yogurt at sporting goods stores? Backpacks at coffee bars? Frozen dinners at video outlets? You get the picture.

The Burton Group, a British chain of retail establishments, came to BrainReserve for help repositioning one of their divisions, Dorothy Perkins, a 563-unit chain of clothing stores for women and girls. Our strategy was called Bonds & Bridges, meaning the stores had to become more Egonomic by creating closer ties with

Zippy Service

Egonomics enables a company to turn a problem into a profit. Case in point: On a recent trip to Hawaii via San Francisco, the zipper on my black suitcase-on-wheels made by Tutto from Hammacher Schlemmer split far beyond the reach of safety-pin repair. Luckily, the luggage company happened to be headquartered right there in San Francisco. Although it was a weekend, Susan Lee of Tutto personally hand-delivered a new bag. That's turning a negative into a resounding positive! Tutto's personalized service (I felt they really cared about my dilemma and were committed to fixing the problem) made me a loyal customer.

the customer. For example, we suggested that they stay open longer to catch working women, unblacken and use their display windows, and move their cash registers from the backs of the stores to the front. But the biggest contribution, related to the strong pull of Egonomics, was to advise them to build a database of all purchases, so that in future selling seasons if a mix-and-match blouse, skirt, jacket, or accessory came in, they could call up particular customers and either invite them to come in or even send the item to their homes for a look. This concept came in part from a premise long-held at BrainReserve: There should be no difference in service between an upper-crust store and an everyday one. Everyone wants the same amount of attention. If you can deliver it, you can get a customer for life.

Dorothy Perkins stores blossomed under this new Egonomic approach. We'd like to think that BrainReserve is partly responsible for a 91 percent increase in their pretax profits over six months.

We recently recommended on a pharmaceutical consulting assignment that it be made possible to hold an individual's medical records for life. Or store the medical records of all prescription drug users in one central file. This could be cross-referenced so that no one would be taking a potentially harmful combination of drugs from different pharmacies—or if someone was taking a calcium-leaching drug, such as prednisone, he or she could be advised to take calcium supplements. The idea: No matter where you move, no matter what doctors you see, there would be one cohesive medical story on you. Wouldn't it be advantageous to know how many times in your life you'd been on antibiotics and which were most effective?

Egonomics says no niche is too small. If you can click with one segment of the population—and click

Ultimate Egonomics

In an attempt to make computer-generated mis-
sives more human and personal, a "Handwritten
Fonts" CD-ROM has been introduced. It features
300 computer typefaces that resemble human
handwriting. Great for thank-you letters. Even
more Egonomically correct, you can send in a writing sample and, in a few weeks, receive a font
that duplicates your own handwriting.

solidly—you'll succeed. After being asked to speak at
a YPO (Young Presidents Organization) CEO Forum
in Berlin, we were amazed at how many of those in
attendance had made their fortunes on highly spe-
cialized widgets. This trend is about making thinner
dental floss for people with tightly spaced teeth and
wider dental "tape" for people with bridge work. Egonomics is behind Hallmark's Personalize It! line of
greeting cards that lets you customize your cards with
special greetings, terms of endearment, and nicknames.

We Americans are the most self-analyzed and self-
important people on the planet. We know ourselves and
we want to define ourselves—not be told how to live and
what to buy. We demand choices and lots of them. We,

and our families, are unique and special and we deserve that rainbow (oh, by the way, we also want to pick the colors). Companies and individuals who click into this concept and market to magnify a person's sense of self-worth (ego) will prosper.

Ergo, Egonomics.

CLICKING WITH FEMALETHINK

The way women think and behave is impacting business, causing a marketing shift away from a hierarchical model toward a relational one.

N ews flash! Women are different from men. Not inferior, not superior—just different. You knew that already? Sure you did, but over the past decade or so, it's been politically incorrect—and maybe even a little socially dangerous—to say it out loud. Well, politically incorrect or not, it's time to get real.

We interviewed over 4,000 men and women and asked them a simple question: "After living and/or working with a person of the opposite sex, would you say that person thinks in significantly different ways than you do?" Every one of them answered, "Yes!"

Science is backing up this thinking. We can hardly open a newspaper or medical journal without reading of a new discovery about the perceptual and cognitive differences between the sexes. Because of breakthroughs in imaging technology, scientists have been able to track our brain activity. And—no surprise to us—they have confirmed that men and women process information in distinctly different ways.

Brain imaging also indicates that women have greater sensory discrimination than men do. For example, they can read the emotional content in facial expressions more accurately and easily than men. Also, when women recall sad events, they exhibit a larger area of neuron activity in their brains than men do. In other words, neuroscientists have proven what we've known all along: Women are more in touch with their emotions, more observant, more sympathetic. Anne Moir and David Jessel, authors of *Brain Sex: The Real Difference Between Men and Women,* wrote that "women are probably 'hearing' much more than what the man himself thinks he is 'saying.'" Does this mean women make better therapists? Better salespeople? Better leaders?

A professor in Canada, Doreen Kimura, has been working on the very different ways men's and women's brains perceive spatial relationships. Think about the way you read a map when you're on a road trip. If you're a woman, chances are you'll turn the map in the direction you're facing so that you, the car, and the map will all be pointing the same way. For most men, however, the direction the map is pointing means little. Men see a destination as separate and apart from them—and navigate by distance and linear direction. (And when it comes to asking for directions, men's stubbornness is legendary—and very revealing.) This fascinating gender difference has implications for the creators of video games, computer programs, even architects.

Here's another little-known fact with interesting implications: Women can actually see better in the dark than men. How can women use this special ability? Would we make better photographers? Private investigators? Graveyard-shift construction workers? The writer Anaïs Nin captured an essential part of FemaleThink and female "vision" in her statement: "We don't see things as they are. We see things as *we* are." That is, through a FemaleThink filter.

In another revealing study, both men and women were asked to empty their minds of all thoughts. The results clearly showed a cultural distinction: Women's "empty" brains were found to be more active in a region where complex expression takes place, while men's "empty" brains showed higher levels of activity in the primitive zone where aggression resides. This strongly suggests a fundamental difference in the response patterns between men and women, and may indicate that nature—more than nurture—determines the way we function in the world.

The fact is, men and women do think differently and have very different emotional make-ups. The sexes don't communicate the same way, don't shop for the same things, don't buy for the same reasons. In fact, men and women view the world in a fundamentally different light. That's the guiding principle of Female-Think, a trend that will have a profound impact on all aspects of business and society in the 21st century.

We're *not* saying you have to be a woman to click with FemaleThink. Nor are we saying you're guaranteed to "get it" just because you *are* a woman (although the right chromosomes do make it come more naturally). No matter what your gender, the key to tapping into FemaleThink is to be aware of and sensitive to the differences between the sexes—and to learn how to respond to women in ways that recognize and respect these differences. Whether you're a young woman clutching a newly minted college degree, a 55-year-old male CEO, or a 37-year-old female determined to quit her job and follow her entrepreneurial dream, understanding FemaleThink will help you click in life and in business (maybe in relationships, too!).

To a large degree, FemaleThink is a function of

evolution. In the past 50 years, sex roles in our society have undergone a sea change—and there's no turning back the tide. In her Pulitzer Prize–winning biography of Franklin and Eleanor Roosevelt, *No Ordinary Time,* Doris Kearns Goodwin looks back to World War II when millions of American women supported the war effort by going to work on production lines. She relates a story about Eleanor Roosevelt visiting the plant where B-24s were being made. "Once again, Eleanor took special pleasure in hearing that women were 'doing a swell job, better than they expected.' Supervisors reported that women were more patient with detail, more capable of handling repetitive jobs without losing interest, more eager to learn, less prone to hide their greenness, more willing to ask directions and take instruction." Goodwin goes on to quote a male executive at the company: "If I had my way now, I'd say 'to hell with the men. Give me women.'" Today, women make up 46 percent of America's workforce and in the ongoing battle for workplace equality have forged a solidarity that is one of the driving forces behind FemaleThink.

This solidarity isn't limited to factories and offices. Women make connections everywhere they go—schools, playgrounds, supermarkets, gyms, trains, or airplanes. Virtually every encounter becomes personal—women care about the human dimension. This has an enormous implication for any business that wants to click into FemaleThink: *How* you sell to women can be as important as *what* you're selling. Women are looking for a relationship before they make a purchase. They want to know that there's going to be support and personal service after they buy, a human being who's out there looking after their interests, someone they can call with a problem—or a word of praise. This desire for a human connection defines not only the way women relate to companies, but how they engage the world, and, ultimately, how they will change the world.

FemaleThink is sweeping into every corner of our society—and shaking the pillars of power from town halls to the United States Capitol.

Women—and FemaleThink—had a major impact in the 1996 presidential campaign. According to every poll, women favored Bill Clinton over Bob Dole by a wide margin, while the male vote was more evenly divided, tipping slightly toward Dole. Clinton's "I feel your pain" comment may have made him the butt of endless *Tonight Show* jokes, but on the whole, women perceived him as more attuned to them—that is, more genuinely caring and more interested in building consensus than waging battles. It's not far-fetched to suggest that by clicking with FemaleThink, Clinton won the election.

She Wants to Talk, He Wants to Eat

A man and woman sit down at a table. The waiter comes over and introduces himself. "Hi, I'm Andre and I'm an actor." (As we all know, there are no real waiters in the '90s anyway.) The woman is fascinated. She wants to know what shows he's been in, whether she's actually seen him act, where he's studied, how many brothers and sisters he has. The man couldn't care less—he wants his dinner, and the sooner the better. He's interested in completing the transaction; she's interested in establishing the relationship. That's the essence of FemaleThink.

Consider Washington's Ellen Malcolm and her brainchild: EMILY's List. EMILY stands for Early Money Is Like Yeast: It makes the dough rise. The long-term goal: to change the face of power by making the government more closely reflect the make-up of the population—which is 51 percent female.

EMILY's List brilliantly tapped a new market, asking mainly women members to pledge $100 to two recommended female candidates. In fact, in 1997, EMILY's List became the largest political action committee in the country. When Malcolm began in 1985, there were only

12 Democratic women in the House of Representatives, and none in the Senate. Five national elections later, EMILY's List has helped elect 42 representatives, 6 senators, and 3 governors. That's high-powered Female-Thinking!

The 7 women in the United States Senate have demonstrated a willingness to work together across party lines and have shown remarkable gender-based support for programs that benefit women and education.

The underlying theory is that the more women there are in politics, the more emphasis there will be on child care, sensitive welfare reform, better health care— so-called women's issues. But aren't they ultimately human issues?

FemaleThink philanthropy looks different, too. It tends to be conducted on a more intimate, human scale. Carole Isenberg, Hollywood screenwriter and producer (*The Color Purple*), paired with Lynda Guber to start a nonprofit organization called Education First, which aims to send educational messages into the community through the media. "Media is an incredible tool," attested Carole. Education First is running public service campaigns with such stars as Richard Dreyfuss, as well as subtly weaving "stay in school" messages into sitcoms and movies.

Carole's own company, Big Light Films, concen-

Ladies Who Don't Lunch

A strong sense of "we can do anything," even elect a president—maybe a *female* president—radiates when a group of concerned women get together. At a Valentine's Day luncheon given by TV news reporter Judy Licht, we were astounded by the power of working women.

Billed as an annual event for "Ladies Who Don't Lunch," the group included television anchorwomen Lynn White and Magee Hickey, and TV personality Donna Hanover Giuliani, the mayor's wife; writers Nora Ephron, Erica Jong, Barbara Goldsmith Perry, and Gael Greene; Manhattan borough president Ruth Messinger; photographer Jill Krementz; fashion people Frances Grill of the Click Agency (you can guess why we like this name), designer Joan Vass, and her PR powerhouse daughter, Sara Vass, among others.

In an amazing touch of FemaleThink, Judy went around the room, generously introducing each of the 60 or so guests by name and by lists of accomplishments—without using notes. Everyone felt terrific to be in the spotlight. And the recitation made us all aware of the enormity of the female talent in the room.

trates on inspirational ideas. "Film is like a tarot deck," she said in our interview. "It's quite metaphysical." Breaking into film used to be incredibly hard for women. In an effort to pay back her good fortune, Carole often takes on female interns and shows them the ropes. "We have a responsibility to help each other," she says.

In the pre-FemaleThink past, when women felt the need to demonstrate strength and resolve, "Iron Lady" Margaret Thatcher's invasion of the Falkland Islands was held up as proof that a woman could be as tough as any man. But maybe it's time we stopped defining "strength" by male standards. FemaleThink suggests that women's true strengths may have nothing to do with waging war—and considering the world's history and the tragic situations of the recent past in the Balkans and central Africa, we're not at all sure waging war is such a valuable strength anyway.

First Lady Hillary Rodham Clinton understands the power of FemaleThink. At a meeting of about 40 New York professional women, she urged the group to remember the power of storytelling. "Think of all the situations each of us finds ourselves in where telling a story could make people think. For instance, I once sat next to a hotel housekeeper whose husband got very sick a few months ago. If it hadn't been for the Family and Medical Leave Act, she could never have

---

Copping a New Attitude

A sterling example of strong FemaleThink role-modeling is Beverly Harvard, the current police chief of Atlanta. Her particular (dare we say female?) brand of leadership—"by example and consensus"—led to her mayoral appointment. Harvard's untough, unparamilitary style means that police officers can fax her with any suggestions or complaints, skipping right over the usual vertical chain of command. *Every* fax gets a response.

---

taken time off from her job to care for her dying husband. She became aware of the act because of dire necessity, but she said, 'Most of the people I work with have never heard of it.'" Mrs. Clinton ended her point by saying, "Women who have a platform in business and the public sector need to assemble an audience and send out a larger message by becoming story-tellers."

When we interviewed White House Deputy Assistant to the President Marsha Scott, she elaborated on the positive ways women can communicate. Marsha tries to bring a spiritual approach to her worldly position. "It's a big and powerful feeling to have everything lined up just right—to be connected in a larger sense to the world. Women develop networks, strengths of communication. It's all there, when we speak our own truths."

When John Gray wrote his monster best-seller, *Men Are from Mars, Women Are from Venus,* he pointed out that women inhabit their own planet: a planet where they are paid only 72 cents on the male dollar (women account for 75 percent of the world's poverty-stricken). A planet that has installed a corporate glass ceiling (although "cement" may be a more accurate description). A planet where adequate and affordable day care is in short supply, where women are under-represented in government, and where the diseases that afflict women are given short shrift by the medical establishment.

Why should we assume that we can speak to men and women the same way when our experience of the world (along with our brain chemistry) is so different?

Linguistic scholar Deborah Tannen, who wrote *You Just Don't Understand—Women and Men in Conversation,* highlighted key aspects of FemaleThink in an interview in *People:* "Men use language to preserve their independence and maintain their position in a group. Women use language to create connections and intimacy."

Tannen and Gray both make the point that we're

talking different languages, and we have to seek a productive new way to communicate instead of shouting at each other across the void. We have to be translators, interpreters, and diplomats. After all, we may live on different planets, but we share the same real estate.

There are many ways you can use this insight to click with women when you're trying to communicate what you do or what your business does.

The way to reach women consumers is to market to their strengths. That *doesn't* mean ads featuring a woman wearing a tie and clunky black eyeglasses, wielding a leather briefcase, mimicking male rules and roles. Nor does it mean trying to convince the world that we're all the same. What it does mean is emphasizing—and then capitalizing on—how women differ.

We hope and believe that female consensus building (often seen as too "soft") and female sensitivity (often patronized) will be embraced as prized attributes of success, not only in business but in all aspects of life. True, women have a *long* way to go to catch up to men in earning potential and material wealth. But it's also true that more women are working—and making decisions about the way they spend their own money. This market cannot be ignored or kept in the second-class-citizen bin for long.

FemaleThink means the whole image of business

What's Clicking Now?

- One-A-Day Vitamins has introduced a new line with one formula for men and another for women. Their marketing campaign proclaims "People Are Different," a key Female-Think theme.

- FemaleThink was also employed in a commercial aimed at changing the previously macho pickup-truck image of the 7-Eleven convenience stores. The company enlisted comedian Brett Butler of the hit TV series *Grace Under Fire*. She walks around the store, surprised to find her favorite bottled water and yogurt, finally asking, "Is this heaven or what? What, are women running 7-Elevens now?"

- Even the sports world, long a bastion of male chauvinism, is starting to play ball. Hillerich & Bradsby, maker of the legendary Louisville Slugger baseball bats, offers softball gloves and bats designed for women athletes. Anne Flannery, manager of women's athletics at Spalding, said it perfectly: "The 'P' word today is performance, not pink."

will be altered—no longer a war to be won by trouncing the competition but rather a complicated mosaic to be pieced together, one relationship at a time. Female-Think will work because it's efficient, economical, and *effective*. It's a way of reaching out, and being reached, a social as well as financial commitment. Here at Brain-Reserve it won't surprise you that we've tailored our company mission around FemaleThink and seek to work with business partners whose corporate mission and corporate values we share.

Gun Denhart is an entrepreneur who also instinctively understands this exciting new equation. She started Hanna Andersson, her $44 million children's clothing catalog company, in her Portland, Oregon, home. She pioneered a clever concept called "Hanna-downs." Customers can return the clothes their children have outgrown for a 20 percent credit toward their next purchase. The returned clothes are then given to charity. Each month, more than 3,000 articles of clothing are recycled—and customer loyalty to the "company that cares" is guaranteed.

The ultimate meaning of this new vision to the business community? No enterprise will thrive without practicing FemaleThink. And companies that have long been dominated by the OldThink perspective are in for a rude awakening if they think this can be accomplished by the token hiring of a few women in high-profile positions. FemaleThink must be genuinely integrated at all levels, and upper management's commitment must be sincere and determined—and backed up by action.

If you think this "women in business" thing is old news, remember that equality is still in its infancy. Look honestly and closely and you'll see that plenty of solid brick walls (and cement ceilings) are still standing.

At a dinner party in Manhattan not too long ago when the man on Faith's right, who happened to own a multimillion-dollar, medium-sized company, blurted out his opinion that the notion of discrimination against women in the workplace was overstated, Faith bet him $1,000 that there wasn't a single woman at his company within seven levels of his lofty CEO perch. The other dinner guests looked on in silence as he mentally ran through his chain of command. It was a risky wager. There's always the possibility of the token female Human Resources director. Finally, the executive, clearly flustered, admitted Faith won the bet. It was both a pleasing and dismaying victory—but not surprising.

What is the cost of "boxing in" women? Some stay and grumble, but many make plans to leave as soon as they have the opportunity. Our belief is that at least 20 percent of women working for large companies will leave to start a venture of their own. Whenever I say this at a corporate seminar, I look up and see lots of knowing smiles and nods.

Don't Box Me In

We know a female executive at a pharmaceutical advertising agency who pulled in a $30 million account for her firm. After the deal was signed, the head of the company stopped by her office to congratulate her. Intending to show her how she fit into the company, he sat down and drew a picture of a box.

"Here is a box," he said, as if talking to a child. "I'm in that box and our other key executives are in that box. Now, where would you place yourself?"

She smiled and pointed at the space outside the box. He was delighted that she seemed to grasp what he was getting at. "You have been outside the box," the CEO agreed, "but we would like you to come into the box with us."

She smiled once again. Shortly after, she gave her notice and took the big account with her.

Moral of the story: FemaleThink doesn't accept the existence of a box. Women think more in terms of the inclusiveness of a circle—smooth, embracing, no beginning or end. This executive wasn't interested in being

The Cement Ceiling

- Only 13 members of the *Fortune* 500 have a woman among their top five highest-paid executives.
- More than 97 percent of America's upper echelon corporate managers are men.
- Some 94 percent of the *Fortune* 500's board members are men.

locked in an airless box with a boy's club. She wanted a team.

How often have we heard women in traditional corporate jobs complain, "There's got to be a better way." That lament is being replaced by the action-oriented declaration: "I'll do it my way." And for nearly 8 million women, "my way," according to the latest figures from the National Foundation for Women Business Owners, is to start their own businesses. Right now, female-owned companies employ one out of every four workers and generate nearly $2.3 trillion in sales. Women are starting companies at twice the rate of men. That's worth repeating: *twice* the rate.

When a woman starts a company, there's a shift in how success is defined. Financially, it is still (and always will be) about survival. But a woman's underlying motivation for having her own company is more about proving herself, recognizing flex-time issues, and doing something for the common good.

Interestingly, women stifled in a rigid corporate environment often retreat to what has generally been considered a female province: home. Today over 18 percent of all working women are running their businesses from home—and that number is growing by megaleaps. Home may be where the heart is, but increasingly it's also a hotbed of savvy FemaleThink.

We could make endless lists of entrepreneurial women (myself included) who had an idea and started a business at their kitchen tables. In her autobiography, *An Eye for Winners,* Lillian Vernon relates how she started her phenomenally successful catalog (in fact, the whole catalog stampede) at her Formica kitchen table—which still sits at corporate headquarters, a potent symbol of the power of FemaleThink.

Advice to Budding Entrepreneurs

Go with what you know. Women have a better chance of launching a successful business concept if it speaks mainly to women. To narrow the focus even further, target a segmented or niche market. If you're Latina, consider the untapped potential of the 27 million Latinas living in the United States—and the 200 million in Latin America. Compare your ideas to the TrendBank, and if you're trend-based in four or more areas you may be the next big-click female entrepreneur.

Create a small office off your kitchen and begin. Women have always viewed the workday not in 8- or 10-hour blocks, but as a 24-hour cycle. Hillary Clinton summed up the steely aspect of FemaleThink: "For many women, it's an act of courage to get through the day."

We're used to going to a job, picking up the kids after school, helping them with homework, reading a report while dinner's cooking, getting back down to work when dinner's over, trying to get some sleep, waking up if the baby's crying, getting the kids off to school, working again, and so on.

You get the picture. We believe this is going to be the work pattern of the future. But this time, women will be doing it to move ahead their own companies. A typical FemaleThink-run company understands that you have to open at convenient times for your customers . . . or go to their homes to make a sale or explain a product. Don't be surprised if the success of the venture gets a husband or significant other to join up. There's a lot of sex appeal in running your own show.

Crow about your ideas. You know the old adage about "giving credit where credit is due." We would change it to "taking credit where credit is due." Know your worth.

Many studies show that when a woman thinks of a great idea, the men in the room attribute it to the man to her left or right (if they attribute it at all). Women, on the other hand, support, credit, and compliment any idea given. One of our common faults, however, is that we apologize too much (on the job, in conversation). We mumble "I'm sorry" when there's no need. We give indirect directions. We stress the words at the ends of our sentences so our commands come out sounding like apologetic questions: "I'd like you to have that report by Tuesday?" There's the problem we call "share/share": sharing the blame when it belongs to others, or overly sharing the credit—even worse, denying any credit—when most if not all of it clearly should be yours.

For Gayle Martz, a flight attendant with TWA, the click came after her fiancé died. Not long after his death, she found herself stranded in Korea on an extended layover, craving the company of Sherpa, her Lhasa apso puppy. Her answer: design a travel bag that would meet airline requirements and be easy to carry. The challenge: to make the pet comfortable and meet safety regulations. Her soft-sided carrier slips under the plane's seat, has side and top zippers for access, mesh vents for ventilation, a handy pocket for toys, treats, and brushes, and a long shoulder strap and short handles for carrying ease.

Everyone who saw Gayle's handsome prototype

wanted one. Working out of her one-bedroom apartment, with $5,000 borrowed from her mother, she launched Sherpa's Pet Trading Company. After a successful national rollout, Gayle exchanged her overcrowded apartment for more space in the same building, where she and Sherpa still work at home. The Sherpa Bag is now the approved carrier for use on board Continental, Delta, Northwest, TWA, United, and others.

In a reverse move, Karen Dubinsky, a corporate strategist, started her firm in a small office and then, after it grew larger, moved it into her newly purchased town house. She believes the change to a home-based environment has made her thinking less corporate, more familial, more FemaleThink—and more successful. Adding to the integrated work/personal picture, she gets to spend much more time with her adopted baby boy, Jack Rose, who stays nearby in the nursery working on strategies for his stuffed-animal menagerie while his mom solves the problems of corporate America.

Although understanding FemaleThink can provide priceless insight into millions of consumers, surprisingly few large companies have fully seized the opportunity. One notable exception is Saturn, the car company with the "no-dicker sticker" policy. The whole idea of no-haggle pricing is directed at women who traditionally have been intimidated by the aggressive, male-dominated world of car shopping. And for good reason. In a shocking Chicago study of car buying, white women were quoted prices that averaged $142 more than white men. More distressing still, black women were quoted prices that averaged $875 more than those quoted to white men.

Is it any wonder that Saturn, with its consistent pricing and an ad campaign that treats women respectfully and intelligently, has clicked strongly with women? How many times have you seen cars advertised with scantily clad women draped over the hood, a come-hither look on their faces? Guess who those ads are aimed at? And guess who they insult?

On a BrainReserve research outing to 14 car showrooms, the Saturn dealership was the only one that voluntarily popped the hood for a female customer. It was also the only one at which the salesperson offered to help calculate the monthly carrying costs, that recommended a woman customer go out on a test drive, and that had a comfortable place to sit and mull things over with a cup of coffee or soda. And it was the only one with a "day care corner" where browsers could temporarily park their youngsters. In addition, the people at that dealership went out of their way to congratulate and make a gentle fuss over a female purchaser who had stopped in to pick up her new car.

Something different is happening at Saturn. And it's working: The company has built a devoted, cultlike following.

After interviewing 500 women for one of our automotive clients, we found that women, if given a choice, would prefer to buy a car from home. That way, they could avoid the "you're invisible" treatment that all our "undercover shoppers" reported: Salesmen tend to look right through any woman and address all their comments to the man accompanying her. One day, throwing caution to the wind, we went to check out a certain German status car and experienced this firsthand. Not one salesman approached us during the 20 minutes we spent in a Mercedes showroom—even though we did everything from opening and shutting car doors to blatantly kicking the tires.

Such treatment seems downright insane—along with outright insulting—especially in light of an article in *Working Woman* magazine that reported women write the checks and sign the leases for 50 percent of all new cars in the United States—a $67 billion segment! By the year 2000, this number will rise to 60 percent. Couple that with the fact that women influence another 20 percent to 25 percent of all new car purchases, and you begin to grasp the cost of treating women like Casper, the Friendly (but invisible) Ghost.

Another retail sector in dire need of FemaleThink

Old Boy's Not-work

Let's take a look at what FemaleThink most decidedly is *not*. The list below compares Old-Think perspectives—the way businesses viewed the world in the past—with New, or *FemaleThink,* approaches to solving both business and relational problems.

OldThink	*FemaleThink*
Establish vertical hierarchies	Build teams
Focus on answers	Look for the right questions
Rigid role identity	Identity adaptable
Single-minded (the number one)	Multi-minded (the numbers two and up)
Resists change	Seeks change
Goal-driven	Process-oriented
Life as a series of destinations	Life as a journey

is the discount appliance store. When you venture into stores such as P.C. Richard or the Wiz, bring along nerves of steel. Slick salesmen, intent only on closing a deal, invariably try to talk you into a model *they* want to sell, seldom listening to what it is *you* want to buy.

Wouldn't it be refreshing to have a salesperson who could talk knowledgeably about which oven is best for baking a cake or roasting a 28-pound turkey? Who would listen to your needs and just maybe recommend a less expensive model that would meet them? Who didn't try to sign you up for the world's longest extended service warranty, which provides nothing more than an easier drop-off point for repairs? A print ad for NEC CD-ROMs sums up the need for an antihustle approach: It shows a serious woman above the caption, "Don't lie to me." That shows that at least one advertising agency has its FemaleThinking cap on.

BrainReserve helped Chesebrough-Pond's apply a FemaleThink perspective to its current and future marketing platform. What will motivate women, we think, is a concept we have identified as Female Realism. The term indicates that women will want to deal with companies that recognize the reality of their lives, not an ad director's fantasy. The name of Chesebrough's double-whammy face cream, Prevent and Correct, simply describes what it does, without the overlay of "alluring" French mystique or mysterious biochemical "breakthroughs." Its introductory ad was a Herb Ritts photo-graph of a woman holding her face in her hands. No glamorous models, no trumped-up promises to stop time.

This concept came about under the guidance of Patrick Choel, the French chairman of Chesebrough-Pond's, Natalie Danysh (who balances her FemaleThink work life with the reality of raising four children), and Mike Indursky. In its unadulterated honesty, this new direction for beauty-product advertising is a style we see clicking for many years to come.

When we talk to usually, but not always, male corpo-rate executives about FemaleThink-based concepts, we sometimes try to jangle their nerves and hopefully, their preconceptions. Often, their main reason for a "no" is firmly rooted in OldThink. "We're not running a social institution," we are told. "We're running a business." They miss the point entirely. To succeed tomorrow, busi-nesses *need* to be run more like social institutions. And guess what? Whether the OldThink old guard likes it or not, businesses are social institutions. They hardly exist in a vacuum, but rather have far-ranging impacts on communities and individuals. FemaleThinkers under-stand this. Companies that espouse and practice caring and sharing principles will earn unprecedented brand loyalty.

Women connect with companies that have "Corpo-

What's Clicking Next?

For a long time now we've been saying that major soap companies could be brought to their knees if a female-run company decided to market a detergent. Its president as spokesperson, appearing in commercials to discuss the ins and outs of stain removal. Her knowledge would be coming from real-life experience. After all, how many of today's top-rung male executives have ever washed a crib sheet, a pair of toddler's socks, or a silk blouse? Our hypothetical soap company—let's call it WASH (Women Are Stain Haters)—would give a percentage of its proceeds to child-care centers and print information on marital counseling and child-rearing on the box, along with an abuse hot line. It would donate a percentage of profits to the much-needed, and neglected, area of female medicine, and support a program to help feed children in low-income households. No major marketer has clicked into this idea yet, although we never stop spreading the word.

rate Soul," that is, those that direct some of their profits to helping women, children, and the environment. Much to the astonishment of some OldThink CEOs, today's women (and increasing numbers of men) don't buy simply because of coupons, jingles, or even a lower price. Witness the success of Newman's Own, Ben & Jerry's, and the entire whole-foods phenomenon typified by New England's wildly popular (and profitable) Bread & Circus supermarket chain.

A FemaleThink approach would also click for a decidedly female-focused business—sanitary napkins and tampons. Wouldn't it be a good idea for a personal-products company to educate while it sells? How about providing age-specific health information on issues relevant to the teen years, postpregnancy, and the onset of menopause? After all, for some time, pet food companies have been putting out brochures on every stage of an animal's life. Are we really that much more uncomfortable about our own bodies than Fido's and Fluffy's? We call this kind of gender-specific consumer education "Sistering." Information on a wide range of topics from raging hormones to breast cancer to pregnancy could be passed on through package inserts, home gatherings, telephone chat lines, and on-line Sistering sessions. Why can't tampon wrappers have empowering FemaleThink info printed on them such as the top 20 female-run companies and their earnings? Or the packaging could even showcase the work of female artists, the way Absolut Vodka uses famous artists to create excitement and cachet for its product.

At one of our BrainJams, someone came up with the click concept of a company such as Disney, perhaps in conjunction with Microsoft, opening a chain of "day-care-tainment centers" across America. With Disney's wholesome image and knack for producing winning child-centered entertainment, what parent wouldn't feel comfortable leaving a child there? Throw in some mind-expanding but fun learning tools from a Microsoft and the possibilities are huge.

At BrainReserve, we've come up with some ideas that would ally companies and not-for-profit organizations to create opportunities that benefit both. How about National Organization for Women Tampons? Or Rainbow Coalition Cosmetics—similar to The Body Shop concept, but contributing to inner-city job creation, Indian reservations (the ones without casinos), and depleted-resource communities. Perhaps Gay Men's Health Crisis Shaving Cream. Sierra Club recycled-paper plates and cups. American Cancer Society Herb-Veg Teas. American Heart Association jump ropes, free weights, and steppers. When the products reflect some of the standards we live by, that's FemaleThink.

Surprisingly, technology has turned out to be one of women's best allies in business today. We might have had trouble programming our old VCRs, but we know how to log onto the on-line Women's WIRE (Worldwide Information Resource Exchange). As Harriet Rubin of

Doubleday put it in *Inc.* magazine, "Technology doesn't get enough credit for being the feminist's friend. Technology has killed hierarchy. When you get into companies that have e-mail systems, you don't have to be the loudest man or the biggest braggart. It flattens gender differences."

Technology may provide the means to alter our basic perceptions about gender roles. Take our friend and ex-client Carol Peters, who has delved into the "man's" field of high technology. Carol was responsible for developing one of the world's most advanced graphic workstations, Iris Indigo, for Silicon Graphics. Soon after, she left to start her own company, daVinci Time & Space. Its mission is to develop interactive television programming that "learns" a child's interests and capacities and then tailors the program to the individual child, instead of dictating to him or her in a one-style-fits-all format. It's fun, yet challenging, and is personalized based on how quickly the child responds to different cues. Very FemaleThink to have the human interest driving the technology.

"I'll only consider it a success if 50 percent of our viewers are girls," Carol says. "I hope my new programming will change the most basic boy-girl perceptions (how to interact, how to view the world). If we can mold a mind while it's young enough to be open, mission accomplished. By the time we grow up and work together, it's too late. As a woman in a company today, you can get passed over because you don't play golf or pee the same way. No matter how smart you are or how hard you work, you can still never fit the form. So it's time to change the form."

Then there's "Jane's Brain," the on-line chat room for girls ages 12 to 19, which, when first blueprinted, banned boys in order to give girls a chance to flourish. Now, as a real-world experiment, 10 young guys have been invited to join the 3,500 members.

Old-fashioned print media aren't immune to the influences of FemaleThink. A magazine called *New Moon* offers an alternative to the usual fashion/make-up/how-to-talk-to-boys articles. Started by parents in Duluth, Minnesota, who were worried that their daughters were underserved—and underestimated—by other magazines, *New Moon* covers political issues, cyberspace, support groups for children of cancer patients, and other weighty topics.

The end result of the FemaleThink trend for both men and women is that people and companies in *every* category can be responsible, caring, and sensitive to their impact on society and on the communities where they're located. Our relationships can evolve from a transactional level to a deeper and more meaningful one. Our lives—business, social, and personal—can grow richer, fuller, and more satisfying.

170

FemaleThink is spreading, not only in this country, but worldwide. The years ahead will see growing solidarity between women in the developed nations and those denied their basic human rights in male-dominated societies.

We've gone through the Year of the Woman and the Decade of the Woman. But evolution (EVEolution) marches on and women are just beginning to come into their own. At BrainReserve, we believe we're approaching the Millennium of the Woman. We think that in the next thousand years, women will find their true strength—and use it for real world good.

FemaleThink: You don't have to be a woman to see its future.

APPLYING FEMALETHINK

A new market for MetLife.

A life lesson that I learned from my grandparents, local shopkeepers, was that the first place one should look for new business was near home. If you can't develop new customers through friends and family, next best is to scan the neighborhood. That's why, one day, when my sister Mechele Flaum (president of BrainReserve) and I were having a new-business meeting, we decided to revisit this family philosophy.

Mechele said, "Wouldn't it be nice to get an assignment right here in New York City?"

I said, "What about looking right here? Literally, right here." (At that time, our offices occupied the 28th floor of the MetLife Tower on Twenty-third and Madison.)

She answered, "Geographically perfect."

A little later that same week, we had already arranged a luncheon meeting with the people upstairs, Ted Athanassiades, president and COO, and Harry P. Kamen, chairman and CEO of MetLife, one of the most innovative insurance companies around. Although we knew that the company was already actively involved with national women's groups, we came prepared with what we felt was an important question, based on FemaleThink: "How many female entrepreneurs do you sell to?"

They had no idea. Even though they had formed a Small Business Center, they hadn't collected data in a way that would let them identify how many of their customers were women. We countered with an ambitious proposal: "Let us look at female small-business owners and work with MetLife to position itself to help these women realize their potential, and we bet it will represent a $1-billion business for MetLife." It worked. We got the assignment, along with the chance to be shepherded by a real future thinker, Jim Valentino, senior vice president at MetLife. The irony of this project was that by the last page of our final presentation, we had shown how and why, if they were to create a Female-Think division, the target number of a $1-billion revenue stream (originally only an enthusiastic guess on our part) was actually a real possibility—and accomplishable within five short years.

Here was our concept for MetLife. After questioning and listening to hundreds of female entrepreneurs, interviewing more than 50 MetLife executives, and brainstorming internally and with BrainReserve Talent-Bank members, we arrived at a premise that we felt could form the foundation of a $1B business! Transform the "insurance" agent into a "success" agent.

We had heard from many women (just like me) who had started their own businesses, despite a serious lack of organizational know-how. Repeatedly they commented it would have been a terrific help to have had a *mentor*—someone wiser and more experienced—to guide them in figuring out what kind of bookkeeping/payroll system to set up, what kind of telephone/computer system to purchase, and what kind of people to hire.

We confirmed with MetLife that this female market was being undervalued and underserved, and, therefore, they were underpurchasing financial services. What an opportunity! The first company to really demonstrate deep levels of concern would be in position to gain market share and loyalty.

We also looked at the price of ignoring this market. Most probably, some of MetLife's competitors would soon be looking at the same opportunities and grappling with the same issues. The fringe benefit was that this move could boost MetLife's overall strength in the insurance and financial services arena, since once women are won, they tend to spread the word.

Our main idea was to create a program that responded specifically to the needs of the female entrepreneur. Its working title is *FemaleThInc.* and its mission is to mentor female entrepreneurs to their successful financial future. Helping to make it possible is Judy Weiss, senior vice president of MetLife's Small Business Center (800-METLIFE), whose experience makes her the perfect person to lead this exciting and revolutionary initiative.

The success agents would be known as MetMentors. The concept of mentoring was developed from more than 10,000 BrainReserve interviews in which women talked about wanting to do business only with companies they can trust. Clearly, MetLife could benefit from offering an entirely different level of service: mentoring support in lieu of traditional selling.

Here's one of our female respondents' typical take: "I am what you'd call an insurance illiterate. The language is always so complicated and confusing. I still haven't found anyone who can sit down and explain the finer details to me."

In essence, women who are running small businesses could be helped greatly by a female-supportive sales force who would offer them information and advice on insurance and other products. Our spin? Compensate this sales force by a different standard—not by the monetary amount of the policy they sell but by measuring how much they grow their clients' businesses.

Our research showed that there are six general areas of concern to the female entrepreneur that need to be addressed:

1. Nurturing/growing her business.
2. Multiple obligations to family/business.
3. Stress of too much work/too little time.
4. Fear of running out of resources in later life.
5. Lack of access to capital.
6. Desire for individual attention to problems.

By understanding and using FemaleThink, it's possible to design a corporate strategy that will meet real market needs. Since MetLife now has the detailed research and strategic plan to better address female business-owners' concerns, it can chart a course to help them achieve their life's dreams.

I'm proud of this—and I'm proud of MetLife.

CLICKING WITH MANCIPATION

Rejecting their traditional roles,
men are embracing newfound freedom
to be whatever they want to be.

Mancipation is a word we coined for a trend that is just beginning to take wing. The flipside of FemaleThink, it refers to the emancipation of men.

Decades of women's lib, the pervasive influence of confessional talk shows like Oprah, Sally Jesse, Rosie; and the "men have feelings too" message of Robert Bly and John Bradshaw have combined to release the American man from the shackles of machoism. Being "manly" no longer means being distant, disconnected, unemotional, toughened, and analytical. Today men are allowed to be sensitive, to admit their fears and weaknesses, even to cry.

What a free-feeling click!

Just as FemaleThink frees women to live up to their fullest potential, Mancipation allows men to be their true selves. Sentimental, if they want to be; silly, if they're in the mood; tender and caring, when the urge strikes. Instead of always being the shoulder to lean on, it allows men to be vulnerable and even needy—to be the leaner.

Mancipation isn't a "movement." It rejects the pack mentality, acknowledging that every man is unique. Mancipation is about celebrating that individuality, wherever it may lead. This means an end to the clichéd assumptions of male behavior. That men only shake hands, but don't hug or kiss. That men can't remember to buy birthday presents or anniversary cards. Forget it. The Mancipated man is released, free to do anything. And click while doing it.

What brought about this 180-degree turn? Complex and interrelated societal, cultural, and evolutionary developments have all contributed. But the primary driving force behind Mancipation has been, you guessed it, women. There has been a revolutionary change in the way women relate to their families, jobs, relationships, and—most important—themselves.

Women, quite simply, will no longer accept secondary citizenship and the tyranny of a patriarchal society. Women are earning their own money and demanding respect, power, and an end to harassment. Their charge to men: Let's get honest here. And men have started to comply.

Women cleared the path to stereotype-smashing self-expression, and men are following in their footsteps. For some men, "Be All That You Can Be" might mean joining the Army. For others, it might mean giving free rein to an artistic sensibility. For others—if the woman in the family has greater earning potential—it might mean staying home to take care of the kids; 3.5 million do. (A surprising number of men find the househusband role fulfilling.) And for many men "be all that you can be" means indulging their vanity in ways long considered unmanly.

The acceptance of male vanity is a big shift, but hardly without precedent. Once upon a time, men were encouraged to be preeners, peacocks, and fops—complete with powdered wigs and beauty marks. Warriors, from Alexander the Great to the ferocious Japanese samurai, were schooled in poetry and the fine arts before they graduated to swords. In her book *The Natural History of the Senses,* Diane Ackerman relates how "ancient he-men were heavily perfumed. In a way, strong scents widened their presence, extended their territory."

In 400 B.C., Cretan athletes anointed themselves with aromatic oils before competition. Egyptian men would attend dinner parties bedecked with garlands of flowers and drenched in perfume. Roman gladiators rubbed on scented lotions. Napoleon went on his warring campaigns wearing rose or violet lotions under his gloves.

Only since the Industrial Revolution—when men trudged off to the factories—has vanity become the province solely of women. You could say that Mancipation lets men reclaim some of the territory that is rightfully theirs.

As a role model for our de-machoed times, once-flinty Clint Eastwood traded in his monosyllables for the talky and poetic Robert Kincaid in *The Bridges of Madison County*. He wore sandals instead of cowboy boots, carried a camera instead of a rifle, and was always ready to help get dinner ready. *The Bridges of Madison County*—which was a phenomenal success as a novel—is emblematic of Mancipation. Kincaid feels no compulsion to prove his masculinity; in fact he revels in the sensitive, empathetic side of his nature.

In popular culture—movies, television, books, and magazines—and on the streets of our cities and towns, we're seeing more men behaving and dressing in ways that blur traditional sex roles. Some men court androgyny by wearing their hair long, their ears pierced, their clothes fashionable, their bodies toned but not muscle-

Trading Places

It's often been said that if men and women could change places for a day, we'd all be more sensitive to each other's problems. Well, *Ladies' Home Journal* took up the challenge. The magazine's copy ran like this: "Have You Ever Wondered What It Would Be Like to Live as a Man? Or Wished Your Husband Could Walk in Your Heels—For Just a Little While? One Couple Carried Off a Role-Switch—With Surprising Results."

After *LHJ* arranged for a makeover, complete with haircuts, leg shaving, professional makeup, and padded body suits, the transformed mid-thirties couple went out in the world as gender opposites. At the end of the experiment, they shared their findings. Mainly, women smile more than men, show more expression, and are more animated talkers, while men have an easier time getting dressed and have more confidence.

The real woman in the article concluded that the best thing about being a man "was the sense of being able to take up space. I didn't have to sit with my arms crossed and my legs together."

bound. Unlike years ago, this style of dress and grooming isn't intended to broadcast a loud political message. It's a completely natural, unself-conscious loosening up. All kinds of men, from truckers to accountants, are affecting this "pretty" look. (Remember the tinted shag haircut and flowing outfits favored by Liz Taylor's construction-worker ex-husband, Larry Fortensky?) This click will only get stronger over the next years.

In these days of Mancipation, men have achieved the rank of sex objects. Now women swoon unapologetically at the sight of male bodies. The permission to ogle started with Chippendale's and its "take-it-off, take-it-all-off" striptease shows. It went on to the graphic posters for Calvin Klein briefs (bulges, bumps, and all). Now shampoos, soaps, soft drinks, and even automobiles are using men-as-sex-objects to sell the goods.

Nudity and sex may be in the spotlight these days, but there's a new shyness surfacing in the Mancipation trend. The classic rite of passage from boyhood to manhood is being delayed. Keeping your virginity is turning into a badge of pride, not a mark of shame. A survey on sex in America shows that the percentage of 20-year-old men who've never done "it" is greater today than it was several years ago. On the streets, these guys are called "Chase," short for "chastity," and, for the most part, get respect—not chiding—from their peers.

In fact, an organized movement called *True Love*

Waits signed up thousands of young kids who have pledged to keep sexually pure until marriage. This is a new click for teens (could this be the start of a shift away from the enormous number of unwanted pregnancies?). Carefree is seen as careless; abstinence is equated with strength of character.

The no-frills men's magazine *Men's Health* has a very healthy 1.3 million circulation, up 400 percent over the past six years. It covers all the basics about health and fitness, plus gives advice on how to have great sex, lose weight faster, dress for success or seduction, and how to prepare a candlelit dinner for two.

The magazine is only one of a growing number of publications devoted to the care and feeding of the male physique. *Men's Fitness, Exercise for Men Only, Muscle and Fitness,* and *Prime Fitness* (for older men) are just some of the titles. Unlike old-style men's magazines that tended to downplay vanity, this new breed revels in it, with glossy photos of buffed and bronzed models to give men something to aspire to. (And admire. If these magazines are any indication, men are less threatened by the idea of admiring another man's body, especially if it shows the virtues of hard work at the gym or on the playing field.)

Susan Sontag once wrote what might be called the Mancipation Proclamation: "What is most beautiful in virile men is something feminine; what is most beautiful in feminine women is something masculine."

But Mancipation is much more than skin deep.

The passing of the Family and Medical Leave Act plays into the trend. This act, signed into law in the summer of 1993, states that all companies with more than 50 employees (including part-timers) are required to give 12 weeks' unpaid—but job-guaranteed—leave for birthing, adoption, or family illness. True, the law isn't working perfectly (early surveys found that almost 40 percent of employers weren't complying) and few workers can afford to lose three months' salary. Still, it's an important start on the road to widespread, legally protected Mancipation. The Families and Work Institute in New York found that 80 percent of the men it interviewed wanted a stronger role in child rearing than their own dads had. And 57 percent of the men at Du Pont said they would like more flexibility in their work schedules so they'd have more time to hang out with their wives and kids. That was up from 37 percent five years earlier. In turn, corporations are responding to these employee wants—Du Pont now offers many employees the chance to design their own schedules.

Mancipation is even growing popular among big-business executives—a notorious old boy's club with rigid rules of male bonding and behavior, and rampant condescension toward women.

Witness Wolfgang Schmitt, CEO of one of this country's most innovative and well-run companies, Rub-

Lookin' Good

American males spend more than $2 billion annually on beauty and skin-care products. And we're not talking about shaving cream. Men are going for facial scrubs, moisturizers, astringents, masks, toners, and all manner of wrinkle reducers. Kiehl's, the upscale but no-frills cosmetics line, reports that 40 percent of its customers are men. Walk into their "pharmacy" on Third Avenue in New York, and you'll see men lined up to purchase Rose Water Skin Tonic and Special Hair Thickening Lotion.

Elizabeth Grady recently added men to their target audience in advertisements for facials and skin treatments. And in Manhattan, Gazelle, a day spa that caters to the special needs of men (with an emphasis on men of color) recently opened in a posh location high above Madison Avenue.

Belly Buster Contouring Gel, at $30 a pop, and Body Sculpture ("with patented lipoceutical technology") at $35 a bottle, are advertised in *GQ* and fitness magazines with promises to "melt fat cells" around the waistline, the "problem area" for most men.

For those hoping to gain (or lose) weight, there's *MET-Rx*, one of the best selling of hundreds of food supplements that promise to shape and tone rock-hard muscle, virtually overnight.

Once considered the province of pampered women, exclusive health spas and resorts (such as Canyon Ranch) now report that 40 percent of check-ins are men.

For those who've let nature takes its course for too many years, there are more extreme measures. Twenty-five percent of the patients going under the knife for plastic surgery are men. That includes facelifts, pectoral and calf implants, liposuction, tummy tucking, butt lifting, and rhinoplasty. And an estimated 10,000–15,000 men in the United States have had their penises enlarged through surgery and fat injections in a procedure called phalloplasty.

bermaid. The last thing this business visionary cares about is rigid rules and traditions. His inspiration? He tries to apply the rules of nature to his work. Inspiration comes from living on an 18-acre arboretum where he can watch the intricate harmony of 3,000 varieties of trees, a lake, and two streams. Studying natural creation, he devised a system of new-product entrepreneurial teams, much like the leaf system of a plant.

There is nothing abrasive in Wolf's management style. No football analogies or belligerence. He listens to unlikely voices: children and his own intuition. An eclectic thinker, he searches for new-product ideas in unexpected places, from the food storage innovations of the ancient Egyptians to a toy based on his son's interest in farm machines. It works. Rubbermaid was voted one of "America's most admired corporations" in a *Fortune* magazine survey.

In an interview with Leslie Wexner, chairman of The Limited, Inc., a leading specialty retailer, we found some real Mancipated attitudes. In reverse of what everyone has been talking about in the past few years—listening to the inner child as an adult—Les listened to the inner adult as a child. He couldn't wait to be in charge. "When I was five," Wexner reminisced, "I taught myself to draw in perspective. I figured out that the furthest place was the smallest by looking down highways and along the lines of telephone poles. Now I have a library of about 3,000 books on architecture and city planning. I would have wanted to be Howard Roark, the architect from Ayn Rand's novel *The Fountainhead*. But my father insisted I go to business school instead."

The concept of balance is Wexner's definition of clicking. "I believe people need a balance in their lives between personal and career. There's also a balance that goes to community responsibility. We have a moral obligation to use our God-given gifts for the benefit of society."

When we first saw the sweater- and T-shirt-clad DreamWorks trio of Steven Spielberg, David Geffen, and Jeffrey Katzenberg, we thought, "Where's the suit?" It's unusual for three creative guys to get together without a pin-stripe heavy in the mix—that older, wiser banker-type lurking in the background to make sure the bottom line is tops. But Mancipation in business is about acknowledging that it's all right to have fun while you work.

Another major Mancipation click came out of DreamWorks. It seems that Spielberg gave his wife, Kate Capshaw, veto power over the deal. And she only flashed the green light after Katzenberg (closest to an Organizational Man) vowed that Steven would still have plenty of home-time to spend with Kate and the kids.

If the old way of doing business is regimented and hierarchical, then the colorful, freewheeling offices of the advertising agency TBWA Chiat/Day are a shining example of a Mancipation business. There are no outward symbols of power. No titles on the doors, just captions on the walls. No big cushy offices with polished wood desks that gleam with brass pulls and locked drawers. No one in this quirky place, not even a top exec, has an assigned office or even a desk to call his or her own (although you can sign up for a room by the hour or day). Nor does anyone have a computer that belongs only to them. The so-called Virtual Office in lower Manhattan, designed by Gaetano Pesce and Jay Chiat, has a pair of giant red lips, behind which is a "store" that dispenses daily computers and telephones for the roll-around workstations. For those inevitable personal items, there are highly stylized lockers that look like sculpture. It goes without saying that no one has to punch a time clock. On the contrary, Chiat/Day has become a successful model of flex hours, and some of the staff works part-time at home.

At BrainReserve we think this kind of "employee empowerment"—acknowledging that responsible individuals should be able to decide "what needs to be done" and "how long it will take"—will become more prevalent in American business.

Millions of men now stay home while their wives go to the office. Being a Mancipated homebody doesn't necessarily mean whiling the days away vacuuming and watching the soaps, any more than it does for a Female-Thinking woman. Like their female counterparts, many of these men start businesses or do creative work at home. John Stegeman is an example. He runs White House Watch, which produces politically satirical wristwatches, out of his home, while his wife Linda charts the future of voice mail as VP of marketing for Octel Communications.

Daddy Dearest

For men who must work outside the home, parenting often suffers. There just aren't enough hours in the day to spend time with the kids. Richard Fairbank, the CEO of Capital One Financial Corporation in Falls Church, Virginia, has some special advice. Before his children were even in kindergarten, he and his wife decided to shift the young ones' sleep schedules so they could stay up later. The kids were put to bed at midnight or 12:30 A.M. and awakened late in the morning, so when Rich returned home after a day at the office the family would have hours to be together—shopping at late-night stores, reading, and playing.

When the children went to preschool, he and his wife found an afternoon program so they could stay on shifted hours. Now his sons are 10 and 13 and his daughters are 7 and 6 months. "I'm somewhat fanatical about being with them," he said. "It's easy to get immersed in work; the pressure is so great, but you need to pull up, get perspective, and spend more time on the things that mean the most. Otherwise, you are mortgaging your future."

To keep this commitment, Rich made up some guidelines to live by:

1. "Exploit the flexibility of your job, whenever possible." Since he often has to travel or work late hours, he takes advantage of any downtime that comes along.
2. "Force yourself to stick to reasonable hours." Rich shared his belief that "work is like your closet—even if you have twice as much closet space, you still fill up every inch. Work expands to fill the time allotted. So if you mobilize your resources effectively, you can get the same quality of work done."
3. "Work on time-creation." You have to be clever to carve out quality time. Use your idle hours to do things that would otherwise interfere with your family life.
4. "Restructure your activity profile." Instead of taking up something solitary and adult-oriented, Rich made a family activity out of canoeing—and now golf. He's also taken up his kids' favorite sports, soccer and hockey, so he can play with them.

5. "Make your home kid-friendly." "The basement of our house is like a sports facility, and it's an open house for other kids. We temporarily put in a basketball hoop when we were remodeling our sunroom. It just stayed there and the furniture never got moved back in." That's a Mancipated man who puts his family first.

In the past, any man who chose to stay at home—working or not working—was misunderstood and looked down upon. In an interview in *Mirabella,* Estée Lauder talked about the stresses she had to face as her family's prime breadwinner 45 years ago. "My husband, Joe, was the dearest man in the world," she said, "but I was moving further and faster than he. Remember, there was no such thing as feminism then, no rules to help a strong women live with a much-loved but gentler man."

There was no such thing as Mancipation, either. Today, Joe could stay at home and Estée could be more comfortable with her ambition and drive. And their neighbors wouldn't think anything of it.

In an interview in the *New York Times,* Gloria Steinem talked about writing a book with the working title *Men Are Mothers, Too.* It would be about "the need

You've Come a Long Way, Daddy

Now that more men are comfortable helping out with the care and feeding of their kids, what's next?

The movie *Junior* gave everyone a good time by taking masculine hulk Arnold Schwarzenegger and creating an incredible story about a male pregnancy.

While the reality lags behind the fantasy, there's already a product on the market that lets men approximate the experience of what the bulk, weight, and awkwardness of being pregnant feels like. Called Empathy Belly, it's a weighted canvas vest that comes preshaped with a large, extended belly and full breasts. Everything but the craving for pickles.

A recent Johnson & Johnson Baby Shampoo commercial featured a big, burly man hand-cradling an infant's head. The voice-over talks about how short a time before the start of ballet lessons and when boys come knocking at the door. Then it cuts to a shot of that father gently shampooing his newborn daughter's hair. The tender side of Mancipation.

A Lands' End print ad shows one adult-sized and one kid-sized turtleneck. The print reads simply: "Like father, like daughter." How's that for a new angle?

A newsletter, *At-Home Dad,* was started by Peter Baylies of North Andover, Massachusetts. There's a support group in Atlanta called Dad-to-Dad (a good idea for many communities), and a comic strip, "Adam," that features a man with three kids and no outside job. The Internet has clicked in with newsgroups such as Full-Time Dads and NFL, the National Father Line, that address issues of particular concern for full-time dads.

for men to be parents. We've proven that women can do what men did, professionally," Steinem said. "But we haven't convinced ourselves, or them, that men can do what women have done."

Of course, not everyone is pleased by this trend. In one backlash article in the *New York Times* entitled "Men Whose Wives Work Earn Less," the writer tried to prove that working women sap husbands of earning power. It was argued that men who don't devote all their waking hours to their jobs are not as successful—simply because they don't accomplish as much as their driven colleagues.

That's anti-Mancipation, and as dated as a Davy Crockett hat.

What's Clicking Next?

Any product or service that panders to a kinder, gentler, but still strong man is bound to appeal to the Mancipated man and his FemaleThink significant other.

Advertising will emphasize that a man's man can also be a woman's man, and a child's man. There is room for more beauty products that work for men, too. For instance, if so many Dads are caretaking their infants, shouldn't there be lotions to make masculine hands softer? Or changing tables that come in adjustable heights to accommodate a taller man?

With more men staying home and doing household chores, advertisers will stop marketing detergents and cleaning products to women only. Some will create products such as cleansers and polishes with unisex scents instead of the stereotypical "powder-fresh" floral fragrances.

Mancipation is spreading, getting stronger, and finding increased acceptance in mainstream culture. In a marriage announcement in the *New York Times,* the bridegroom, Joseph Baumer, 27, a securities trader at J.P. Morgan, was very offhand about his future plans:

"He talks about family life as excitedly as some men talk about hanging out at bars with models. 'I'm a trader, a job I picked partly because the day is over at 4 P.M.,' he said. 'I plan to be home at 5 with my kids.'" Another Mancipation Proclamation, and one we can expect to hear echoed in boardrooms and locker rooms from coast to coast.

The American male is no longer afraid to express his inner needs and wants. He has been freed, ironically, by his female counterpart. With women busting out all over, living full and actualized lives, seizing power, making money, and having a terrific time—well, men are starting to feel a little bit like the parade is passing them by. And so they too are busting out of the straitjacket of traditional sex roles. They're exploring all aspects of their souls and psyches—and discovering that there's a lot more going on in there than they had imagined. And that, yes, it feels good to openly express your feelings, to allow yourself to be tender and caring. That there's a deep satisfaction to be gained by expressing your creative urges, even by pampering yourself. Not macho, Mancipated.

CLICKING WITH 99 LIVES

Consumers are forced to assume multiple roles to cope with the time pressures produced by ever busier lives.

The highly charged 99 Lives trend, once careening ahead at breakneck speed, has settled down into a somewhat less frightening and more manageable mode. The idea that we have too little time, too many responsibilities, and not enough of ourselves to spread around is now a given. How many times have you heard the lament, "I wish I could clone myself?" Or the exasperated, "I just can't be in two places at one time." It's a fact—being overscheduled, overcommitted, and always on the run is a fundamental part of our late-20th-century lives.

What's new is how we're coping with what sociologists are calling our "time-compressed lifestyles." We've learned to use every moment efficiently, often with the help of our high-tech toys. These days, no one starts at the beep-beep-beep of pocket data organizers, or stares at a harried executive walking down the street barking orders into a phone. We at BrainReserve admit to being completely addicted to those two-minute, credit-card-sized Voice It recorders, using them for quick meeting recaps or reminders. The contents can be turned into a memo before you can say "click."

Consumers have also become accustomed to stores that do double duty—Laundromats that sell videos and supermarkets with ATMs in their aisles. And speaking of supermarkets—those emporiums where we used to buy the ingredients for a meal have undergone a 99 Lives remake. Today we are just as likely to walk out with a steaming hot repast ready to take home and eat (or devour in the car on the way to yet another commitment). And many times, even the supermarket seems too daunting (there may be a long checkout line). So we head for junk-food central, the inevitable strip mall lined with every fast-food chain in creation. Those who still insist on using their kitchen stoves clip magazine recipes that promise scrumptious meals in 20 minutes or under. At our Clicking seminar, one of the biggest laughs comes when we flash a cartoon of a kid watching his mom putting something into the microwave and complaining, "Two minutes? I thought you said it was instant."

We are a bombarded people, assaulted with thousands of images, messages, and enticements. But . . . if you can do something, make something, or license something that stands out in this hall of mirrors, it can definitely click. The secret: Zip into the fast lane—products and services that save time and/or effort. It's that clear-cut.

In the coming years 99 Lives will steadily accelerate. Time will be measured not in minutes but in nanoseconds. A coveted watch in Europe and Japan is the German-made Junghaus, the most accurate timepiece on the market. It's guaranteed to lose no more than one second in a million years.

Madison Avenue is a good gauge of how entrenched we are in the 99 Lives trend. Advertisers continually remind us that they know just how busy we are: "You have such precious little time, you even pay someone else to smell the roses," one TV spot announces. Whirlpool empathizes, "If only you could duplicate yourself," in a print ad featuring photos of a mother doing her daily tasks—holding the baby, lugging bags of groceries, walking the dog, cooking, talking on the phone. Just a routine nonstop day, clicked into 99 Lives.

Another approach used by advertisers: Products

that help you "get things off your mind." The prescription birth-control product Depo-Provera made by Pharmacia & Upjohn Inc. now comes in an injection form, with the enticement, "Introducing Birth Control You Think About Just Four Times a Year."

Every time Lys has to fill up her hefty gray Ford Explorer, she invents new ways to speed up the long, boring process of standing and hand-squeezing the nozzle while 20 gallons of gas is pumped into the tank. "Until we go electric, why can't some advances be made?" she wonders as she plays the "what-if" game. What if, for instance, you pulled up, pressed buttons for octane/amount, and an automated nozzle reached out to quickly pressure-pump the gas into your car? Or what if the tank opening was underneath the car, and fed in from the ground? What if you could slip your credit card (or debit card) into a slot on your dashboard to pay for your gallons?

A service station in Coconut Creek, Florida, came up with an entertaining way of making double use of the time spent filling up the car. The owners installed mini-TVs right into the pumps so customers could watch while they gassed up (and perhaps pump a little longer).

Several states are moving to shorten the aggravation associated with driver's license renewal. The New York State Department of Motor Vehicles has "adopted the attitude of the private sector." It has an office in mid-

Faster Food

Another sign that the 99 Lives trend is not abating is the success of even faster ways to get fast food. Now, drivers in a hurry (what other kind are there?) don't have to get out of their cars. Drive-throughs have become the biggest source of sales for many of the major fast-food chains, accounting for over 40 percent of sales in Southern California. Both McDonald's and Taco Bell say that drive-through customers account for 60 percent of their sales. Anyone starting a restaurant should know that one meal in ten is now eaten in the car. And more than 50 percent of meals are taken out, not home-cooked. Research from the NPD Group finds takeout meals eaten with the kids are among the fastest-growing categories of restaurant fare. And kidless meals eaten at restaurants are expected to become the industry's key growth sector.

Wouldn't it be nice if someday you could fax in your fast-food order, pay by credit card, and have the food ready when you arrive? It's on the drawing boards. There is a tracking feature that lets you scan for oncoming gas stations, rest rooms, and such—the first step in fulfilling that 99

Lives fantasy—although it's expensive—about $1,800 per vehicle.

In that same vein is a system written up in *Business Week* magazine that turns a "car's computer into a restaurant guide on wheels." By analyzing your past eating patterns (what restaurants you've gone to before, when, why, and with whom), the "smart" program, designed by Ray E. Eberts of Purdue University, can predict where you'd like to eat at any given moment. Next? We'd like a similar personalized guide to concerts, dances, movies, and other happenings.

town Manhattan called License X-press that promises to renew your driver's license in no more than eight minutes. Your mug shot, stored digitally, only needs to be updated once a decade. Increasingly common around the country are automated E-Z Pass tollbooths that "read" your car's identification sticker, then deduct the toll from your prepaid account.

Traffic jams are a hated fact of life in larger cities, but in Houston, the City Traffic Center has started a program to transmit information via television monitors to the larger office buildings, letting workers know how to avoid rush-hour tie-ups before they ever get into their cars.

Recognizing that we will never be able to escape *every* traffic delay, it behooves 99 Livers to spend unavoidable "aggravation time" in some activity that is more productive (or relaxing) than the traditional stew-and-simmer. In an interview with Diane Sawyer, the ABC television newswoman talked about her antidote for being stuck in a car: "I like to keep a book of poetry in my purse for traffic jams." Calling time, or rather the lack of it, "one of the big problems of the '90s for two-career families," she observed that "no one has the time anymore for extended conversations. My husband [Mike Nichols] and I get in the car just to be able to finish sentences."

When budgeting time (and money), it's helpful to see where you're wasting it. Write out a timed activities chart for your day and you'll be surprised at how long mundane things take. Project that timetable out to a year, or ten years, and you'll really be shocked. A daily shower could mean a quarter of one of your precious waking hours gone. Add ten minutes or so to blow-dry your hair and the time really gets eaten up. (No, we're not suggesting that you forgo personal hygiene.) Watching television is the number one time-burner in America, with video and computer games coming in a close second. If these activities are crowding out more productive endeavors, a reevaluation may be in order.

Another way for those living 99 Lives to save time is

Helping Hands

One of our favorite clicks is designed especially for second-home owners. A central outfit does *everything* for you—not just the standard pre- and postvisit cleaning, but food shopping, event planning, repairs, even waiting for delivery people—all hassle-free and at a fixed hourly rate. A weekend spent in Deer Valley, Utah, at our pal Audrey Friedman's "ski-in, ski-out" house opened our eyes to this clickably ingenious idea for catering to harried 99 Livers.

What makes the idea so special is the care given to details. First, Polaroid snapshots are taken of every corner of your house so as to assure that when the cleaning staff finishes, everything is put back in the right place. Even your bed pillows are arranged exactly as you like them. You are interviewed about your preferred brands so that the larder is stocked with your favorite honey mustard, not the grainy kind.

Before you and your guests arrive, tickets are purchased for the local symphony or reservations are secured at popular area restaurants. Appointments are made with massage therapists, aerobics instructors, or perhaps a trail guide for a mountain hike. All that's left for the host and hostess to do is to relax with their guests and share uninterrupted time exchanging ideas and life plans.

Another small example of the helping-hand concept is the Elephant Secretary, a 24-hour service that remembers all your important birthdays, anniversaries, and holidays, then selects and sends out cards in *your* handwriting.

Or how about a lawnmower that works without you to guide it around the yard? The solar-powered Turtle, a green robotic mower from Sweden, crawls around on its own cutting your lawn. The click here is the unspoken promise: It takes over one of your 99 Lives while you concentrate on something else (hopefully something more enjoyable).

to call ahead—to your doctor, hair stylist, mechanic, or whatever—to make sure your appointment is still on schedule. You can save hours of waiting time if you know ahead that someone else is running late.

Technology is often viewed as a time-saving savior. Think again. Often we rush to embrace something new without considering all the consequences. In fact, so-called advances often make certain tasks more complicated. Take voice mail. Remember when you strolled into your office and were handed a packet of little white or pink message blanks that told you who had called? You could view them at your leisure or shuffle through them, prioritizing the messages as you cradled the phone on your shoulder. So is voice mail any more efficient than a receptionist? And as for those endless electronic menus you have to sift through when calling just about anyplace nowadays—why can't they all include a "scroll through" feature so we can cut to the beep?

Gadgets have become an integral part of our daily lives, helping us connect in all sorts of ordinary, and even some bizarre, ways. A few years back, a distraught man called radio talk-show host Howard Stern and announced that he was standing on the George Washington Bridge, contemplating a fatal jump. Stern and several of his listeners tried to calm the man down. Then some of the responding police officers called in to say a few words to the listening audience. Several passing drivers who had stopped to offer their assistance also called in with updates. Using a cellular phone to participate in a "group-therapy session" is taking 99 Lives to the max—and, in this case, it helped to save a life.

Another gadget that's often time-saving (and almost always addictive) is a fax machine. It's faster to scribble a note than get involved in a phone conversation. It's clearer to mark an "X" on a map of your town

Noise Neutralizers

This is probably the next "must-have" appliance for your home, your car, and your 99 Lives. Imagine being able to blot out the ear-splitting din of leaf blowers, power mowers, chain saws, electric generators, low-flying jets, cement trucks, car alarms, vacuum cleaners, washing machines— well, you get the idea. The microchip technology exists that can compute the pattern of the offending sound waves, then duplicate the direct opposite pattern, which cancels out 50 to 95 percent of the irritating noise. The principle of yin and yang miraculously reduces loud sounds to a quiet hum. This technology can already be found in some automobiles such as the BMW 5-Series.

Japan Air Lines passes out noise-canceling headphones on some of its flights to enhance the movie experience. Small companies in Stamford, Connecticut, and Phoenix, Arizona, are working on developing lightweight headsets for consumers. The best part about "active noise reduction" is that, unlike stuffing your ears with cotton or plugs, it allows you to still hear conversation, music, or a ringing telephone while blanking out the nerve-jangling blasts of modern living.

and fax it to someone than to give lengthy directions to your house. It's more fun (and infinitely easier for some of us) to fax a roughly drawn heart and flower than to say something mushy. And it's a lot quicker and cheaper to fax a letter internationally than to mail it.

As millions of us embrace the accoutrements of 99 Lives, there's a distinct undercurrent of trend backlash. For many, this means taking a breather from the barrage of information that assaults us daily. Don't you ever feel like screaming at the endless litany of call-waiting interruptions and faxes and E-mails? The arrival of still another magazine, newsletter, or catalog can make us want to light an information bonfire. The communications avalanche is adding to the stress of trying to simultaneously live 99 Lives.

We crave downtime, private time—unbuzzed, unbothered, unbewildered time. But finding peace of mind isn't easy when you can be reached 24 hours a day. Clicking with the backlash is the manufacturer of Gotta Go, an interruption gimmick to end unwanted phone calls quickly. Gotta Go is a call-waiting imitator that emits a tone exactly like a phone company tone, only it's under your control.

You also know there's a 99 Lives backlash when the classifieds carry ads for late-model, barely used television sets. It's a badge of courage to be able to say, "I don't have a television in my bedroom" or "in my week-

CLICKING WITH 99 LIVES

The Living Is E-asy

The Electronic Messaging Association estimates that the number of E-mail senders will leap by 50 percent this year to a very well-connected 60 million. As of March 1997, there were 40 million E-mail addresses. About 30 percent of U.S. households now have a PC and—with prices falling dramatically—the numbers are multiplying faster than bunnies. America Online and Shoppers Express have joined forces to provide interactive home grocery and pharmacy delivery services. Streamline, a new interactive venture located in Boston, reports 500 orders a week for home delivery of groceries, plus many once time-consuming chores like film developing, dry cleaning, even FedEx mailings. Banking and bill paying by home computer is becoming commonplace. Even "tele-medicine" is teetering on the edge of a virtual explosion, with networks linking doctors, patients, nursing homes, and even prisons. Hollywood is getting instant feedback on movies via Prodigy. Artists are painting, dancers and choreographers are working out their movements, and musicians are composing—all on-line. And now Echo on-line is soothing psyches, offering on-line group therapy with a board-certified social worker for about $100 a month.

end house" or "where I go on vacation." We're certain there's a backlash under way when friends who have always prided themselves on being well informed shrug and say, "I can't read [see, hear, view] everything." The overriding feeling is, "Enough already. Turn off the assault." Staying informed takes too much energy.

If we are going to keep our sanity, the key challenge in the next few years will be how to manage information and communications tools. We're already seeing consultant companies with names like Internet Navigators and Network Buddies that are clicking by helping us deal with *information overload*. The best of the new on-line consultants will not only help you make connections but also *dis*connections. We're calling this "DeTeching."

It's not unusual to hear of people running up thousands of dollars in monthly on-line charges. There are some college kids who don't want to shut off their computers and leave campus for spring break (ugh! the boring old sun and sandy beaches of Cancun) because they're "mudding"—exploring Multiple User Dimensions (MUDs). These are computer programs that serve dual and triple purposes. Users walk around, chat with other characters, explore monster-infested areas, solve puzzles, socialize. Very addictive. The day is around the corner when there will be a recovery program to wean people off-line. "Hi, I'm Bob. I'm a computer-holic."

Enough Already

Out on the eastern tip of Long Island, there's a club for cranky, old-fashioned types who solemnly pledge to hang up on voice mail, avoid faxes, and never utter the dreaded word "interface." They believe that if any computer should catch a virus, no one should seek a cure. This group of curmudgeons calls itself the Lead Pencil Club (a self-described "pothole on the information superhighway"). One of its leaders fired off an editorial to the local paper complaining that American culture has gone "Gizmo Gaga." The writer, Bill Henderson, said he overwhelmingly favors "the lead pencil—simple, erasable, light, portable, and responding immediately to the greatest computer of all, the mind." He fears that unless something is done, we'll all be facing a cold and lonely future. "We won't write letters to friends because we won't have any friends—just electronic images approximating faces on screens. 'Handshake' and 'hug' will become anachronisms." But since it's impossible to turn back, we have to click into ways to live with the gadgets while retaining our human connections.

Another big issue to click with: the concept of how well you work as opposed to how long you work. For living proof that a slower pace and higher concentration can be more valuable to clicking than frantic, longer hours, take note of one of the movers and shakers in the business world: powerful billionaire John Malone, who became president and CEO of Telecommunications Inc. at the tender age of 32. Malone, 55, works only five hours a day as TCI's chief executive and always goes home to eat lunch with his wife. Professionally nicknamed the "Darth Vader" of communications, he has miraculously managed to keep his private world private.

The quest for a respite from 99 Lives reminds us of those times in kindergarten when we would put our heads on our desks and rest after cookies and milk. It's also similar to the search for the dreamy solitude that Thoreau found on Walden Pond: "A cabin on a pond a mile away from your nearest neighbor." One way to find your own Walden Pond is to do something totally different from your routine. Peter Roaman, a New York textile executive, recharges by playing the bass fiddle in a small band called the Cool Jerks. The band's motto: "Legends in Our Spare Time."

The lucky among us can drop out momentarily, unplug, or set our own limits, but others have a much tougher road through their 99 Lives. Filling the fractured hours with fun and games is seldom, if ever, pos-

---

Quiet Time

Some companies are trying to slow down their own little worlds—using employee meditation breaks, *t'ai chi* exercise groups, and simple doodling. A California company encourages everyone on staff to take a deep breath when a phone rings, then answer it casually on the third ring instead of compulsively on the first. We've heard of another laid-back place that has instituted a companywide Quiet Time. Every workday morning, between the hours of 10 and 11, all phones are turned off and messages routed to voice mail. The fax and copy machines are unplugged. Quiet Time has reportedly become the most productive time of the day.

---

sible. Today, over 7 million Americans are holding down two jobs just to make ends meet. Most of these multiple-job holders are married, and, for the first time, there are statistically as many women as men in this category.

Rebellion against 99 Lives can lead to an acceptance of our imperfections (which may be healthier anyway). It's the white-glove housekeeper who finally overlooks those dust bunnies multiplying in the corner. The workaholic who starts playing hooky from the job. The control freak who learns to delegate. With the time line accelerating, we must find ways to impose speed limits on our lives. Or, if we can't do that, we must at least understand the boundaries.

We've all started to take a good hard look at our 99 Lives. Yes, we're doing more. But are we happier? More fulfilled? Isn't that, ultimately, what it's all about? Is it time to shed some of our personas, responsibilities, and gadgets? (See next chapter.) What should our goal be as we race through 99 Lives at breakneck, stress-filled speed? We think it's obvious—to cut the craziness in half, and get back to a mere 49.5 kinder, gentler, happier lives.

CLICKING WITH CASHING OUT

Stressed and spent out,
consumers are searching for fulfillment
in a simpler way of living.

For years the American dream was epitomized by *more, bigger, better,* and *faster.* No longer. Today we dream of less. No boss, no red tape, no climbing or clawing your way to the top. Working the hours we want, with the clients we choose. Setting our own schedule and calling our own shots. Making do with last season's car, boat, computer, or evening dress. It's what we call Cashing Out, the low-keyed trend that recognizes that quality of life is more important than the title on the door. We know we'll be happier in the long run if we like what we're doing—rather than doing it just for the paycheck or because that's what we've been educated to do.

Cashing Out isn't about dropping out or copping out. We've actually thought of changing the name of this trend to "opting out"—out of a boring job, a bad neighborhood, a deplorable school system, and, most important, a corporate mind-set that doesn't appreciate mavericks, doesn't applaud loyalty, and has no demonstrable will to help us survive.

When we at BrainReserve first coined the term "Cashing Out" back in the '80s, it centered on, as we said in *The Popcorn Report,* "some fast-track, hard driver —maybe a Wall Streeter or a corporate executive—who suddenly (it seems) leaves his briefcase in the out-box and resurfaces making goat cheese in Vermont. Or running a small New Hampshire newspaper. Or a dude ranch in Montana. Or an environmental action group ten blocks from his old office. Or a classical guitar lover's newsletter ten steps from his bed."

Cashing Out still embodies this same idea, but the trend has evolved to a higher level for many reasons. First off, we have even less trust in the corporate life— and less desire to wear the old gray flannel suit. We're less scared to take a chance. Also, advances in technology have made it easier to set up a home office, put together a professional-looking newsletter on a laptop, and contact people by fax and E-mail.

If you've done your homework, and selected a dream so strong that the thought of *not* doing it makes you really unhappy, then you're ready to lay your cards on the table and Cash Out. One Casher Outer we know, Steve Bromberg, formerly of the *New York Post,* said he figured out it was time to work at home when the paper had its third or fourth management shift. Steve felt he'd do better helping his wife, Linda Kallman, grow her public relations business—and would rather be editing her corporate newsletters than the *Post*'s sports news anyway. Besides, Steve figured, in the event it didn't work out, he would still have spent a year with their kids (a benefit he never dreamed of pursuing when he was younger). Timewise, he thought that if he needed to, he could bounce back into the corporate world at his same level if he gave less than two years to the experiment. It's seven years now and Steve and Linda are still the epitome of this trend.

In his book *Entrepreneurs Are Made, Not Born,* Lloyd Shefsky points out that the typical entrepreneur perceives risk differently than a more traditional, buttoned-down businessperson. The "worst case" means going back to the corporate world. Shefsky mentions one study that showed that even though entrepreneurs may work long hours and get very little sleep, such self-starters claim they get a better night's rest than when they worked for others. Talk about fulfilling your dreams.

Flowering Dreams

We read a true story in *New Age Journal* that perfectly exemplified this click. Doug Self told about using Shakti Gawain's book, *Creative Visualization,* to try to find a way to change his life. After doing the exercises, he became convinced that he and his ad-exec partner should go to Hawaii, look for land, and become flower farmers. Even though he thought it was "the wackiest thing I could have come up with," his visualization work gave him five specifics about the land: two acres, near the ocean, fertile soil, a good growing climate, and a great neighborhood.

They flew to Maui and knew after a day of looking that they'd found their dream spot overlooking Waipio Bay. But, alas, someone else had already sealed a deal on the land. On their last sad night there, not only did they find out the name of the owner—the author Shakti Gawain (small world, big coincidence)—but that same evening, the phone rang with the shocking news that the original buyer had just been killed.

Doug and Guy got the land they'd envisioned for their flower farm and settled in to till the soil. It wasn't all a dream come true. When their short-term debt overwhelmed the bank's long-term trust, the partners quickly turned a glassed-in meditation and yoga space into a bed-and-breakfast. Doug explained that "by sharing the land, we were able to stay here—and this also allowed us to bring the special energy of the place to others."

Ranching is another daydream category. Kim and Sue Fowler closed their small construction firm in San Diego and opted for a life in Oregon, where they began Skyline Bison Ranch and raise herds of buffalo. Very low-maintenance animals, buffalo are becoming popular with the American consumer because their meat is lower in fat. After the initial investments, it's even possible to turn a profit as a bison rancher. But the main reason to go into the herding business is far simpler: open skies and open minds.

All over the world, the corporate system is undergoing radical change. As the global economy takes hold, corporate loyalty to the United States—not to mention individual communities—is fast disappearing. What was previously one of the main selling points of a big-business job—security—now seems like a quaint anachronism. Increasingly, college grads are shunning big companies. Smaller businesses are taking over as the chosen places of employment. According to *Inc.* magazine, the five-year growth rate of the country's top 100 small businesses is over 3,000 percent, a figure the magazines states "approaches the incomprehensible." One reason that small businesses are flourishing is because talented people want to work for them.

In *Powershift*, Alvin Toffler tells us we're moving away "from an economy of monoliths. The small business entrepreneur is the new hero (and often heroine) of the economy." Toffler sees an "economy built of boutiques, rather than behemoths (though some of the boutiques remain in the belly of the behemoth)," by which he means those small firms that stay in a "power-mosaic" arrangement with bigger ones. A good example would be the small bioengineering labs that have been partially acquired by large pharmaceutical companies. Likewise, start-up computer-component firms often align with Microsoft, Apple, and IBM.

Toffler goes on to talk about a new breed of people he calls "business commandos," who know how to build businesses on their own terms and work by a whole new set of rules. If, as Toffler believes, "the power of the market is downshifting into smaller businesses where opportunities seem much more unlimited," it will become commonplace for every person to Cash Out at least once during the course of his or her career.

Margery and Larry Nathanson, parents of Erica, an assistant project director at BrainReserve, made their exit from the advertising and design worlds to successfully pursue what had been their hobby. They opened Grass Roots Garden in New York City's SoHo neighborhood, doing plant-scaping for interiors and terraces. Also in this category would be Michael Jordan, the Chicago Bulls' basketball superstar who took time off from the team and his megabucks contract to fulfill a lifelong dream of playing pro baseball. (So what if Jordan's foray into baseball paled in comparison to his hard-court escapades?)

Doctors and lawyers, as well as corporate types, are ardent about Cashing Out. Dr. Hy Lerner gave up a career as an epidemiologist to open Baldwin Hill Bakery in Massachusetts. He sells thick, chewy, stone-ground whole-grain breads. We also heard about an orthopedic surgeon in Florida who traded in his rubber gloves for boxing gloves. At one point, Dr. Harold Reitman's record of eight wins and two losses actually made him the International Boxing Council's 12th-ranked heavyweight. Pow! A click punch.

Cycle Time

The Cashing Out bug bit Richard Dittmar while he was working at GTE as a computer technician. Since he spent his spare time bicycle racing as part of the U.S. Cycling Federation, he knew all about taking bikes apart quickly and efficiently. So, without leaving his job, Dittmar went to bike repair school and started a service-oriented home business in Tampa called Bike Ambulance. Dittmar picks up, fixes, and returns bicycles in need of repair. To get his venture off the ground, he cultivated new customers by placing fliers on every bike he came across, especially targeting the bike racks at the nearby college campus. When the business started to look promising, Dittmar quit his computer job to concentrate on his passion. Now he's fixing as well as selling bikes. His latest offshoots? He partnered with Weight Watchers to offer trail-riding jaunts, and advertises his three-day, long-distance "bike road trips" nationally and through local hotels. In an interview with the *Tampa Tribune*, Dittmar said, "It's everybody's dream to have their own business, especially something they love so much. I'm living that dream."

There's even a magazine based on the idea of repri-
oritizing your life. Called *Simple Living,* its Cashed Out
editor, Janet Luhrs, has a law degree but chooses instead
to spread the word about consuming less and enjoying
life more. In fact, this lifestyle choice has a movement
attached to it: Voluntary Simplicity.

There's also a new wave of 20- to 30-year-old children of fairly well-to-do boomers who have their minds
set on starting out as entrepreneurs. They're what we
call "Earlypreneurials"—people between the ages of 25
and 35 who aren't afraid to take the risk. In many cases,
these are young women whose moms had personal
experience with hitting the glass ceiling and warned
their daughters of the frustrations of a corporate career.

Look at the unusually named Me and Mom
restaurant in Greenlawn, New York. It's owned by a
mother/daughter team, both runaways from corporate
America. There's also Best Friends Cocoa, started by two
female friends in Massachusetts who took their favorite
recipe for cocoa and managed to sell it to restaurants
along the East Coast. Or Gooseberry Patch, a mail-order
catalog of inexpensive country nostalgia items developed by two friends. It reads like a chummy newsletter,
offering cookie cutters and cinnamon-scented candles
(the best-selling home scent by the way, followed by
gingerbread), and now has $4 million in yearly sales and
up to 75 employees during the holiday rush.

Just looking at the numbers of those we can safely label Cashing Out/Cocooners makes for quite an amazing picture: 1.4 million U.S. jobholders are working for themselves. The vast majority run single-person businesses out of their homes, with varying goals and results. Marilyn Ross, of Communication Creativity Inc., which publishes books on small businesses, makes a distinction between part-time, $20,000-and-under entrepreneurs in vocations like crafts and repairs and those $60,000-and-up professionals who are probably using technology to run their companies.

We think that statistics for the nontech businesses may be artificially low due to the enormous amount of bartering that goes on. Part-time home-business owners often trade goods for services (or for a combination of services and money). Who can keep track of an exchange such as "I'll prune your bushes into topiaries if you paint a mural in my kitchen?"

So popular has the give-and-take of bartering become that it is even getting organized. Networks of small companies, such as Barter Basics and Barter Advantage in Manhattan, publish newsletters and take a small cut on transactions. How quintessentially Cashing Out to build a small business out of helping other small businesses! Bartering is also recognized as something other than a tax dodge; the exchange can be reported to the IRS as equivalent dollars and taken as a legitimate business expense.

Publish and Prosper

For a new profession close to our hearts, you can always Cash Out and write a book—or start a newsletter, such as *Plain,* a plain-talking monthly from Amish editors that is attracting readers with its Cashing Out philosophy about living simply and sensibly without modern interruptions. With all the computer programs geared to desktop publishing—and a wee bit of imagination—it's easy to find some quiet spot and just begin to write. We've noticed that there's a trend toward entrepreneurial business books indulging in extra-long titles, such as *When Friday Isn't Payday: A Complete Guide to Starting, Running—and Surviving in—a Very Small Business,* by Randy W. Kirk, as well as another mouthful, *The Ultimate No B.S., No Holds Barred, Kick Butt, Take No Prisoners, and Make Tons of Money Business Success Book,* by Dan Kennedy. Or, if you decide not to write anything yourself but just publish others, the first thing you should think of is a clever name—such as Upstart Publishing of Dover, New Hampshire, or Ten Speed Press in Berkeley, California. We're sure you'll be inundated with plenty of manuscripts.

At BrainReserve, we refer to the entrepreneurial split as the Tech-Knows and the Tech-Nots. Both groups are simultaneously driving the Cashing Out trend to ever-greater popularity. The Tech-Nots believe they offer something that's lacking in the corporate world: hard-to-find personal attention, whether it be in home repair, child care, beauty services, or pet maintenance. The Tech-Knows have formed businesses using the latest in technological support, such as answering beeper calls on how to install Windows 95.

There's a great and growing demand for computer know-how. BrainReserve sees a window of opportunity for Tech-Knows in which Tech-Nots will pay big bucks for in-depth assistance to overcome their technological gap. And it will be well worth the expenditure; on average, the self-employed person using a PC makes $70,000 versus $42,000 for nonusers. There's also some very Cashing Out software available, such as LegalPoint, which offers more than 75 basic business contracts and documents—from noncompetes to partnership agreements to purchase orders. It's very handy. Click.

Telecommuters have Cashed Out and clicked into a global village where you commute to your job electronically, never leaving your home office. It's estimated that almost one-third of the adult workforce is putting in some part of its working hours while at home. Advancements in home-office supplies have facilitated this change. Staples, the office superstore, is now a $2 billion business, and according to its buyers' profiles, 25 percent of Staples customers have a family member in a home business. Kwik-Kopy has 873 locations; Sir Speedy, almost 900. Catalogs, such as Reliable Home Office, out of Ottawa, Illinois, can set you up in business in a flash, even if you're a hundred miles from nowhere. That's clicking with Cashing Out.

At BrainReserve, we've been helping our *Fortune* 500 clients get a clearer picture of the entrepreneurs of the future. Targeting the Small Office/Home Office (SOHO) types isn't quite as easy as targeting other distinct market segments. To avoid higher deposits and business-line charges, some home workers are reluctant to alert the phone company about what they're up to. Apartment dwellers might not want landlords or co-op boards to know they're running home-based businesses; the same goes for home owners up against strict neighbors or zoning laws.

This SOHO marketplace is going to grow even bigger over the next ten years. Interestingly enough, to the vast majority of those we've talked to, Cashing Out is strongly associated with packing up lock, stock, and barrel and moving to the country. Away from the hot, asphalt streets and smog-filled cities, and back toward all things green and natural, where one can say "good morning" to the butcher, the baker, and the FedEx driver. It

Strength in Numbers

The Home Office Association of America (telephone: 800-809-4622) was formed in 1994 in response to the needs of this massive workforce. For yearly dues of $49, members can access numerous services including group discounts on health insurance and package delivery. The association has a monthly newsletter, *Home Office Connections,* and a firm in Washington, D.C., that lobbies for home-office tax deductions.

It's no surprise to us that *Fortune* reported in an article entitled "Kissing Off Corporate America" that many business school grads are taking a different route now. *Fortune* said that "as recently as 1990, a quarter of Columbia University's new MBAs joined large manufacturers: last year only 13% did so." Stanford's grads were similarly disenchanted about going corporate. In '89, 70 percent went to work for big companies; five years later, the numbers dropped to 50 percent. Plus, many of the ones who have signed up have plans to "make big money for a few years and then find a small company to buy. . . ."

was no surprise to read in *EDK Forecast* that, in a study querying American women about where they would like to live if money were no object, only a paltry 8 percent said they would be happy in a city setting.

The nostalgia for all things country is especially strong in the big cities. As mentioned in *New York* magazine, many Manhattanites are decorating their downtown dwellings with weathered barn siding, whitewashed chests, old oak buckets, hand-sewn quilts, carved rooster statues, and folk art.

The popularity of country music with city folk is another symptom of Cashing Out. We can sit in traffic jams dreaming of the golden hills of our mountain home (even if we've never been farther west than the flats of New Jersey). There are more than 3,000 all-country radio stations today, and at least two or three cable television stations where you can watch couples two-stepping around the dance floor. Deep in the heart of London, staid Brits are getting away from their usual reserve and lining up for line dancing. It's the fad to slip into Levi 501s, tie on a bandanna, and prance around in high-heeled cowboy boots doing the Tush-Tush, a shake-your-hips country strut. Landsake!

Perhaps the ultimate Cashing Out fantasy is to open a country inn. What's different now is that really high-powered corporate types are taking the leap. An article in the *New York Times* mentioned William Schreyer, for-

Outside In

The current mania for outsider art is directly related to Cashing Out. We have romanticized these quixotic dreamers (some of whom are more than a little crazy). They are the ones following their private stars—giving shape through art to their unique visions. There is a magazine called *Raw Vision* devoted to outsider art, and the American Visionary Art Museum recently opened in Baltimore. A common thread among these artists seems to be little, if any, schooling. Some of the names are William Hawkins, Mamie Deschillie, Jimmy Sudduth, Mose Tolliver, "Professor" Eddie Williams, and the Reverend Finster, who related, "The Lord spoke and said: 'Give up the repair of lawn mowers . . . give up the preaching of sermons; paint my pictures, and that's what I done."

Haven't we all dreamed of giving free rein to some deep inner calling? This longing to live a pure life in touch with our best selves is one of the major forces driving this trend.

mer chairman of Merrill Lynch, who purchased an inn in State College, Pennsylvania, to add "a little extra spice to life." Then there's Robert Mnuchin, former Goldman

4-Wheel Freedom

We're following the country pipe dream with the cars we've been buying—from four-wheel-drive Jeep Cherokees, Ford Explorers, GMC Jimmys, Land-Rovers to sporty pickups. However, nothing can outdo the Hummer for Cashing Out souls. Ads describe it as the "Most Serious 4x4 on Earth," and continue on with unadulterated Cash Out–speak: "In an environment where only the strong survive, some species refuse to be compromised by a world of glass and concrete. For them, freedom is the ultimate privilege. The highest premium. So, go ahead. Move. Run. Drive a Hummer. And find out what freedom feels like." The $70,000 vehicle, a civilian version of the Desert Storm hero, is made of aircraft aluminum, and can climb cliffs, creep up sand dunes, and jump from boulder to boulder. Inside is a plaque with the only instructions—"deflate tires when fording rivers." That's tough with a capital "T." We have two in our neighborhood: a red convertible and a dark green tank, and if we predict this one correctly, plenty more will be on the way. You have to see one to believe it. It moves like a magnificent turtle—wide, low, flat and invincible.

Sachs partner, who owns the Mayflower Inn in Washington, Connecticut, with his entrepreneur wife. Pick any inn, and it's a good bet the proprietors are happily into their second career.

Keeping with this return to a simple, honest life is the experiment that Citibank has initiated for small businesses: its "character loan" program. Loans of up to $50,000—the seed money needed for many a Cashing Out dream—are being granted on the branch manager's assessment of the applicant's character. Some $10 million has already been lent to 460 "good character" companies, and so far only two of the loans, totaling $30,000, are in default.

One thing you can be sure of is that masses of us are looking for a slice of life that's easier, happier, and more straightforward. Wheeling and dealing is out. Personal satisfaction is in. In the reality of Cashing Out, even though you may become shackled with loans and work harder than you did as a nine-to-fiver, you're doing it for yourself. As John Donne quilled, lo, so many years ago, "Be thine own palace, or the world's thy jail."

CLICKING WITH BEING ALIVE

Recognizing the importance of wellness,
consumers embrace the concept of
not only a longer life but a better
overall quality of life.

W hen we wrote *The Popcorn Report,* BrainReserve had been tracking the Staying Alive trend for more than eight years. This trend, which concerned an aging population and its quest for longevity, dealt with eating right, exercising correctly, and even meditating to the right *Om.* Today, the sands have shifted under our feet, from Staying Alive to Being Alive. No longer interested in longevity alone, we want to enhance the quality and value of our lives right now.

Where before we were saying, "I don't want to die. Keep me alive at all costs," we now recognize that mere "survival" isn't enough. Quality of life is the more important goal. We want to feel good and we're beginning to understand that every *body* is different. That the key to vigor and wellness is understanding the way our own body works—and taking the measures that keep it tuned and humming. Is there any high that matches that marvelous feeling of being fit, energized, wholly alive?

An integrated vision of health is emerging that embraces what nature has to offer. People in our country are finally beginning to do what cultures all over the world have done for eons: medicate themselves naturally. Herbs are an important source of primary health care for 2.5 to 3 billion people in the developing world. It's interesting to note that aspirin, digitalis, and morphine were all folk remedies long before they were "discovered" by modern medicine. According to the botanical experts, only 10 percent of plant life has been cataloged. Wonders await us.

Some 42 percent of British doctors have begun to routinely make referrals to homeopathic physicians. One-third of family physicians in France prescribes homeopathic remedies, as do more than 20 percent of German physicians. Even here in the United States, botanist-turned-MD Dr. Andrew Weil says, "For every

Gone to the Dogs

There's an American Holistic Veterinary Medical Association, which is exploring the use of such alternative treatments as herbal therapy and homeopathy in treating four-footed patients. We watched a local chiropractor give an arthritic, almost paralyzed Dalmatian a massage and manipulation treatment, after which the dog friskily rose to his feet and walked away.

single prescription that I write for pharmaceutical drugs, I probably give out 40 or 50 for herbal remedies." Sure enough, sales of homeopathic remedies in this country increased from $2 billion in 1991 to $3.77 billion in 1996.

As homeopathic medicines become more accepted in our society, we expect to see these remedies dispensed through neighborhood vending machines or delivered door to door. Better to pass out bee pollen and crushed violet petals than tranquilizers. Honeysuckle wards off feelings of homesickness. Elm is good for self-assurance. Maybe a mélange of wildflowers for mega-energy, and crushed essence of crabapples for confidence. Not to worry—all are nontoxic and non-habit-forming.

Some other natural remedies:

- Rosy periwinkle. This is a Madagascan plant from which scientists have developed the most effective treatment yet for Hodgkin's disease, and one that has also upped the survival rate for kids with leukemia by 60 percent.
- Calophyllum lanigerum. A Malaysian tree was found to yield this compound, which seems to work against an AZT-resistant strain of the AIDS virus. (Horribly, when researchers returned to gather more samples, loggers had razed all the trees.)
- Aspidia. After watching chimpanzees chomp on it to relieve stomach problems, researchers discovered that aspidia not only killed nasty parasites but also slowed the growth of cancerous tumors.

These plants could save our lives (if we don't kill them first). Only a tiny percentage of the world's plants—some say as little as 1 percent—have been tested for their therapeutic potential.

It's not only exotic plants from the far corners of the world that can promote Being Alive. Did you know that mangos may inhibit the spread of the herpes virus? A bunch of bananas may prevent ulcers? Onion juice may lessen the wheezing of asthma? Tofu could work against the development of prostate cancer? And now that you do know, are you a believer? And if you're a believer, will you partake?

We're still in the infant stage of sensory understanding. The scent from a mixed bouquet of flowers may hasten learning skills, helping us solve problems faster. Of course, aroma persuasion has been around for a while. (A piece of insider real-estate knowledge: The homey smell of bread baking in the oven will sell a house faster.) A whiff of vanilla or jasmine will lessen stress. One New York hospital has actually been releasing vanilla fragrance under patients' noses before performing MRI scans—it helps them relax. Lavender oil, with its mild sedative powers, is being seriously tested as a drug replacement to treat insomnia in older people.

The wildest take on food scents comes from a *Times of London* magazine article about a study done by Dr. Alan R. Hirsch, director of the Smell and Taste Treatment and Research Foundation in Chicago. He found that the powerful combination of pumpkin pie and lavender increases blood flow to the penis, causing erections. Other exciting flavors? Licorice and donut. The center's conclusion is that these experiments may be useful in curing impotence or in deprogramming sex offenders.

Adding fuel to the Being Alive trend is a growing mistrust of "big medicine." We've all read and seen the horror stories of misdiagnoses, botched operations, fly-by-night doctors, and greedy pharmaceutical companies.

Supplemental Knowledge

In Harvard Square in Cambridge, Massachusetts, you'll find Harnett's, a large store that sells nothing but vitamins and homeopathic remedies—and is always filled with customers. Founded by Anthony Harnett, the retailing wizard who built and then sold the phenomenally successful Bread & Circus supermarkets, Harnett's is a harbinger of health care's future. Similar stores are opening all across the country as people educate themselves and take responsibility for staying healthy.

One of the first clickers into homeopathy was Edward Bach, a physician who worked in Britain in the early 1900s. Sometimes he would walk through the countryside, work himself into emotional states, and then taste various plants and petals, noting the effects on his mood. He went a step further and packaged these natural remedies. And so was born Bach Flower Remedies, now marketed in the United States. Sales have doubled every year for the past decade.

In a triple whammy, Rainbow Light Nutritional Systems, partnered by Tom O'Leary and Linda Kahler from beautiful downtown Santa Cruz, has managed to combine the good-health benefits of herb, vitamin, and food therapies. Their 3-Way Stress System offers not only the more usual B vitamins and minerals but also herbs such as valerian and kava for natural calming and therapeutic effects. Rainbow Light also has an advanced nutritional system, a daily supplement full of potent herbal extracts that draws on the best of the world's vital traditions: Ayurvedic for balance and longevity (using gotu kola and gymnema sylvestre); Chinese for digestion and detoxifying (ginseng, sausserea, reishi); and European herbalism (ginkgo for mental vigor). Although these herbal helpers sound strange now, someday soon they might roll off your tongue as easily as aspirin and benzocaine.

The potent powers of these herbs, garlic in particular, are being taken so seriously that New York Hospital has opened a Garlic Information Center with its own Garlic Hotline and Garlic Research Network (all this is good for Listerine sales). In the Glendale Galleria in Southern California, a huge mall near central Los Angeles, there's a store that sells only—and everything—garlic: oils, condiments like garlic salsa, cookbooks, wreaths, foods, and roasters.

For those who want in-depth knowledge of herbal medicine, there's a CD-ROM program called the Herbalist, which provides more information than you could ever imagine on the subject—from homeopathy's uses to classifications of all medicinal plants.

And there is a *major* backlash against the managed-care companies, many of which simply don't inform patients of available treatment options. The reason: The companies don't want to pay for them. Americans are literally dying because their medical insurers are withholding critical information. This is an outrage of the first order, and it's causing many of us to take increased responsibility for our own health.

Just recently, Mutual of Omaha, the nation's largest provider of individual health insurance, announced it would reimburse patients participating in a preventive program that combines diet, medication, exercise, and support groups to reverse heart disease. It's only a matter of time before other alternative treatments—acupuncture, biofeedback, transcendental meditation, hydro-relaxation, craniosacral therapy, reflexology, and chiropractic adjustments—will be fully reimbursable. Consumer spending on nontraditional therapies is esti-

The R$_X$ Restaurant

An article in *The Wall Street Journal* described the always-crowded Yat Chau Health Restaurant in Hong Kong. There, "the restaurant's thoughtful host listens sympathetically and jots things down on an order pad. But unlike your conventional maître d', Mr. Wong doesn't recommend dishes, he *prescribes* them. Have swollen glands? Try chicken and sea-horse stew. Feeling dizzy? Perhaps some fried rice with wolfberries."

mated to top $14 billion a year, yet 75 percent of those expenses aren't reimbursable by our health plans.

Dare we hope that Congress is becoming more progressive? In spite of the way big medicine torpedoed Bill and Hillary Clinton's health care overhaul, we remain optimistic. Federal legislators passed a bill in 1994 that allows general health claims to be made for vitamins. Even the National Institutes of Health has an Office of Alternative Medicine, which has pumped millions of dollars into investigating nontraditional medical treatment options ranging from massage to prayer.

Of the 53 major drugstore chains—including Payless, Walgreen's, and Thrifty—almost half now carry some homeopathic products. Even your local supermarket and K mart are expanding the shelf space allotted to good-for-you natural remedies.

A presidential proclamation declared the 1990s as the Decade of the Brain. Evidence has finally shown that the brain should be treated like a muscle: The more you flex it, the stronger it gets. The brain's ability to change and adapt well into old age is encouraging to the Being Alive trend. It shows that old dogs *can* learn new tricks.

Certainly we have something to learn from our more than 50,000 centenarians, one of the fastest-growing segments of the population. It's definitely survival of the fittest. If you get through your 80s without a life-threatening illness, there's a good chance you'll make it to 100. The point is not just to be alive and kicking, but alive and *thinking*.

We saw a television program about a man named Sidney Amber, who was born on January 26, 1886, when Grover Cleveland was President. Amber had started a new job when he was 104—as a maître d' at a San Francisco restaurant, meeting and greeting customers for more than four hours at a stretch. If asked to guess his age, people would venture "75," or "82," never dreaming that he was well over 100 (Amber died at the age of 109). His secret, besides stimulating work? Amber said he ingested three tablespoons of Worcestershire sauce every night for 90 years. Thank you, Lea & Perrins.

For years now, doctors have been studying a group

of retired Minnesota nuns, many of whom have the distinction of living well beyond the age of 100. The research shows that those nuns who have earned college degrees, teach, and actively use their minds live longer than do those who spend their lives doing only manual work. The ones who continue to tease their brains with crossword puzzles, reading, or card playing have significantly lower rates of dementia and Alzheimer's.

There are other ways to stay alert and enhance Being Alive. Chinese ginseng is said to boost the powers of concentration and memory. L-tyrosine converts into mental stimulants known as neurotransmitters, which, in layman's lingo, means that if you need to be sharp before a meeting or an exam, you should gobble up a plateful of high-protein food: fish, skinless chicken, or tofu. Extracts from the ginkgo tree supposedly spur short-term memory, which is very helpful if you're one of the millions who misplace keys, glasses, and, most aggravating of all, the TV remote control. Piracetam, a central nervous system stimulant, is reported to unclog the flow of data between the brain's hemispheres. Now available in Europe, it's one of those things that certain in-the-know travelers are smuggling back into the States. Hydergine, an extract from the fungus that grows on rye, is believed to increase blood supply to the brain—and is already being used to treat memory problems in the elderly.

Many centenarians age gracefully, attributing their

longevity to maintaining a low level of stress. To reduce everyday tension no matter what age you are, these simple stress-buster exercises are perfect for Being Alive. Hysterical? Grab two fingers of one hand, take a deep breath, and release the fingers as you exhale. To calm yourself even further, try breathing in 10 or 12 times through your left nostril only. Or, even more pleasurable, just dig into a simple dinner of a baked potato, or pasta with red sauce. This combination will stimulate the brain into producing serotonin, a mood-relaxing chemical. Don't laugh. These easy remedies can help you cope and, hence, live longer.

There are so many unexplored ways of keeping the mind fit and at its peak. As the baby boomers age, better brainpower will definitely become the next challenge.

Chinese medicine differs from Western medicine and clicks with Being Alive because the Chinese focus on "health" rather than "disease." People in China not only go to the doctor when sick, they also keep going when they're well—to keep their bodies harmoniously balanced with nature. How fundamentally different this is from Western medicine, which focuses on finding a magic bullet to shoot down the problem. Our obsession is killing the disease—even if we kill the patient in the bargain. Just think about chemotherapy. Chinese medicine says it is more important to support the body's natural-killer immune cells and leave the body's vital growth mechanisms intact.

What's Clicking Next?

Foods that foster the total package of physical, emotional, spiritual, and mental health will grow in popularity. Why not fruit chips rich in sun vitamins, or ultrathin waffles and pancakes with pure-fruit fillings for breakfasts on the go? We already drink certain beverages with this in mind: coffee for energy, herbal tea to calm us down, and isotonics (Gatorade, sports drinks) for stamina.

More likely, the next big health breakthroughs will be in the realm of medications, perhaps a shot that dissolves fat cells or one that fools the chemical balance of the brain into suppressing the appetite. Headlines of late have trumpeted reports of promising new antiobesity drugs and genetic research pinpointing causes of this all-too-common disorder.

Watch liquor sales turn around and go right through the roof again if a patch is made available that makes you instantly sober or keeps you at a reasonably safe, one- or two-drink high (a light buzz) all evening long—while completely eliminating the morning-after blues.

Needle injections may soon become obsolete. No more being lunged at with long, pointed hypodermics. We can expect the painless delivery of drugs via a gas-fueled "pen" that fires the right dosage into the skin at three times the speed of sound. We've heard about a vitamin B_{12} gel named ENER-B that cleverly goes into the bloodstream from a tiny dab in the nose. Why shouldn't other medications be administered this way?

Have we watched too much *Star Trek,* with its handheld medical scanners and futuristic operating techniques that make the methods of the 20th century seem hopelessly slow and outdated? We want to use laser light, sonic vibrations, and digital imaging to detect microscopic tumors or weakened blood vessels. Someday soon, operations will take place right in our own homes with Virtual Surgery. A Rent-a-Robotic arm will follow the surgeon's instructions or arm movements via computer. In this virtual operating theater, the doctor will feel as if she is working with real flesh and blood, while the patient will feel as if a top surgeon is right in the room. A win-win proposition.

A good click with Being Alive would be the start-up of Dr. Nature Clinics, an organized, nationwide group of doctors who would promote wellness through nutrition, stress reduction, energy balancing, and meditation—the smart new medicine of the late '90s.

In a recent brainstorming session, a new click was discussed. Wouldn't it be comforting if you could own shares in a few farms in your area, so you could actually check out the conditions under which your family food—from vegetables to dairy to meat—is grown?

Another click idea: What about a chain of SourceSmart restaurants that could serve all-organic, pesticide-free, low-fat meals created by top chefs. Even though the food might end up being expensive, it would be the eco-experience of your life. (This is probably as close to the Chinese experience of "better-health dining" as we can reasonably get in the near future.)

As SourceSmart consumers are busy Smart-Dining, they might desire something safe, yet delicious, to drink. Most of us have heard how many wines are saturated with sulfites and antifungal sprays from the vineyards. There's a wine store in Amsterdam that is owned by two men trained in the science of wine toxicology. The store sells only pretested bottles, guaranteed pure. Why not bring the concept here?

A further click idea: SourcesMart. A chain of supermarkets in which the origin and composition of *everything* is disclosed.

Magnetic field therapy devices could be slipped into lots of things, such as phones, headsets, and massagers. There could be headbands to combat migraines, a bracelet for arthritis, an ankle bracelet for gout, and chairs and car seats for back pain, or magnetizers could be set into home or office doorjambs—anyplace you pass through at least once a day—to provide overall good health.

Another example of an older, wiser Chinese medical treatment is acupuncture, which is still in its infancy here. Yet when you meet people who have firsthand (first-needle?) experience with a good acupuncturist, you hear rhapsodic stories. Whether it's the almost instant disappearance of the redness, swelling, and sharp pain of a herpes viral sore or the freeing up of a spasmodic hand, this artful science has the ability to solve problems that Western medicine can't touch.

Acupuncture is now being used for the treatment of drug addiction, according to Dr. Michael Smith of Lincoln Hospital, in New York City's Bronx. Patients say they prefer acupuncture to going on methadone. A good-news side effect: Acupuncture was found to also

Magnetic Attraction

A Japanese company, Nikken, is creating a U.S. sales network for its Magnetic Field Therapy products. In a technique similar to acupuncture (only without needles), rubberized magnets are placed on the skin. By generating heat and energy, the magnets are said to help heal aches and pains. The same company also makes magnetized shoe inserts, mattress pads, and pillows—all de-stressers.

make patients more cooperative and more inclined to continue drug counseling.

Another alternative science we'll be hearing more of is called naturopathy. Naturopathic physicians are thought of as the "generalists" of alternative medicine. That's because they're quite eclectic, combining clinical nutrition, herbal medicine, homeopathy, behavior modification, manipulation, and physiotherapy along with a combination of Oriental and Ayurvedic (ancient principles of natural health and beauty) medicine. The goal is to bolster the immune system with natural remedies, and make changes in diet and lifestyle—all to help the body heal itself. A far cry from quackery, naturopaths are highly trained, and actually receive about ten times more training in clinical nutrition than do regular Western MDs.

A galloping mistrust is making us anxious about what we're eating and where it's all coming from. Sometime in the near future, we're going to be increasingly interested in identifying what particular cow the milk in our container comes from.

We're also seeing the start of the pass-along-the-benefit chain. We're already producing hyperimmune milk, yogurt, and cheese from cows vaccinated against human diseases. The animals pass along the antibodies for human consumption, providing what is essentially a passive vaccine. Besides storing antibodies, chickens and eggs are being used to pass along the benefits of the fatty acid Omega 3. Although Omega 3, which helps prevent heart disease, is found naturally in oily fish such as salmon and bluefish, Americans just don't eat enough of those fish to gain the benefits. A biologist from Omegatech came up with this solution: letting chickens feed on an algae source of the nutrient so that, when you dine on either chicken or eggs, you'll get a dose of heart strengthener. What do you think will be the next pass-along benefit? Anticancer? Antiaging?

To combat the negative publicity stemming from the overuse of antibiotics and unknown substances in cows and other farm animals, both Land O Lakes and Marigold Foods, two major milk suppliers, are launching brands certified as being free of any genetically engineered hormones.

Vegetarian Delights

The recent outbreak of Mad Cow disease in England has heightened fears of eating meat. There's a new organization at work, the Vegetarian Education Network, that is trying to spread the word and pressure the educational system (especially grammar schools) into offering vegetarian meals. In a Danish department store emporium, we saw shoppers grabbing up a product called Selleribof, celery burgers that are made up of 34 percent celery combined with onions, rice, potatoes, bread crumbs, and spices (there are also carrot burgers). TGI Friday's, the restaurant chain, says that its Garden Burgers are among the most popular choices on the menu. Even the big, beefy Hard Rock Cafe does a big business in them. Boca burgers, whose main ingredient is soy, were the winner of the *New York Times* Tofu Burger contest. In just four months, over 6,000 of these flavorful patties were served in the White House. Bambi and Cinderella have forsaken meat, too. At both Disneyland and Disney World, the veg-and-grain Nature's Burgers are selling well.

Some unscientific polling by *Veggie Single News* (the magazine for vegetarian singles) as reported in Adweek points out people who ingest a "non-violent diet" are viewed as being "more gentle and giving and more highly sensitive to their lovers' needs." Conclusion: Meat eaters are selfish.

Exercise may not be the be-all and end-all of our lives, but it certainly helps. Those who do exercise know how terrific it makes you feel, and that's the essence of Being Alive. It also helps us stay alive. Stanford University researchers conducted a study in 1996 that concluded that runners have lower death rates, fewer joint symptoms, and take fewer medications than nonrunners. And we all know that people who get regular exercise look better.

Our drinking water, the elixir of life, is contaminated. That's a fact, and the latest statistics from the EPA are shocking. During 1993–1994, some 53 million Americans drank substandard water, causing 400,000 known cases of illness and almost 1,000 deaths. How much those numbers will go up if environmental restrictions are diluted, no one can even guess. Already, one in five of us drink tap water that contains poisonous lead, radiation, herbicides, or even fecal contamination. This is a national disgrace—and the reason that sales of bottled water are soaring.

Sweat Shops

In 1996, membership at health clubs in the United States reached 20 million. And these spandex-studded emporiums are always looking for new and exciting ways to help customers feel the burn—or de-stress. One of the hottest new activities is spinning.

Spinning uses a sleek stationary cycle, modeled after a real racing bike, and has a Virtual Reality feature. Even at over $7,000 a bike, it's catching on. Unlike using other exercycles, spinning is anything but boring. Spinners can choose road conditions, locale, and atmosphere. Ready for a hairpin turn on the Swiss Alps in a rainstorm?

Another hot ticket is gravity training. No music, no mirrors, no walls—just unforgiving angles. Speed is not the point; it's technique, technique, technique.

Bored with bikes and laps? How about running an obstacle course. Crawl-through tunnels, monkey bars, ropes for climbing, and other mixes of exercises are utilized. The exhilaration comes from the sheer exhaustion. It's the closest thing to an adult playground.

We're feeling vulnerable—as well we should—but we're also feeling hopeful. Being Alive is transforming our environment by the day. We've looked around us—and inside our bodies—and we're taking charge. We're demanding no retreat on environmental standards, we've joined local community clean-up groups, we're shouting for improved health care, and most important we're taking responsibility for our own health. We're working to understand the specific and unique needs of our bodies—and we're responding to them. We want to live long lives—and we want to feel terrific, with a clear head and a jaunty step, almost until the day we drop. There are so many ways that you, your family, or your company can Be Alive. Whether it's taking up woodworking on your 92nd birthday, stocking healthy new drinks on the coffee wagon at work, or turning to holistic remedies for that nagging backache, Being Alive is ripe for exploring and set for clicking. Are you ready?

CLICKING WITH DOWN-AGING

Nostalgic for the carefree days of childhood,
consumers seek symbols of youth
to counterbalance the intensity of their adult lives.

O n March 25, 1997, George Bush took a fall—
from an airplane at 12,000 feet over the Arizona desert. After free-falling for a mile and a
half, the former president pulled his rip cord, and out
puffed a rainbow-colored parachute that the intrepid
ex-Navy pilot hand-guided to within 40 yards of his target painted on the desert floor. Asked about his experience, the 72-year-old Bush gestured with a thumb's-up
and exclaimed, "I'm a new man!"

Down-Aging is about rejuvenation, renewal,

rebirth. In a culture in which 60 often feels like 40 and 50 like 30, the reality about how we live, love, work, and play at a certain age is amazingly different from what we imagined or expected. The demeaning taunt "Act your age, not your shoe size" has no meaning: Why *not* act your shoe size when it's so much fun? And acting funny, foolish, and footloose is a great release from the stress of our all-too-serious adulthoods. Smiling at the reporters standing around like cacti in the desert, Bush bloomed in the warmth of his stressful, yet stress-releasing feat.

Think about the last time you really laughed—not a snicker, not an amused sigh, but a deep, rolling belly laugh. *Reader's Digest* has it right: Laughter *is* the best medicine. If Jim Carrey can make you laugh like that and shuffle off those cares, he's a bargain at $20 million per picture.

Down-Aging ignores those social conventions that say that age should dictate behavior. At BrainReserve, we recognize that "should" is one of those words we should try hard to forget: "Should" conjures up notions of other people's expectations, which invite us to preserve the status quo, resist change, and avoid clicking.

Today, 80-year-old marathon runners compete with thousands who are decades younger. Sexually active seniors now experiment with tickler condoms and lubricating creams. Daytime talk shows feature 60-year-old women who marry men in their 20s. Not uncommonly, second-family fathers sire at 70-plus; and now there's new mom who got pregnant at 64. Fully 40 percent of the students now enrolled in colleges and universities are over the age of 25.

One 40-ish friend of ours, Mary Nealon, is just starting the long haul of going into the medical field. It makes perfect sense: She'll be hanging out her shingle at age 50, armed with knowledge of all the latest advances, *and* the life experience to make sounder decisions.

Another woman we met, Colette, told us about her struggle to find a school that would "take a chance" and admit her. In her early 60s, she felt a calling to become a rabbi. Logic says, "It takes six years to complete rabbinical studies, and that makes her too old." Clicking says, "It's never too late: Older is wiser, and wiser is what a rabbi should be." Reconstructionist Rabbinical College in Wyncote, Pennsylvania, agreed.

And what about high-tech mothering? Now that science has handed women the capability of giving birth after menopause, what does this do to our concept of age?

So-called elder-mothers and elder-fathers adopt at a ripe old age. In China, people are encouraged to adopt into their 40s and beyond, whether they're married or not. In the course of writing this book, Lys journeyed to Shanghai, China, and returned with her beautiful adopted orphan daughter, Skye Qi. When questioned about the advisability of adopting so late in life, Lys quipped, "I might be the only one buying Pampers and Depends at the same time." Today more than ever as long as you have the energy and good health, neither the desire to be nurturing nor the ability to do it well goes away.

Credit Willard Scott on NBC's *Today* for making us aware of the ripest old-agers. In his daily recitations of centenarians' birthdays, he not only shows their photographs but also shares their individual secrets for long life. Leading the list is those elders' attitude that they are never too old to start something new. In his enthusiasm for Elsa's gardening or George's carpentry, Scott reinforces the concept of Down-Aging, which redefines what is appropriate behavior for a person who has lived a century or more.

The number of centenarians is expected to grow: In the next 50 years it's projected that there will be 2 million people in this country over the age of 100 (see "Clicking Through Being Alive" for more on this topic). Think of it. What will it be like? How can you click into marketing to this group? How will you click if it's you who is trying to blow out those eight-and-a-half dozen candles?

Be a Sport

Sports are a clear window to Down-Aging. Go to any gym and check out the over-55 set tracking on the treadmills. We have grandfolks who are cross-country skiers, triathletes, and long-distance swimmers; most are in better shape than their grandkids. It's estimated that the largest numbers of exercise walkers (not *on* walkers) are over 65. Indeed, since 1988, the number of Americans over the age of 55 who have joined health clubs has *doubled*.

Organizations such as ElderTreks and Backroads (call 1-800-GO-ACTIVE) now sponsor camping trips, bicycle tours, snowmobiling, and climbing groups for people over age 55. A televised documentary, "Height of Courage," chronicled the feat of Norman Vaughn, who at age 89 climbed an icy 10,302-foot mountain in Antarctica—with an artificial right knee and an unbendable right ankle. He was accompanied by his wife, 37 years his junior.

Warren River Expeditions in Idaho runs whitewater rafting trips for seniors only. A recent Nike ad quotes 72-year-old Beatrice Brophy and 74-year-old Barbara Anderson, canoeists and guides in the Boundary Waters of Minnesota: "Some people look at you and think you should stop now, rest now, grow old now, gracefully. But if you live gracefully enough, you don't have time to grow old. You have a canoe. And that canoe has a river. And that river does not end. You hike thirteen miles at the end of the day and that is how you rest." Two who Just Do It. Nice job, Nike.

Where do forever young NBA wanna-bes go? At the Swept Away pro basketball fantasy camp in Negril, Jamaica, you get to compete against former Knicks and NBA All-Stars from the 1970s and '80s. Coaches share their strategies; trainers and conditioning experts instruct you about caring for injuries and prolonging your dribbling days. You even get to take home a videotape of your game with the good old sports to show to your b-ball buddies. Your own personal *Hoop Dreams*.

That sports and Down-Aging make perfect partners is a marketing lesson that many a company has learned. Keds, for example, recently ran a two-page ad showing a black-and-white photograph of two little girls superimposed over a four-color picture of two grown women. The headline read: "Your childhood isn't lost, you just misplaced it." The copy went on: "It's probably in a closet behind an old Concentration game or buried under a pile of mortgage payments somewhere. So dig it out and use it. Do something incredibly un-adult."

Keds has clicked perfectly into this stir-up-the-memories trend.

The trend of Down-Aging, however, isn't limited to those old enough to have welcomed in the 20th century and to be still active as it departs. Down-Aging is not forgetting about your age or railing against it; rather it is tossing away the old ideas of what chronological age is and what it means.

The best advertisers and marketers know this lesson well. Madonna, that consummate marketer, started a fashion look by posing for *Vanity Fair* in pigtails, calling up images of the seductive and seemingly innocent Lolita. Designer Anna Sui pushed it further with a recent spring collection that featured baby-doll dresses, anklets, and Mary Janes. Now we're seeing slews of fashion ads for mature women dressed in pleated plaid skirts or schoolgirl jumpers along with rubber-cap sneaks. Their message is clear: Don't let age dictate your life. Give in to some of your youthful, even childish, impulses. Go for the sprinkles!

Fun and Games

When Blockbuster canvassed adults and heard them wishing for someplace to go "to hang out with other adults, play high-tech games, and act like kids again," the company heard a great Click. It responded in 1994 with Block Party, amusement centers in Albuquerque and Indianapolis for middle-aged children. No one under 18 is admitted—without parents.

The young, body-pierced, and dreadlocked set frequent a café and bar in New York's East Village called BabyLand. The place looks like a nursery: There are toy telephones, rocking horses, and wooden blocks to play with. Patrons sit on crib sofas and order malts, floats, and apple pie, or move to the bar and try the specialty drink of Mother's Milk, a Kahlúa-laced concoction in—what else? A baby bottle.

Trend watchers look to language as a reliable gauge of what's clicking. In the so-called good ol' days (were they *really* all that good?)—when adults were adults and kids were kids—people learned a way of talking appropriate to their chronological years. Folks in their 60s did not say "Daddy-O." During the 1940s, jazz musicians used the word "cool" to refer to the smooth, unemotional tones of extended improvisations. Beat musicians in the 1950s adopted the word to mean "fine" or "excellent." At the other end of the language thermometer, some people said, "Hey, man, that's hot" or "This is dy-no-mite!" when they wanted to indicate approval. Each generation has appropriated words and phrases to form its own secret lingo, its "code." But today, in part because of the widespread sharing of communication channels, such language is no longer the strict prerogative of one group or generation. Words cross the generational boundaries: You are just as likely to hear octogenarians at the retirement center exclaim "Awesome!" or "No W-a-a-a-y!" as to hear their great-grandchildren saying these words on the basketball court. Terms such as "Mr.," "Mrs.," and even the more recent and politically correct "Ms." aren't used as much as they once were. They seem too stiff and formal.

Many children casually call their parents by their first names. In high schools and colleges, students address their teachers in similarly informal ways. My godchildren, Sean and Chad, have taken a shortcut and refer to me simply as "God." Guess what? I like it.

Computer visual imaging is also mixing up and blending our perceptions. Ads for The Gap feature a young Andy Warhol, looking perfectly natural, wearing this season's khaki pants. The unstated message of that ad comes through loud and clear: "We are every age, not our chronological age. We are how we see ourselves." Andy may have died before his time, but his youthful image—thanks to the miracles of computer enhancement and manipulation—lives on. It's downright Down-Aging.

In short, Down-Aging changes expectations, dreams, desires, and visions. It offers us a perpetual state of growing, a way of saying "Yes" to life and all its possibilities. A recent ad seen on the subways in New York quotes British novelist George Eliot, who once wrote that "it's never too late to become what you might have been." The irony and import of that sentiment are underscored by the fact that "George Eliot" was the pen name of Mary Ann Evans.

Call it what you will: Splitting your sides, guffawing, chortling, roaring, cackling, falling out of your chair—the ability to throw back your head and laugh uncontrollably is a necessary and pleasant part of the Down-Aging process. A group in La Jolla, California, has formed the University of Light Hearts. Their motto is "A day without laughter is a day wasted." At their once-a-month meeting, the so-called Laugh for Lunch Bunch goes over such stress-busting tricks as "Create and invent funny nicknames for your family" and "Find a silly toy—put it on your desk."

The search for laughter is why comedy clubs draw standing-room-only crowds. Ditto for the Comedy Channel, with its terrific cartoons such as *Dr. Katz, The Tick,* and *The Critic*, which specifically target adults. It's why we're reading all those books—more like comedy routines on paper—by stand-up comics. Jerry Seinfeld's *Seinlanguage*, Tim Allen's *Don't Stand Too Close to a Naked Man*, and Ellen DeGeneres's *My Point, And I Do Have One* were all major best-sellers. It's why *Liar, Liar*, the latest Jim Carrey movie, made over $32 million in its opening weekend.

You can Down-Age by wearing comic T-shirts that remind you of your youth. Interestingly, there are just as many adult-sized T-shirts with silly cartoon characters as there are kids' sizes. Dr. Seuss's *Cat in the Hat*, Casper the Friendly Ghost, Betty Boop, Batman, and the Muppets are still popular shirts. Kermit, the Muppet spokesfrog, is a major imprint. (What's fascinating to a ClickWatcher is that on average these characters are about 40 years old, which shows the incredible staying power of a successful cartoon figure.)

Retail stores selling those cartoon characters are proliferating and doing well. The Walt Disney Company has opened some 600 of its exclusive stores, and Warner Bros. operates about 150. They sell everything from cartoon-y caps to mugs to posters. It's reported that 80 percent of sales at the stores are to adults for adults.

You can get Pepe Le Pew oven mitts, or athletic socks announcing, "I Tawt I Taw a Puddy Tat!" These items can run into big bucks; for $450, you can walk out wearing a sequined bustier of Tweety, or for a mere $4,500, you can bring home a desk-sized bronze sculpture of Road Runner.

Have you read any exciting comic books lately? It isn't only those freckled-faced 10-year-olds who are plunking down their allowances. As any comic book salesperson can tell you, close to half of all comic books are now bought by men over the age of 25.

Down-Aging sells at the bookstore. The fastest-growing group in America (and over one-quarter of the population) is already over 50, and these people want to read about themselves and the issues they face. To learn about age, not give in to it.

In her midlife memoir *Fear of Fifty,* Erica Jong writes that "sex is not a matter of life and death anymore. . . . It's gentler, perhaps less intense and definitely better." At age 60, Gloria Steinem, writing in *Moving Beyond Words,* addresses the "hormones within" instead of the subject of her previous book, the "child within."

Betty Friedan wrote *The Fountain of Age* in an attempt to change society's negative image about aging. She extols the benefits of being "older," equating it with growing "wiser." Other books, such as *Age Erasers for Men* and *Love and Sex After Sixty,* cover similar topics to recharge the batteries of their readers. Their authors tell you how to look younger, feel better, develop greater vitality, and enhance your sex life.

Games People Play

In this era of rapid hand-eye coordination video games, it's interesting that the laid-back board games—Scrabble, backgammon, chess—are enjoying a healthy revival. People of all ages gather on street corners around the country to play these satisfying games. The provide a chance for the older to feel young again, and the young to feel grown-up.

Television is also jumping on the Down-Aging band-wagon. In the spring of 1996, a cable channel called Prime Life Network debuted. It addresses issues of interest specific to the over-50 crowd. In the privacy of the home, mature folk can now click in and out to watch *Gourmet Cooking* and *Our House* instead of *Kidfest* and *The Muppets*.

In contrast to the film industry, television doesn't let age get in the way of major stardom. Perennial favorites Ed Asner, Mary Tyler Moore, Carol Burnett, Bill Cosby, Della Reese, Beatrice Arthur—to mention just a few—all work well into their 50s and beyond. And they're not given clichéd grandparent roles. Often they play physically, mentally, and sexually active characters.

Products that help us Down-Age our looks are

Bennett Rules

The quintessential generation-blender is Tony Bennett, who at age 70 has definitely been born again and is flying higher than ever. This crooner of decades past was taken in hand by his son, Danny, who is managing his renewed career and following a strategy for promoting the singer over the next decade. What's so interesting is that this is classic marketing repositioning: to take something out of synch with today and make it click. How did a smooth-singing square with gray hair, who wears white jackets and black bow ties, make it happen in a time of grunge and violent rap lyrics?

Much of the credit for Tony's turnabout—besides his son's management style and a general warm feeling about him—is due to a new willingness to change. From his 1962 Grammy to his 1992 Grammy, he had stayed fixed in his "I Left My Heart in San Francisco" lounge-lizard mode. Then he decided to cut *Perfectly Frank,* an album of Sinatra's saloon classics, and it went gold. The next year, Tony made an album of the great Fred Astaire songs, *Steppin' Out;* an MTV appearance with new pals, the Red Hot Chili Peppers; and a

> video and special, "Unplugged," complete with
> duets with k.d. lang and Elvis Costello. He did
> everything right: Old reliable became internation-
> ally supercool. Tony Bennett has done what few
> else have: He clicked into the music tastes of both
> parents and their kids. He clicked so well, in fact,
> that he won another Grammy in 1995 and
> received a nomination in 1997.

intensifying as baby boomers get older. Clairol's once famous ad for hair coloring—"Does she or doesn't she? Only her hairdresser knows for sure"—is OldThink. Men and women gleefully color their hair today, and they don't try to keep it secret.

Not a day goes by without some new elixir to try, a new number to call, a new doctor to see. In California, you can dial 1-800-BEAUTIFY for a free referral to a plastic surgeon. Face-lifts look more natural now that muscles are lifted as well as skin. Thanks to advances in the study of wound healing, you can go under the knife without the telltale scars. (Doctors operating on a fetus discovered that when the *in utero* surgery was performed during the first five months of pregnancy, there was no noticeable scar tissue. Now work is being done to isolate the prenatal cellular compound that makes this miracle possible.)

Collagen injections are popular for quick fixes, those lasting four to six months. So are electric shocks to energize and give a lift to tired skin cells. Next step after Retin-A: the youthful effects of skin-smoothing glycolic-acid creams. Avon's Anew sloughed off $70 million in sales in its first year. A patented emulsion called Hydron Care broke the record for TV shopping sales, luring more than $750,000 during a one-hour program. From Vita Industries, we now have GH3, an antiaging formula based on a product developed by a famous Romanian clinic that Hollywood stars such as Marlene Dietrich and Cary Grant frequented.

You can choose a lympho-drainage massage that helps move internal waste materials toward the lymph nodes and then out of your system, thus improving skin tone. Christian Dior's new cellulite remedy, Svelte, is causing a stampede at cosmetic counters. The forecast for one year's sales is 500,000 bottles.

At training workshops based on ancient Tantric and Taoist beliefs, men are taught techniques for controlling ejaculations in order to promote a stronger, more youthful appearance. The instruction relies on the ancient belief that having a climax weakens a man. (Hollywood rumor mills turn out scads of stories about male stars who are trying in vain to pursue this new beauty treatment.) There's little doubt that this will prove to be one of the most difficult attempts to Down-Age.

What's Clicking Next?

What could be more fun and trigger more flash-backs than resorts and health spas that remind us of summer camp? We see this as a logical exten-sion of the booming interest in adventure travel. Travel to another place—and another time in our lives. A little bit of "roughing it" makes us all real-ize we're not as stuck in our ways as we thought.

Now that fashion designers are creating entire lines for plus-sizes, it makes sense they'll be creating attractive, flattering, even sexy clothes for the older adult. Down-Aging consumers are far from giving up their efforts to look their best, and they're not content to drag their old duds out of the cedar closet. We see specialty boutiques with gorgeous clothes cut to fit the older, more settled body.

Along the same lines, why do sensible shoes have to look so sensible and dull? Safe, comfort-able, even orthopedic shoes can also be alluring. We see a promising future for the shoe manufac-turer who can shake up expectations for what older adults should be wearing on their feet.

The world of kitchen appliances is on the verge of many breakthroughs. No, not more electronic slicer/dicer/grater/shooters that are impossible to use and too much trouble to clean. We're talking about good old-fashioned, low-tech egg beaters and mixers, garlic presses, and can openers.

With its emphasis on de-emphasizing generational differences, Down-Aging holds great potential for any business that can cross age barriers and appeal to youngsters and oldsters. If you can appeal to both at the same time, so much the better.

Good old-fashioned "nostalgia" has a major place in the Down-Aging trend. The past—no doubt romanticized—holds powerful sway over our imaginations. The ad campaign for Levi's 501 jeans plays on this by stating, "Don't know why Levi's 501 jeans have stayed in style for 150 years. The first jeans. The last great mystery." Coca-Cola's ads include an old-fashioned bottle cap, perpetuating its classic image with the tagline, "Always Coca-Cola."

Music lovers are again requesting vinyl LPs, and 45 RPMs are making their own comeback. Album sales increased in 1996 to over $25 million, thanks to popular groups such as the Beatles, the Fugees, and Pearl Jam releasing vinyl. *Vitalogy,* a Pearl Jam hit, made it to *Bill-*

board's top charts, despite (or maybe because of) the fact that it was pressed originally on vinyl. Although a CD soon followed, only those who bought the LP had a real understanding of the album's single, "Spin the Black Circle," which pays homage to the old technology and reminds us how easy it was to scratch a record's surface. Disk jockeys at hip clubs now spin these records, often faster or slower as the mood strikes, something they can't do with CDs. Eddie Vedder sings, "See this needle . . ." and "pull it out of the paper sleeve." Mariah Carey's hit song, "Dream Lover," had intentionally added needle scratches.

The same toys you played with as a pup are making a steady comeback for this upcoming generation. Only now they are called "Classics." And they're consistently antitechnological. Radio-controlled cars, planes, and boats can thrill away your Down-Aging hours. Stamp collecting has returned as a hobby. You can share your exotic favorites by sending Say It With Stamps cards, decorated with real canceled postage stamps that have been steamed off and applied to greeting cards.

Down-Aging playthings can benefit many generations. The remake of the 1933 Schwinn Classic Cruiser bicycle with its one gear, foot brake, and retro curves appeals to younger kids, who like the simple lines, as well as to Down-Agers, who appreciate the charm and the memories.

Kathleen Matthews, of "Working Woman TV," told us what a click it was for her to get yo-yos and marbles from the Nature Company for her two sons and a Madame Alexander doll for her daughter. "The doll is traditional and dressed beautifully, and exactly like one I played with when I was a little girl," she said nostalgically.

Yes, we all want to recapture the past and hold on to our youth as long as we possibly can. We refuse to be inhibited by traditional notions of age and its limitations. We Americans are an optimistic people at heart—we believe anything is possible. Including turning back—or at least slowing down—the clock. Down-Aging is a trend that will blossom in the years to come as our population ages, or refuses to.

CLICKING WITH VIGILANTE CONSUMER

Frustrated, often angry, consumers are
manipulating the marketplace through
pressure, protest, and politics.
They cannot be taken for granted.

E ver watchful. That's today's consumer. We're tired
of being tricked, cajoled, hoodwinked, had. We're
out to protect our interests, and pity the poor
company or group that tries to pull a fast one on us. It's
not just the angry few who are protesting with raised
fists (and phone calls, E-mails, faxes, and protest
marches). Vigilante Consumers are everywhere. We all
carry within us the seeds of discontent.

Every time you've written an angry letter to a company about a disappointing, overpriced product or ser-

vice, you've been a Vigilante Consumer. Every time you decide not to make a purchase because you don't like a corporation's policies, you're exercising your right as a Vigilante Consumer. Every time you've clicked off a channel because you find a certain program too violent or offensive, you've clicked onto Vigilante Consumerism.

The underlying theme here is a lack of trust. Vigilante Consumers are suspicious of corporate motives, corporate sales pitches, and corporate bigwigs. We're tired of being wooed by advertisements full of false promises. When we see yet another sticker announcing "New" or "New and Improved," we roll our eyes. "Who are they trying to kid?" we ask with skepticism. "They're just trying to give us less and charge us more."

After all, we've been watching the number of tissues in the same-sized Kleenex box shrink from 95 to 85 to 70. We've realized that some of those higher priced candy bars with "40 percent less fat than the regular" are simply 40 percent smaller than the regular.

We Vigilante Consumers seek substance over style, truth over packaging, answers over press releases. We translate feelings into action, wallets into weapons. For us, shopping is war. The enemy is whoever doesn't meet our needs—and we reserve our strongest wrath for those who promise what they can't deliver. Vigilante

Consumers know there's strength in numbers. We're often fighting to preserve something that's dear to our hearts (family time, the ecology, animal welfare) or to promote a point of view (vegetarianism, free speech, so-called "family values").

With high-tech "protest tools" at our fingertips, speed is on our side. Tens of thousands can send off their not-so-humble opinions by "fax zap" or by "flooding voice mail."

Now that third-graders can E-mail the White House with any number of questions and complaints, Vigilante Consumerism has become a part of growing up—which means it's likely to get even stronger in the future, when today's kids come of age. You know it's shaking up corporate America when certain *Fortune* 500 companies (Lotus, for one) hire special chief ethics officers to handle delicate problems such as sexual discrimination. You know it's part of family life when parents and kids get together to decide which brands have an acceptable moral track record.

And speaking of family life, the Vigilante Consumer trend has given birth to a subgroup we call warrior parents. These parents are absorbed with fighting for their children's future. We see evidence that they're bringing together issues such as literacy, childhood immunization, nutrition, toys, television, and music, to form a powerful national movement.

Two-Footed Friends

Ultrasensitive readers of *Vegetarian Times* who've raged against using goose or swan's down plucked from birds may be inspiring a whole new cash crop for farmers. Milkweed, wild and woolly, is being tested by the Natural Fibers Corporation of Ogallala, Nebraska, in combination with cotton, for pillows and comforters. The floaty, flossy-soft weed might also be used to make tissues and baby diapers, thereby saving trees.

With more women in the workforce—currently about 45 percent and projected to rise to 50 percent by the first decade of the next century—motivated mothers are bringing their job experience into play to shake up school boards, consumer product companies, and entertainment providers. Barney, the purple dinosaur, a $500-million-a-year business, was originally created by a mother from Houston concerned about the over-acceptance of aggressive toys for kids. One group of warrior parents, upset about the sexist messages in the computer chips behind the voices of Talking Barbie and Talking Ken, raided toy stores and opened boxes of the dolls to switch voice mechanisms: Barbie bellowed gruff, rough commands while Ken demurely made luncheon dates. The manufacturer learned about the switcheroo—an unequivocal message had been sent.

Warrior parents can—and frequently do—take an active role in actual and suspected drug problems. After his son died of an overdose, actor Carroll O'Connor swore to avenge the senseless loss by pressing charges against the pusher who sold the lethal dosage. The unexpected outcome? He won. Parents in a working-class town in Massachusetts bonded together to form support groups when the members of a cheerleading squad took nearly lethal doses of a muscle relaxant for "fun." The concern over drugs prompted warrior parents to demand availability of at-home drug-testing kits.

One of the obvious characteristics of the '90s consumer: a high degree of impatience, almost at the boiling point. Ever look closely at people who wait in line at the movies, the supermarket, at restaurants, or at the post office? Don't you sometimes think that any minute some explosion is going to occur as a result of aggravated restlessness? Not necessarily violence, just maybe a severe temper tantrum from normally normal people who have reached the end of their tethers. Impatient with companies that don't seem to care about consumers. Irritated with service providers who provide anything but service.

Testing One-Two-Three

A simple envelope holds an easy method for detecting the presence of nonprescription drugs on your child's body or in his room. Without samples of blood, urine, or hair, Barringer DrugAlert can give an extremely accurate reading just from picking up invisible traces of drugs on everyday objects—such as a desktop, a computer keyboard or phone, the steering wheel of a car, or the handle of a school locker. There's a small "collection" cloth you use to "dust" over the surface, along with a sealable sample bag and ID number. You send these to the company and wait for a confidential lab report, which, if positive, can even pinpoint what specific drugs are being used: cocaine, heroin, methamphetamine, LSD, PCP, THC (marijuana, hashish), and any of their derivatives such as crack cocaine. Call 800-378-4942 for more information.

Of course, such techniques send the message to kids that we don't trust them and could very well backfire with a reverse click: Will Vigilante kids take their parents to court for invasion of privacy?

Prescription for Safety

Getting a doctor to prescribe the right drug is only part of the battle for health. You have to be able to read the label on your medication and then speak to someone knowledgeable about side effects and drug interactions.

A pertinent K mart advertisement clicked with the concerned Vigilante Consumer, strongly suggesting the necessity of shopping around for a pharmacist. It said, "My pharmacist wasn't checking for drug interactions, so I decided it was time to interact with another pharmacist." K mart sent this frightening message: "Not talking can cost you. Did you know that 30 percent to 50 percent of prescriptions dispensed each year are taken incorrectly? And 11 percent of all hospital admissions are due to patients improperly taking their drugs." K mart has a click going here. Besides providing customers with a take-home computer printout of medication information, it also has an 800-number to call for answers.

CVS, the chain of drugstore superstores, advertises a "quiet corner" in each store, where a customer can have a confidential chat with the pharmacist and ask personal questions about the medication and its effects.

When violence does break out, there's always the use of citizen's arrest—another form of Vigilante Consumerism. Remember the couple on a cruise ship that videotaped the crew hurling bags of garbage overboard? That couple received a reward of $250,000 for their vigilance. Now the Center for Marine Conservation (202-429-5609) has created kits for passengers, explaining procedures for policing the seas. Called a Citizen's Report Form for Observed Marine Pollution, it lends a hand (and spying eyes) to the U.S. Coast Guard. Nobody owns the oceans; they are a shared resource, and Consumer Vigilantes are going to make sure they're not abused. The flip side of this attitude is the angry consumer who insists that he has the right to do as he likes and resents any regulation or government interference in his life. Fair enough, the Vigilante Consumer answers, as long as it's on your property and stays exclusively on your property— which pollution most decidedly does not.

There is such free-floating angst and consumer anxiety in every corner of the country, a Seattle-based magazine called *Boycott Quarterly* was founded to help Vigilante Consumers decide where to direct their rage. It spells out the reasons you should actively join forces with any number of boycotts occurring at any given time.

Another rile-upper, the *Bottom Line* newsletter, pokes and provokes with undercover information such as how to check out your accountant's competency, which is the dirtiest airline, how to get VIP treatment in hospitals, and so on. It also warns against some of life's little risks: Would you believe those whooshing airline toilets can be dangerous to your health? According to the newsletter, the hindquarters of an obese person could create an airtight seal around the toilet seat. Flush and . . .

Computers can also rally the troops. Take the case of Bill Knutson, a freelance technical writer, who was asked to take a drug test by Hewlett-Packard before he could start on his next home-office-based job for the company. It was a new policy, he was told. He refused, on grounds of privacy, and didn't get hired. Chagrined, Bill logged onto the WELL to share his frustrating experience. Almost immediately, someone suggested a boycott of HP. Some wrote letters of protest, while others looked for replacement opportunities for him.

Bill's tale of protest fanned out from the smaller WELL to the entire Internet. Others have joined in to say no to drug testing—especially for freelancers. It's very satisfying to know that your complaint is reaching a potential audience of millions. Even *Spin,* the hippie-zippy music magazine, has launched an on-line service called *Night Whine* that gives computerphiles a venue to nag and complain.

Ralph Nader could be called the Father of Vigilante Consumerism for showing America that having a big mouth can do a lot of good. He clicked as a consumer hero when he announced to the auto companies, in a loud and clear voice, that the cars we were driving were *Unsafe at Any Speed*. That Nader book came out in 1965, in an aura and era of tumult: student protests, sit-ins, and the rising growth of the women's movement, gay liberation, and civil rights. Now, 30 years later, we're protesting everything in our paths, from mere bad service to monumental moral decisions that go against our beliefs. And let's not forget that the car companies tried to destroy Ralph Nader, investigating his private life and spreading malicious rumors. Do we have *any* reason to believe that large corporations today won't resort to similar tactics? In early 1997, the infamous Texaco tapes came to light, revealing blatant, institutionalized racism at the highest levels of that corporate behemoth. Thousands of Vigilante Consumers tore up their Texaco credit cards in response.

An example of a Nader-like Vigilante Consumer—with a wry '90s sensibility—is muckraker Michael Moore. After taking on General Motors in his low-budget, highly scathing documentary *Roger & Me,* Moore was given the NBC summer news magazine series *TV Nation*. With his wild sense of audacity, he created outrageous segments such as one showing that New York cabdrivers are more likely to pick up a man in a clown suit than a well-dressed black man. He even offered a viewer call-in to pick the next country for the United States to invade. "I want people to be angry," says Moore. "I want them to get up and do something." On one show, Moore camped outside Ford Motors headquarters and prodded its CEO, Alex Trotman, to show on camera that he knew enough about his company's cars to do something as simple as change the oil in a Bronco. "Prove it," in front of our very eyes, is now the name of the game.

But you don't have to be a Ralph Nader or Michael Moore to make a difference. Ordinary citizens are more than up to the job. In the music being marketed to the public—especially, tender young ears—a consumer outcry forced Michael Jackson to rerecord a song on his CD *HIStory,* deleting certain anti-Semitic lyrics. Time Warner felt the heat about obscene language and offensive actions promoted in gangsta rap. Indeed, the company decided to sell its 50 percent interest in Interscope Records, which has produced many of the gangsta hits, although that decision is unlikely to have much effect on future productions in this genre. (It helps that prominent politicians have spoken out in favor of censoring phrases that promote rape and violence.)

You can click with the specific Vigilante Consumerism that suits your frustration by finding a vigilant group with your interests. Look at some of the narrow-niche groups. There's the long-named, small-focused Safety for Women and Responsible Motherhood group in Colorado, which has 1,500 women banding

Hey, Mr. Postman

If you're thinking of stopping all mail delivery because you can't deal with the 40 pounds of junk mail you receive every week, there's help available. You can join the 50,000 people a month who write to the Mail Preference Service, Box 9008, Farmingdale, NY 11735, to have their names taken off mailing lists for five years. It cuts down—but doesn't cut out—the reams of unsolicited catalogs, flyers, sale announcements, charity requests, and so on. You can also ask for your name to be deleted from telephone lists (same address, different box: #9014).

Unwanted telephone calls always come at unwanted times. Michael Jacobson, cofounder of the nonprofit Center for the Study of Commercialism in Washington, D.C., says, "People are angry about intrusive calls. I hope that people file so many lawsuits that telemarketers finally understand that a nuisance call at dinnertime is not the way to do business."

In an episode of *Seinfeld,* Jerry tells a telemarketer, "I'm sorry, I'm having dinner right now. Why don't you give me your home number and

> I'll call you back later." We tried doing that. The caller started to sputter and said, indignantly, "*You* can't call *me* at home!" "No?" we said. "Then don't call us." Click.

together because they want to carry concealed handguns. And there's a network for kids who want to rally against things they don't particularly like in their schools. Originally formed to protest being forced to watch the commercials in the classroom on Channel One, Unplug sends out a video on how to effect change on such common complaints as school rules, old textbooks that are falling apart, and yucky cafeteria food.

One citizen action group that clearly shows the power of a click is MADD, Mothers Against Drunk Driving. It has changed the way America parties. By applying both political pressure for tougher laws and social pressure for appointing a designated driver (now a part of everyone's party vocabulary), this group has contributed significantly to the reduction in alcohol-related traffic deaths. In the decade that ended in 1994 those deaths declined by 30 percent. For reasons yet to be explained, the number of deaths from alcohol-related accidents began rising again in 1995, despite the fact that public awareness about the dangers is high. Which only proves that Vigilante Consumers can't let down their guard.

Another area in which the Vigilante Consumer is making noise is health. The members of the group at the Center for Science in the Public Interest think of themselves as "Food Cops." First came their exposés on the high fat and salt content in typical Chinese and Italian restaurant fare. They were the ones to describe fettucine Alfredo as "a heart attack on a plate." After that, they sounded the nutritional alarm against those buckets of greasy, salty, finger-lickin'-good popcorn at the movies, and, via public pressure, got many a movie theater to offer the air-popped variety. Exposés of Mexican food, mayo-laced tuna sandwiches, and even the ubiquitous muffin (basically a cupcake, but with more fat and sugar) soon followed.

Food Cops of another kind are fighting thinness rather than fat. Boycott Anorexic Marketing, founded by Mary Baures in the Boston area, focuses on a struggle against the practice of featuring skeletal models in advertising. Companies that use young skin-and-bones models (notoriously bad role models for adolescent girls) are identified, and consumers asked to boycott their products. Among the early targets are Diet Sprite for its underweight imagery and, of course, Calvin Klein for its jeans ads with the model all normal-sized women love to protest—Kate Moss.

Bucking Starbucks

A perfect example of a sour courtship (or Vigilante Revenge to the max) exists between Starbucks and Jeremy Dorosin of Walnut Creek, California, who bought an espresso machine at his local branch of the chain coffeebar. After complaining of a malfunction with his machine, he was given a "loaner" by the store while his was being repaired (so far, so good). Liking the one on loan, Dorosin purchased a like-kind to give as a wedding gift. But something was also wrong with that machine. Consumer Dorosin felt his inexpensive gift machine should be upgraded for all the trouble.

When Starbucks balked, he took out four ads in regional *Wall Street Journals,* costing many thousands of dollars. In the ad Dorosin included his toll-free number. So far, 3,000 other disgruntled Starbucks consumers have called in with their stories, and the Vigilante Consumer has been interviewed on TV (including CNN), on radio, and in major newspapers. Starbucks has tried to right the wrong, sending two new machines, gifts, and apologies, but too late for Mr. Dorosin. He now wants them to take out a two-page ad in the national edition of the paper (they refused). He's also asking the company, which is involved in community service, to open a center for runaway children in San Francisco.

When we spoke with Mr. Dorosin, he explained his tenacity. "With all the moral decay and level of dissatisfaction in this country, someone has to say, 'This has gone too far, and I'm going to stick up for myself.' If we walk into a store which touts customer service as their highest standard, pay for that service, and still not get it, how can we expect anybody to adhere to what is right vs. what is wrong? . . . At least, the runaway center could make a bad situation good. Even though I'm not getting any pleasure out of this, I'm going to follow it out and make it my life's mission to finish what I started."

Good luck, Starbucks, on ending this public relations nightmare. For many injured consumers, J. Dorosin is a Vigilante Consumer hero.

In New York and elsewhere, angry consumers scrawled "Feed Me!" over bus stop and subway posters of the pale and hollow Ms. Moss. When the protests began drawing more attention than the ads themselves, Calvin Klein quietly replaced them.

Another eating-oriented consumer group, Vermont-based Food & Water, has taken up the banner against toxic pesticides in food production. Members feel that the federal government has really fallen short by allowing the use of carcinogenic pesticides if they pose only a "negligible risk" to human health. "No risk" has a healthier, longer-life sound to it than "negligible risk." F&W is collecting signatures on Declarations of Opposition to Negligible Risk—about 500,000 in all—and is backing this up with local Neighborhood Networks for additional education and action. Think of all the other Vigilante Consumer causes that could model themselves after this well-thought-out campaign.

The point is: Vigilante Consumers are mad as hell and aren't going to take it any longer. And any company that tries to sneak something past them is bound to be sorry—and sooner rather than later. Instead of trying to pull the wool over consumers' eyes, it's best to take a hard look at what's happening out there and address some of the concerns.

In many cases just a small amount of basic common sense and a willingness to service your customer will make all the difference between anger and appeasement. What ever happened to a spontaneous gesture to please? That's the smart way to approach a Vigilante Consumer.

In business, you can easily deflect the wrath of a Vig-

Transforming Tragedy

Vigilante Consumers can be born out of tragedy. Maybe it's from watching too many episodes of television shows like *ER* and *Chicago Hope*, but you'd probably feel relatively calm if your loved one suffered chest pains when already in the safe haven of a modern hospital.

That's what Myra Rosenbloom thought: The experienced doctors with the Code Blue team would leap into action and make everything all right. But when her husband died in an Indiana hospital that had not one doctor on duty, she went on a quest to try to right that wrong. After investigating the laws, she found out that Indiana, as well as 20 other states, simply did not require hospitals to have doctors physically present 24 hours a day. Cost was the reason.

Rosenbloom kept pestering the politicians, and even went on a six-day "sleep in" at the capitol until a form of her measure passed. Click for her. And for anybody in a hospital in the state of Indiana. Now, what about the other 20 states?

ilante Consumer (before an apology is needed) by being a Vigilante first. Anticipate problems. If you know that an integral part of your product isn't working up to snuff, think about sending out a replacement to a customer's home before you're forced to make a recall. Even if you are working out of an old, precode building, why not consider putting in a handicapped ramp even before you're required to by law? Look closely to see if your business is treating all minority groups equally and fairly.

Look to click down a new avenue of integrity. Start by being forthright and admitting your faults. The recent "honesty is the best policy" ad campaign for Jaguar cars confronts their well-known past mechanical problems: "We've kept what you've loved. The rest is history."

Vigilante Consumers are out there in force and they're not going away. Don't think you can dodge them forever. Remember this: *Anger* is only one letter short of *Danger.*

CLICKING WITH ICON TOPPLING

Skeptical consumers are ready to bring down
the long-accepted monuments of business,
government, celebrity, and society.

Is nothing sacred anymore? The Lincoln bedroom is
for sale and the Speaker of the House is fined
$300,000 for unethical behavior. Ma Bell is ancient
history, and trying to pick a phone company has
become an exercise in anxiety. The three oldest television networks are losing market share faster than the
Edsel. The Royal Family (pre–Diana's untimely and sor-
rowful death) was behaving like tabloid trash, and sports
heroes sulk while collecting $20 million a season. The
Evil Empire is floundering in crime-ridden chaos. The

Catholic Church keeps more dirty secrets than J. Edgar Hoover. Supreme Court Justice Clarence Thomas makes regular appearances on right-wing televangelists' TV shows. A higher percentage of Americans know that Howard Stern has a small penis than can name the vice president. Doctors are feared and mistrusted, schools aren't doing their job, and everyone knows that a blood transfusion can kill you.

What is happening to the good old U.S. of A.?

The political, business, and cultural bedrocks that anchored our lives are crumbling like stale scones. Authority is something we question as a matter of course, and dismiss as often as not. Civility is a thing of the past and integrity, patience, and faith are starting to look like quaint anachronisms. Corporations are greedy organizations without allegiance to any country or loyalty to employees.

Welcome to Icon Toppling—the socioquake that's transforming mainstream America and the world. Over and over, the pillars of society are being questioned and rejected. Who or what can we trust if we lose faith in government, corporations, marriage, religion, education, medicine, advertising, retailing, heroes, and even our own families? Not much.

We no longer sheepishly follow authority, accept the old rules, or only buy name brands. The larger the entity, the more suspicious or resentful we are. Even institutions that have been around for a long time can't bank on touting their heritage anymore. Too many companies earned our trust and then abused it. Ford and GM thought they could get away with shoddy products, and for a while they did. But after too many lemons rolled off the line, consumers got wise. Winning us back hasn't been easy, and we'll never blindly trust these and other corporate turncoats again.

Business as usual has become a prescription for extinction. American corporations are trembling. The broad generalizations of the past aren't working anymore. Big business needs new ideas and new paradigms. When highly conservative companies started knocking on BrainReserve's door for help, we had our first inkling that the by-the-books business world had turned upside down.

Remember when department stores were fun and satisfying places to shop? Today they are in real danger of becoming relics. The list of departed stores reads like a who's who of American retailing: A&S (after 112 years), Alexander's, B. Altman, Bonwit Teller, Gimbel's, Ohrbach's (the best of imported "collection" clothes), the venerable I. Magnin, and scores of others. In *The Popcorn Report,* we reviewed BrainReserve's 1985 prediction that department stores are the "dinosaurs of shopping," and that they could be replaced by catalogs and interactive television. Now it's happening.

One master of the dinosaurs came to us a few years back to try to find out why his chain of department stores was steadily losing customers. BrainReserve went into project-action: setting up a team, probing our TalentBank, doing scores of one-on-one interviews, and scanning the culture to come up with some answers. One major reason, we deduced, was that women simply did not have time to shop in a poorly laid-out, poorly staffed, and poorly stocked environment. Department stores can be eminently unfriendly or even hostile, with merchandise tethered to the walls on metal cords to prevent customers from stealing. I call it clothing on leashes. (Tip: If you're frustrated by being ignored by the sales help and want instant service, just yank one of those security tethers. Bells and whistles go off and you'll get the immediate attention you deserve.)

Our department store client turned to me halfway through the BrainReserve presentation and said, "Honey . . . " (My own informal analysis shows that everyone who calls me "honey" goes into Chapter 11 within one year. He did.) "What would women do if they couldn't shop?"

That's how Icons Topple—by not seeing what's right in front of their eyes. His corporate setup hadn't noticed that things had changed. Women, like men, are time-stressed, busy juggling home, career, relationships, children, health, exercise, repairs—life. No one finds it fun anymore to waste hours trying to buy one needed item. As a quick alternative, it's too easy to dash into a specialty store that has a concentration of focused merchandise or to dial up a catalog's 800 number (or log onto an Internet site) at any hour of the day or night.

The supermarket is next. The men (mostly) who run them haven't realized yet that the women who regularly shop there—with two screaming hungry kids in the cart and a strict budget to adhere to—don't *really love* food shopping.

American business—indeed our culture as a whole— is paying an enormous price for the recent rash of downsizing. Companies are unilaterally rewriting the social contract, and if we don't like it, well, they'll just take their jobs to India, thank you very much. It's pretty hard to trust the folks at GE, H-P, and AT&T when that seems to be their prevailing attitude.

Icon Toppling has made us aware that corporate giants can become corporate monsters and turn on us at any time. When you total it all up, corporations announced over 475,000 job cuts in 1996, most in the fields of telecommunications, retailing, and computers. More than 17 million of us have been downsized, right-sized, and reengineered out of jobs since 1990. That adds up to a lot of disgruntled people—and a lot of Toppled Icons.

The workplace is far from the only venue where our

Net-working

A recent advertisement for the Cable & Wireless Alliance boldly announced its concept: "The corporation is dead. Long live the federation." The ad read, "The traditional, lumbering, top-heavy, and multi-layered corporations of today cannot survive in the new chaotic marketplace. . . . And what do they [business advisers] predict in their place? Federations of smaller companies and groups free to move quickly and efficiently in an ever changing marketplace." This is the basis of the Cable & Wireless partnership—to put together a network of more than 50 organizations worldwide, forging the fifth-largest telecommunications group in the world.

When you think about this, there's something savvy going on here that hearkens back to the ancient concept of trade guilds. Where cooperation, not backstabbing, reigns among like interests. It's not about creating a new icon, a monolithic organization that claims invincibility—it's about delivering great service on a dime.

social contract has frayed. The World Trade Center and the Murrah Federal Building in Oklahoma City are bombed, fanatics attack family planning clinics and

Cleaning House

Nike, stung by allegations that it uses sweatshops across Asia to produce its highly profitable sneakers, recently hired Andrew Young to review its labor practices. The former mayor of Atlanta and U.S. representative to the United Nations is only the latest example of corporate-icon polishing cum damage control. Mitsubishi brought in former secretary of labor and congresswoman Lynn Martin to investigate charges of sexual harassment at its Normal, Illinois, plant. The company agreed to act on her recommendations. Texaco has hired former federal judge A. Leon Higgenbotham to help overhaul personnel practices after the debacle of the "racist tapes." Dow Corning, GM, and Bausch & Lomb are other companies that have brought in high-profile outsiders of unimpeachable integrity to help them answer allegations and make positive changes. In those cases where action backs up recommendations and abuses are corrected, this is clicking at its best.

their staffs, the Tokyo subway is gassed. Open anarchy and hatred spew over talk radio and the Internet. A hate-radio host in Arizona broadcasts that "Hillary Clinton should be taken to the vet and put down like a dog that yaps too much." How does that kind of disrespect and language affect our national psyche? The fact that there is so little outrage is evidence that we have turned into a nation of cynics, bullet-fast.

Remember when the cop on the beat was a friend? How do we reconcile this with the videotapes of police beatings and brutalities, disclosures of evidence tampering, the gutter language and lying of a Mark Fuhrman? Four police officers in New Orleans are charged with murder, and it's discovered that for years the Philadelphia police framed literally thousands of citizens for crimes they didn't commit. In one Harlem precinct alone, 28 officers were arrested for drug dealing. As Jesse Jackson eloquently explained to Charlie Rose, "The youth have been drug running; the police have been drug dealing. When there is no distinction between cops and robbers . . . [we] discredit the entire judicial system, and we are very vulnerable." Filmmaker Sidney Lumet delves deeply into these problems in his thought-provoking movie, *Night Falls over Manhattan.*

When a nation starts to view its law upholders as lawbreakers, an important Icon is Toppled, and the social fabric further tears.

The nightmare is on Elm Street, too. As women enter the workforce in record numbers, even that most unassailable American icon has come under fire: motherhood. Yes, we've all learned that even Mom is

Cop In

In New York, Mayor Rudolph Giuliani, a former federal prosecutor, has revolutionized the police department. A computer now tracks crime street by street on a daily basis. Police brass study the results, discern patterns, and take a proactive approach, sending extra manpower to specific neighborhoods, streets, and even buildings. Giuliani has also instituted strict enforcement of quality-of-life laws such as those restricting loud radios, littering, and begging. The results: Crime is down in all categories, the murder rate is the lowest in 30 years, and a sense of order and control has returned to the city. Yes, Icons can be rehabilitated.

human—she's stressed, she's cranky, and the last damn thing she wants to do is bake a batch of cookies. And Dad—who has his own problems—is hardly picking up the slack. These days, the American parent is largely absent, leaving the latchkey kid home alone much too often. An average parent (in a two-parent household) ekes out only a total of seven hours per week with her or his children. Bye-bye, American pie.

If parents aren't available, at least there are schools, safe havens where our kids will get educated and socialized. Hello?! These days, nobody's minding the schools and the new reality is a generation of kids raising themselves on a combination of junk food, junk movies, and just plain junk. Former New York school chancellor Raymond Cortines told *Newsday,* "Sometimes, I think we should be handing out medals for bravery instead of diplomas." My own cousin, Maureen Rosenkrantz, a New York City teacher who has dedicated 30 years to kids, was pushed down a flight of stairs at Washington Irving High School and required 53 stitches on her face.

It's not just a problem in urban areas. Police are being sent to athletic events in almost 90 percent of schools. For children, there's daily anxiety generated by walking through metal detectors, witnessing slashings, stabbings, and shootings, and slinking around in fear of gang intimidation. The old three "Rs" of our school days have turned into three "Gs": Gangs, Guns, and Getting high.

There was a time when a college diploma was a passport for getting a job. Today, that piece of paper doesn't guarantee anything. Some 30 percent of graduates between now and 2005 will "march straight into the ranks of the jobless," according to a recent study by the American Management Association. A full 15 percent of law-school grads are still pounding the pavement six months after graduation. The college-degree-as-job-entry Icon has Toppled.

Special Ed

Two key new directions are emerging out of the rubble of our public education icon. Home or alternative schooling, now a reality for 1 percent of America's children, is part of a push for more safety and stronger family ties. Then there is the privatization of schools (kudos to Chris Whittle for trying). Big click opportunities exist here.

Remember when the church represented a sanctified space, a shelter from the hustle-bustle of life that provided an opportunity for reflection and spiritual growth? Icon Toppling is redefining exactly what was meant by the concept of "the sins of the fathers."

In Australia, the pope's joyous 1995 visit was overshadowed by a child abuse scandal. Six Catholic clergymen and teachers were jailed, one for a term of 18 years, for the flagrant molestation of underage victims.

The Church tries hard to keep its secrets—at a price. It's been estimated that approximately $400 million has been quietly paid out in legal fees and settlements to cover sexual abuse lawsuits. In Chicago, there's even a support group called SNAP—Survivors Network of those Abused by Priests—which has compiled a list of several hundred pedophile priests. These days,

Driving Forces

One bureaucracy on its way to a user-friendly click is Connecticut's Department of Motor Vehicles. A cost-cutting program has actually led to improved service. After closing eight branches, the DMV opened 16 *rent-free* offices in shopping malls. The mall developers saw it as a traffic-builder, and the consumer sees it as convenient. Many large companies are also paying the DMV to send clerks in mobile units to serve their employees on-site.

Other states are letting go of control by allowing car dealers to register the new cars they sell. Arizona's DMV has cut down on paperwork, offering new drivers a license valid until age 60 with no need for constant renewals. California and Virginia are experimenting with ATMs for ordering plates and renewing registrations. In Massachusetts, you can even pay for a speeding ticket by entering your credit card number over a touch-tone phone. Everything the state agencies are doing works toward the dual goal: customer *and* worker satisfaction.

churches can't get full-coverage liability insurance anymore because of the risk. The policies are beginning to exclude any clauses covering minors and pastoral liability. This fear has spilled over to coaching and summer camps as well. New rules are the norm, stating: "A counselor must never be alone with a camper," or "Never tickle or wrestle with . . . "

For decades, Saturday's biggest thrill was going to a double feature or a doubleheader. Where are the heroes we can still believe in? We know all too much about movie stars—their romantic entanglements and health problems are lead stories on tabloid television shows. And sports heroes have been tarnished by drug and assault scandals, and their unbecoming habit of whining about fans and management while cashing mind-boggling paychecks. That sound you hear is Icons Toppling. According to a Video Storyboard survey in 1996, the approval rating for featuring celebrities in commercials has dropped because they dilute/distract from the message of the product. Yet advertising agencies still keep looking for someone fresh and viable to be a hero. Unlike the past when a celebrity endorser was likely to be a tried-and-true face, today seven of the top ten are newcomers, less likely to be tainted by scandal or have any skeletons waiting to burst out of the closet.

Watch any one of the over 15 television news magazines—including *20/20, 48 Hours, Prime Time Live,* and *Hard Copy*—and you'll quickly find the answer to our opening question, "Is anything sacred?" Murder, may-

Gap-lash

The first evidence of a backlash against The Gap came on the hit sitcom *Ellen* when Ellen DeGeneres dubbed her squeaky-clean neighbors "Gaps."

The Gap is fighting back. It was one of the lead sponsors of the New York City AIDS Walk in which millions of dollars were raised. Red ribbons were prominently displayed in store windows. This is an example of what a big national company can do to make a local connection. We could point to this as a rule for how a chain store can stay in the click-zone and not topple off the popularity cliff. Can keep from getting lost in the sheer mechanics of being an organization. Can work together as a sum of parts and not one big, unmanageable whole.

hem, and malpractice reign. Gennifer Flowers gets a half hour on *Nightline* and JonBenet Ramsey's murder supplants O. J. as our national obsession and reveals girls' beauty pageants to be thinly veiled child porn. A supermarket tabloid lures Frank Gifford into extramarital sex and videotapes the proceedings. Why this endless deluge of sensationalism and sleaze? Because Icon Toppling pulls in Nielsen ratings. We love seeing our gods revealed as mere mortals, and not particularly savory mortals at that.

In an age of information overload, Icon Toppling is, without a doubt, the best entertainment going. Forget the formula thrillers and action-adventure films that Hollywood churns out like clockwork. Everyone knows Tom Cruise is going to win in the end. Real life is a lot messier—and more interesting. Court TV, the ultimate insider's view into the judicial process, has the same pull. It advertises itself with the tag line "Real Drama, No Scripts."

We want the gossip, the dirt, and the intrigue, yet we also want the truth. We've been lied to and misled for so long, that we've developed highly sensitive B.S. detectors. There's an insatiable craving for the unvarnished truth, even if it isn't pretty.

Take two melatonin and *don't* call the doctor in the morning. Remember when the doctor knew best? When medicine promised a magic pill that would cure all ills. AIDS, malpractice horror stories, generally shoddy care, and astronomical medical bills have combined to destroy our faith in health care. When women are told one year that they should get an annual mammogram and then told the next year not to, and then told, "Well, maybe you should after all," is it any wonder faith in conventional medicine is at an all-time low? These days, we'll do just about anything before subjecting ourselves

What's Clicking Next?

The post office is making a valiant effort to play catch-up. Subscribers buy rolls of stamps or call for fast pickups. How about personalized vanity stamps: your own picture, your dog's, a company logo? And why can't the P.O. expand its services—become an information and tourist bureau, a ministorage unit for documents, an IRS headquarters (after all, it's always been a place to pick up tax forms), and a Social Security office.

Watch for a growth spurt in publicly traded, for-profit higher education colleges or grad schools. There is the still-small but growing DeVry, which now has 13 campuses throughout the United States, and Keller Graduate School, which has spread to 17 locations. Run on tight budgets with no fat (saving on everything from lower electricity bills due to solar heating to less fancy campuses), these accredited institutions charge about half the tuition of a large state university and a third that of a private school.

to the medical establishment. Is it any surprise herbal medicines and alternative treatments are the rage? According to Tom Rawls, editor of *Natural Health,* there

Down with Cynicism

Icon Toppling is a fact of our lives. But it's not the only fact and it most emphatically is not an excuse to just give up. Cynicism is easy, boring, and profoundly unfulfilling. You can make the world—and your life—a better place.

- Lost your belief in big business? Start your own small one, based on your expertise and your beliefs.
- Lost your belief in formal religion? Create your own brand of ritual through Zen, yoga, meditation, or even chanting. Look into Anchoring and find yourself.
- Lost your belief in the traditional family? Gather your own extended families through Clanning ties or on-line connections.
- Lost your belief in leadership? Get Vigilante Consumer political and make it a priority to get everyone to vote.
- Lost your belief in doctors? Take control of your own health. Educate yourself. Be Alive.
- Lost your belief in the police? Get involved in a local community-policing effort. Clan.
- Lost your belief in men? Find a Mancipated one.

- Lost your belief in people? Volunteer at a homeless shelter, hospital, or animal rescue. Meeting other volunteers will renew your faith.

  Click your life.

are two types of people who turn to alternative medicine: "Those who have had zero success with conventional medicine and those who are simply taking responsibility for their health. . . . People are tired of being blindly led by traditional medical practice." (See "Being Alive.")

Icon Toppling is about the failure of belief systems and institutions that have dominated our thinking and way of life for decades upon decades. But where there's failure there is also opportunity. That's why, as much as Icon Toppling is about tearing down, it's also an opening for creating something that works better. As citizens and as consumers, we *want* to trust, we yearn for honesty, for personal heroes, and products that delight us by delivering on their promises. Create those products and you will become that hero.

CLICKING WITH S.O.S. (SAVE OUR SOCIETY)

Concerned with the fate of the planet, consumers respond to marketers who exhibit a social conscience attuned to ethics, environment, and education.

The alarms are sounding. They're going off in Idaho, Brazil, and Belgium. Their shrill warning can be heard above the din in London, New York, and Tokyo. They're jarring us out of our sleep, as Bob Marley did when he sang, "Get up. Stand up. Be heard." These alarms are a global wake-up call, telling us that we must rise up and take action to Save Our Society.

A collective awareness of the threat of environmental degradation has taken hold. It is particularly strong in the United States, Germany, Japan, and other industrialized nations. In underdeveloped parts of the planet, the environment is a less pressing concern. When your children are hungry, the dangers of pollution seem distant and relatively insignificant. However, as nations such as India, China, Brazil, and (hopefully) Russia grow and prosper, look for a global sense of environmental urgency to grip the new world community. After all, a radioactive cloud escaping from a faulty nuclear power plant has no respect for national borders. The alarm grows louder.

What are *you* going to do? Go back to sleep or leap out of bed and join the battle to save the world? That's the question underlying the trend of S.O.S.—or Save Our Society—which BrainReserve first identified twelve years ago. It's a trend that we'll be tracking for decades to come. Like the ship's distress call from which it takes its name, S.O.S. means that nothing less than survival is at stake.

We've put emission controls on our cars to help clean up the air, but what about the other kinds of gas motors? On summer weekends, up to 50 million lawn mowers send out clouds of pollution (the EPA estimates that mowers and blowers account for 20 percent of *all* air pollution). The noisy gas guzzlers do as much damage in a half hour as a car does in four to five hours. The easiest answer: fit lawn mowers with $100 tax-deductible pollution controls.

We can safely say that in a few short years recycling has become a way of life. After a brief period of balking, we're separating out glass and cans. We tie up our newspapers and break down our cartons. Twine sales are soaring. So are prices for recycled newspapers. You can't walk into a major corporation or building these days without seeing the recycling label on the garbage pails. Some communities are holding monthly garage sales at which citizens can swap or sell their discards. Others have an area at the dump where throw-aways, many of them perfectly usable, can be claimed. Supermarkets routinely offer reusable or recyclable shopping bags. CDs, once the poster child of overpackaging, have been stripped of their enormous outer layer. The reusable string-mesh shopping bags ubiquitous in Europe are starting to catch on in the United States. And have you noticed how many people are sending faxes with small Post-its instead of cover pages? It's become ingrained in our social consciousness that it's smart—and crucial—not to waste.

After switching to a plain-paper fax machine, Lys was appalled to see the size (and waste) of the toner cartridge that had to be replaced every couple hundred pages. Click! Computer Friends of Portland, Oregon, has introduced a universal system (cost: $80) to recycle used toner cartridges and ribbons from 23,000 models of printers, photocopiers, and fax machines.

Musical Boxes

A friend turned us on to a terrific, simple way to cut back on waste. When someone gives you a boxed gift, use the box next time you give a present. Like musical chairs, the last person to end up with a battered box gets stuck with the task of crushing it and taking it out for recycling.

The long-term answer to Clicking into S.O.S., however, is to cut back on *creating* waste. In our resort area of the Hamptons the population surge can be estimated by the garbage collection: It goes from 18 to 20 tons a day in winter to over 120 tons a day on peak summer weekends. There's something scary about walking around New York City on a large-item pickup day. So many people, so much stuff. Mattresses leaning up against parking meters, three and four per street. Where can it possibly all go? We need to concentrate on making more products that can last a lifetime or be easily repaired, recharged, or reconstituted.

One problem is that the cost of repairs comes mighty close to replacement value. Whenever our appliances—TVs, VCRs, fax machines, even toaster ovens—break, we feel justified in tossing them and buying a brand-new one with all the latest features.

And then there are the small things—which quickly add up. Americans toss out a zillion batteries of the AA, C, D, and 9-volt types, all filled with leakable mercury, lead, lithium, cadmium, zinc, and other minerals. Why can't it be mandatory to use solar rechargeables only? Every little bit and bristle helps. A German company, Monte-Bianco, has come up with a method of putting new bristles on old toothbrushes, so if you like the handle you never have to throw it out. Seems minor, but it sends a major message.

Instead of using Styrofoam pellets, there's a protective packaging fill called Eco-foam made by American Excelsior composed of 95 percent starch and a small amount of organic polymer. It simply dissolves in water or on your compost pile. Environmental groups are even pushing the use of real popcorn for packing and protecting breakables. Besides being delicious (an admittedly biased opinion), popcorn is biodegradable and can be composted later on. Formerly one of the world's biggest users of polystyrene packaging, McDonald's has turned to cardboard for its carryout food. The fast-food chain's latest effort for S.O.S. is composting its scraps and leftovers to cut down the volume of excess garbage.

Even the Pentagon has been thinking green. Beyond adding more trees and grasses around the geometric building and its parking lots, a 1995 renovation included acres of natural fiber carpeting and insulation materials, nontoxic paints (why did it take so long?), and energy-efficient lights and computers. It's been estimated that because of lower energy costs, the environmentally sound materials and new designs will pay for themselves in three years.

It helps an S.O.S. cause to click if famous folks get personally involved. In our celebrity-obsessed world, it's the fastest way to get publicity. Ted Turner and Jane Fonda try to effect change by being members of the Environmental Media Association board of directors. Robert Redford lends his support as president of the Institute for Resource Management and a board member of the Environmental Defense Fund and the Natural Resources Defense Council. Sting works for the preservation of the rain forest, giving star-studded benefit concerts to raise money. Greenpeace has a CD for sale called Alternative NRG, featuring such stars as Annie Lennox, REM, and U2, which was recorded and mixed using solar power. The fabulous funny lady Bette Midler has started a cleanup group in New York that targets trash-littered culverts, stream banks, and highways. The Divine Miss M lends more than her name—she rolls up her sleeves and gets down and dirty for a cause she believes in.

Kids, too, pitch in with enthusiasm and a knack for getting news. Remember, it was a child-led boycott of

Mobile Electricity

Electric automobiles have finally become a reality—prodded along by state laws. General Motors introduced the EV1 in Arizona and Southern California in December 1996 and it has been selling briskly to celebrities and businesses eager to further efforts to lessen air pollution.

Toyota has gone a step further—the company recently announced plans to bring a vehicle featuring a hybrid gasoline and electric engine to the Japanese mass market. The engine gets 66 miles to the gallon (twice as many as the best-selling Corolla), reduces carbon dioxide emissions by half, and the emission of other gases by 90 percent. Audi, GM, Ford, and Chrysler are all following suit, with the Big Three receiving funding from the Department of Energy for their R & D efforts.

tuna that led to the voluntary banning of tuna nets that killed dolphins. Children today are growing up with a strong awareness of our planet's fragile ecological balance. According to Response Analysis, which surveyed 27,000 citizens in 24 countries in 1997, young Americans age 18–25 express stronger environmental concerns than virtually any other citizens in the world. They

Planet Pals

Spain has its own version of "enviro-cops," Seprona, a public watchdog association that sniffs out anyone who pollutes the land or seas. Seprona also publicizes an easy-to-remember phone number—091—so ordinary citizens can report polluters. A tough global "eco-patrol" that is on guard against big-company misdeeds—such as leaking barrels of radioactive materials or illegal ocean dumping—goes under the moniker of Earth Alarm and is headquartered in Amsterdam.

want action and believe the environment should be preserved even at the risk of slowed economic growth. The generations that come will no doubt have even less tolerance for pollution and polluters than we do.

Even though endangered animals are still disappearing, they're not going without notice—or a fight. The peregrine falcon is perching on the tops of New York skyscrapers and soaring around the helicopter lanes. Ospreys have returned to the swampy areas of the East Coast. On the beaches, too many piping plovers are still being run over by the increased traffic of four-wheel drives, despite the roping off of nesting sites.

> **Winning Goal**
>
> The Florida Panthers, an NHL hockey team, is determined to save its namesake. Because of habitat lost to development, the state's sleek panther population is endangered, with as few as under 50 animals left alive. Hockey fans and local corporations pledge money to save the cats each time a Panther goalie makes a "save" at a home game.

For too long many in the business community have resisted a wholehearted embrace of environmental sensitivity. They have played on people's economic insecurities with the cry: "Jobs are more important than trees." These irresponsible, short-sighted prognosticators are being proved wrong. If ever there was a paper tiger, it's the argument that the environment/economy is an either/or proposition.

Remember the famous spotted owl controversy in the Northwest? The prevalent economic fear was that if the owls were saved, the timber communities of Oregon would become ghost towns. It was assumed there would be a rippling wave of foreclosures and a crippling recession. "We'll be up to our neck in owls, and every mill worker will be out of a job," then-President

Bush forecast while campaigning in the region. But the calamity never happened. Even with deep curtailment of logging in the federally owned forests, Oregon posted its lowest unemployment rate (under 5 percent) in many years. One ex–mill worker who had switched careers after going through the state retraining program said, "I never had any other options in my hometown but the mill. Now, a whole new world has opened up."

It's time for the antienvironmentalists in the business community and the political arena to stop their fear-mongering and embrace long-term, integrated solutions. Because without a livable planet, jobs and other economic benefits will be meaningless. This is not about tree-huggers—many of the world's most *cautious* scientists are raising their voices in alarm about the deteriorating state of world's ecology.

Making the necessary changes will not be easy. The Commerce Department has halted commercial fishing in almost 20 percent of the Georges Bank fishing grounds off the New England coast. This emergency action is targeted at protecting the schools of cod, haddock, and yellowtail flounder being rapidly depleted from one of the richest fishing areas in the world. The state and federal government have both initiated programs to help the out-of-work fishermen adjust to their loss of livelihood. It's a wrenching change for this proud

Winning Business

Business for Social Responsibility is an organization dedicated to promoting ethical business policies and procedures. The group has over 800 members, including Levi Strauss, Reebok, Time Warner, AT&T, Edison International, and Sony. Its annual conferences are crammed with meetings that cover such topics as "Social Responsibility Research," "Daycare in the Workplace," "Business and Children: An Agenda for Our Future," "Environmental Tools for Small Business," and "Recycling and Waste Management: Making It Pay."

Hewlett-Packard, the undisputed leader in printer and printer products, has gone one step beyond expectation in implementing programs in the U.S. and abroad for recycling toner cartridges. At no cost to themselves, consumers may send used toner cartridges back to the local HP plant for reuse or disposal. In the U.S., a mailing label is included in the packaging.

3M has discovered a new item for recycling—transparencies. The company runs a program dedicated to reclaiming overhead transparency film. In its test phase in early 1996, the program received

57,000 pounds of film. This is an effort to redirect the estimated 15 million pounds of transparency film that end up in landfills.

Although several organizations participate in the program, the largest supporter is Milliken & Company of Spartanburg, South Carolina. The company is dedicated to zero waste contribution to landfills and feels that the 3M program dovetails beautifully with its goal.

3M is preparing to expand the program nationally now that they're sure that transparencies can be recycled safely and efficiently.

breed, and they need our unqualified support. However, we all have to accept the fact that had the ban not been instituted, they—and the entire planet—would have lost these fishing grounds forever.

The S.O.S trend isn't limited to environmental activism. There's a serious interest in volunteer vacations—a book by that name describes opportunities. Listed are such high-flying items as how to help the Audubon Society track migrating birds and how to volunteer for a stirring stint at a soup kitchen. Years ago, Lys's father, Allen, a surgeon/urologist, volunteered one month a year on the hospital ship, the *Hope*. He

Don't Bungle the Jungle

Conservation International is an innovative Washington, D.C.–based organization that develops commercial enterprises based on the sustainable use of natural resources.

The Tagua initiative is an example of the CI approach. An alternative to ivory, the tagua nut makes terrific buttons. It has enjoyed tremendous popularity with upscale casual clothing manufacturers such as J. Crew and The Gap.

CI has also partnered with Subway Sandwich Shops and a Peruvian trade organization to introduce a Brazil nut cookie. Hard Rock Cafe and Ben & Jerry's Ice Cream have also gotten into the act using these versatile nuts in their culinary creations.

Covering all bases, CI is involved in personal-care products. It has developed a line of shampoos, soaps, and lotions in conjunction with companies like Forest Pure and Nature's Gate. These winning products are made from raw materials found in the rain forest but which can be harvested without adverse ecological effect.

Much of the money generated by CI's innovative partnerships is directed to raising the quality of life of the rain forest's indigenous population through social and economic opportunities.

The World Bank and Walt Disney became two of CI's most powerful associates in 1995. Disney has footed the bill for the organization's annual report, and CEO Michael Eisner is on the board of directors. The World Bank president, James Wolfensohn, is spearheading a movement to transform the bank's existing development policy and practices to ones more favorable to sustainable and renewable resources. Harrison Ford is also a board member of CI. For more information on this worthwhile organization, call 1-800-406-2306.

traveled to different ports of the world and operated from early morning to late at night, often on people who had never seen a doctor in their lives. What happened to that floating mercy ship? It became a casualty of insurance liability. Wouldn't it be wonderfully S.O.S. to send forth another? For medical attention closer to home, more doctors (and other caregivers, like nurse practitioners) could donate an afternoon a week to the desperately needy.

One of America's great national characteristics is generosity. We are a country of people who care about

Cool Kids

Nickelodeon, the children's network, deserves major kudos for their Big Help-a-thon and Big Help Day. The campaign, launched in 1994, connects kids to volunteer efforts in their communities. In 1996, more than *8 million* kids pledged their time during the eight-hour Big-Help-a-thon. Those pledges will be fulfilled in all 50 states and overseas. Some of Nickelodeon's partners in this exciting effort are the Earth Force, American Humane Society, Feed the Children, Second Harvest, Points of Light Foundation, National 4-H Council, and the United States Department of Education.

What a powerful antidote to cynicism this endeavor is. Marva Smalls, Nickelodeon's senior vice president of public affairs, puts it like this: "Today's kids are not a disinterested or disenfranchised generation. They constantly see and hear about problems and they're taking active roles in their communities to bring about change. Big Help Day is about recognizing kids' volunteer efforts as they prove they're ready, willing, and able to help."

our neighbors. As our society has grown more transient and complex, we have lost some of our sense of community. Charitable giving used to be a part of everyday life. In the movie *Little Women*, even though the March family was quite poor and needy themselves, the girls voluntarily gave up their coveted breakfast oranges and sausages to an even needier German family nearby. Acts of charity were considered a moral obligation and civic duty, not only for the upper and middle classes but for the working class as well. Charity meant devoting time, money, and energy to better the lives of others. While this spirit still exists across our land, it needs to be revived, renewed, and celebrated.

Part of "doing good" is also "spreading good" each day. Like a pebble tossed into a pond, goodwill and kind intentions fan out in ripples. The "Perform Random Acts of Kindness and Senseless Acts of Beauty" movement—and its popular bumper sticker—are manifestations of the S.O.S. trend. These acts can be as simple as stooping down to pick up a piece of trash on the street, or dropping a quarter into a stranger's expired parking meter. Or slightly more complicated, such as organizing a group to clean up a beach, riverside, or highway shoulder.

S.O.S. isn't an isolated trend. It is profoundly linked to our culture, to our hearts, and to many of the other trends discussed in this book. As a true global society

Slate of Winners

Not long ago, Ted Turner created a furor by criticizing the *Forbes* 400 list of richest Americans. He accused the famous compilation of dampening philanthropy because its wealthy members were afraid of falling off the list if they gave away too much of their fortunes. Turner suggested issuing a list of the country's biggest givers to encourage philanthropic competition. Not to be accused of not putting his own money where his mouth is, Turner has pledged $1 billion over the next 10 years to the United Nations' charities, which spread help worldwide.

Slate, the Microsoft on-line magazine, took up Turner's challenge and in late 1996 published the *Slate* 60 of the 60 largest donations of the year. The largest was $100 million given to San Diego's Scripps Research Institute by Samuel and Aline Skaggs. The smallest was in the $10 million range and there were dozens of honorable mentions who didn't quite make the cut, in spite of multimillion-dollar generosity. Even more mind-boggling are the ten largest anonymous gifts—excluded from the list—that ranged from $50 million pledged to New York's Museum of Modern

Art to an eight-way tie for tenth place at $5 million (stretching the list to seventeen). Three cheers for Ted Turner and the generosity of all the givers and for *Slate* for initiating an important annual event.

emerges, we're on the threshold of great ethical debates. Not since the heyday of ethical philosophy has there been as much focus on moral principles. How do we instill a sense of right—or what is wrong—in today's youth? In a global village, where does responsibility to others begin—and end? How do we raise the ethics of journalism and all areas of communication? Of commerce? And, of course, last but first—of politicians? It's the hot topic and hot course at grad schools and colleges. More and more regional and national business organizations are gathering together to debate issues of social and environmental responsibility.

Much of this is consumer-driven. Many people, willing to put their money where their beliefs are, are tracking which companies are socially and environmentally responsible. Green consumers report that they're willing to spend more for products they believe are better for the environment. Supermarket chains like Bread & Circus and Whole Foods are growing at

House Smarts

Ryan Homes, a Maryland-based home builder, has responded to the S.O.S. trend by developing two prototypes for an energy-efficient town house. The buildings use novel materials, including steel, for structural support—as opposed to the traditional wood frame. The town houses are designed to maximize the use of natural light. Innovations in insulation, layout, and mechanical systems result in an energy efficiency increase of 30 percent over the norm. Some of Ryan Homes' partners in the effort include Owens Corning, Weyerhauser, Whirlpool, and Westinghouse.

an astonishing rate. Shoppers are clamoring for organic produce and minimally processed food. Sales of organic food have exploded from $631 million in 1989 to $3 billion in 1996.

In great American tradition, we're responding at some gut level to protecting the underdog—and the underdog is the earth. Yet the planet will likely survive, even if we humans are dinosaured out of existence. (In fact, both the planet and its four-footed inhabitants would likely celebrate our demise.) Note that the trend is called S.O.S., Save Our Society. Although it's deeply

Plastic Fantastic

In just a few years, we've gotten clever about product recycling. Clothing manufacturers are using the darndest things. Polyester fibers are being made out of plastic soda bottles that are sorted, sliced and diced, washed, heated, pelletized, and extruded. Malden Mills uses over 140 million recycled bottles in one year (about 15 large bottles per jacket) for its popular outerwear fleece fabric, the warm and cozy Polartec. (Malden Mills is headed by that true American Hero, Aaron Feuerstein, who continued paying his workers their salary and benefits after a disastrous fire shut down the mill. This is big-time S.O.S. clicking. A note to all businesspeople: Malden Mills makes a big-time profit every year.)

Patagonia, which pledges 10 percent of total profits to environmental concerns, has its own beverage bottle fabric, Synchilla. The company has developed a "Coat of Many Colors" program that donates Synchilla jackets to needy children. So far, more than 6,000 jackets have been shipped to southern Chile alone. NatureTex is using still another recycled plastic to make hiking boots. Green bottles are being spun into fluff that's filling

the Rising Star futons. Called Cloverfill, it's lightweight and doesn't bunch up.

Then there is ever reliable Evian. To make
more space in the recycling bins for all those clear
plastic Evian bottles, the French marketer has
made a commitment to gradually change over to
a newly developed collapsible bottle. It squishes
down into a small ball shape, and will provide
hours of amusement for your kids.

Freddie Heineken, head of Heineken beer,
has invented a different beer bottle for the Dutch
Antilles, where many of the poor live in shanties.
The so-called World Bottle is squared off, unlike
the usual green rounded one, so it can be used as
a glass building brick when emptied. This gives
new meaning to the old song, "A Hundred Bottles
of Beer on the Wall."

concerned with and committed to saving the planet, this
concept should be pushed to its ultimate conclusion:
saving ourselves.

The click for the future will be making the world
safe for our children. Probably the greatest challenge
S.O.S. faces is having to decide what to save. Our
resources are limited, so each of us will have to make

What's Clicking Next?

Soft-drink dispensers in supermarkets, where we'll refill bottles of sodas, fruit juices, and drinking water.

A fleet of hospital airplanes manned by on-call volunteer doctors and nurses. These Flights of Hope will fly to crisis and disaster areas around the globe on a moment's notice to provide humanitarian care.

A universal S.O.S. 911—one number we'll be able to call from anywhere in the world to report ecological problems and abuses. Dispatch teams and cleanup crews will be ready to swing into action, and law enforcement will move quickly to prosecute offenders.

Global environmental laws. Since pollution doesn't stop at the border, why should the laws against it?

choices. And all of our choices will reverberate through society. What will be the fallout from the current budget-cutting mania that is sweeping Washington? Will the money be there to build and upgrade treatment plants? To acquire and maintain parklands? To prosecute polluters? These are tough questions without easy answers. But asking them is an important first step.

As Sinclair Lewis wrote long ago, "The trouble with this country is that there are too many people going about saying, 'The trouble with this country is. . . .'" Threats and alarms only make people feel anxious and paralyzed. Blame and shame aren't exactly great motivators either. Yet, even though doomsayers control the headlines, there are many success stories. There are vectors of change for the good. If we each make the effort, for real, relying on facts and not scare tactics—the results will become collective. It's not overwhelming. Like our all-time favorite bumper sticker says: "There's no hope, but I may be wrong."

NEW DRIFT: ATMOSFEAR

Polluted air, contaminated water and tainted food
stir up a storm of consumer doubt and uncertainty.
How safe is anything?

S omething is in the air. Can you feel it? We can. It's
a chill, a blast of anxiety, a real sense that fresh air
is turning foul, that we are surrounded by invisible enemies—E. coli (and even worse) lurking in our
fast food, fiberglass particles spinning in our air, listeriosis breeding in our hot dogs.

This goes beyond a general sense of uneasiness. It's
deeper. It's more wrenching. It's AtmosFear—a new
national nervousness that comes from continual assaults
on our health and well-being. It's not a Trend yet, but

it's on the way to full-fledged Trend status. Right now it's a powerful drift we need to watch carefully.

We know trouble is afoot when the U.S. Centers for Disease Control launch a Web site solely dedicated to "the prevention and control of traditional, new, and reemerging infectious diseases."

The once-nurturing natural world is turning on us—and it's making us insecure, shaky. We're not Chicken Littles or hypochondriacs. Both corporations and countries have been over-stressing the environment and messing with the ecosystem for so long that we are right to be desperately worried about the consequences to us all. It's not just a single threat here or there—it's a synergy and symphony of assaults.

We are feeling threatened by the air we breathe, the water we drink, and the antibiotic-resistant viruses that are being spread by the person sitting next to us at the movies.

We shudder when we read statistics that predict one airline crash per week by the year 2010—based on extrapolations from current data.

Then add the facts that millions are made sicker by the hospitals that are supposed to cure them, the growing "road rage" that makes even driving to the supermarket a life-threatening experience, plus dozens of other dangers, and you have the gale winds of Atmos-Fear.

A Smorgasbord of New Fears

Food-borne illness strikes when a virus, a bacteria, or fecal material contaminates the innocent-looking meal on your plate. It could happen at the most suspicious-looking greasy spoon, or the 4-star restaurant where you're celebrating an anniversary. The Centers for Disease Control estimates that bacteria in food kills as many as nine thousand Americans a year and poisons millions of others. The cost of treatment and lost productivity tops $10 billion per year. Why can't scientists at the CDC pin down the numbers? Because so many cases go unreported. Restaurants used to have atmosphere, now they have AtmosFear.

E. coli is today's and, even more, tomorrow's news. Recently, in the largest U.S. recall, 25 million pounds of possibly tainted beef were found to be distributed to such unsuspecting national chains as Boston Market, Wal-Mart and Sam's. Unfortunately, the Government lacks the authority to trace the nasty bacteria back to the breeding ranches, where E. coli starts off in the intestines of an animal. And there's campylobacter (a microbial foodborne pathogen) and the more common salmonella in so many chickens and eggs. Amazing, isn't it, how quickly we get used to danger?

Perhaps the biggest food-borne-illness scare was (and is) Mad Cow Disease. The economic consequences to Great Britain were enormous. Experts say we aren't out of the woods yet, that this virus can spread to pigs, other animals, and even humans worldwide. And, with beef consumption in the United States on the rise, it makes the chance of contamination even greater. Here's a seriously overlooked Mad Cow risk: The bone meal that millions of gardeners use so liberally (and often inhale without any second thoughts) could very well have been made from the skeletons of animals that carried the virus.

Blame our fast-paced lifestyles. Convenient take-out food can also contain diseases-to-go. Listeriosis, a food-borne illness that is especially dangerous to pregnant women, AIDS sufferers, and immune-suppressed individuals, is found in ready-to-eat food that hasn't been properly reheated. But don't rely on heating as a safety measure. Even steamed oysters can contain a stubborn, heat-resistant virus that will make you sick.

We need to beware of more than the usual suspects—even seemingly benign foods like iced tea can be a contaminated time bomb. During the heat of last summer in both Ohio and Washington state, some restaurant goers got sick, and the health department traced it to brewing iced tea using too cool water, creating dangerously high levels of coliform bacteria.

As for our water, it's a liquid question mark. (Coleridge must have seen it coming when he wrote

"Water, water everywhere and not a drop to drink.") Erin Olson of the Natural Resources Defense Council was quoted as saying, "Over 90% of the water systems in the U.S. use pre-WWII technology to clean their drinking water." Unsafe at any sip.

It's not just the big, industrial states that are in danger. In Alabama, half the lakes register the highest levels of nutrient pollution ever recorded (boats that dump raw sewage are to blame). And the runoff from fertilizers is causing even bigger problems, from cancer-scares to turning once harmless microorganisms into sci-fi monsters. In one case, a formerly-benign microbe is wreaking havoc along the Eastern sea coast, killing over a billion fish in the last six years. Now the so-called "cell from hell" is thought to be infecting people who are eating the local fish, causing ailments from itchy sores to minor brain damage.

And our water worries are deepening. In the United States, the National Toxicity Program is beginning a two-year study to examine whether chlorination creates a cancer-causing by-product called MX. A previous Finnish study showed MX is a carcinogen. The irony: Chlorination has its good side, preventing the spread of water-borne diseases like dysentery, cholera, and typhoid.

We see that all too often. What does good can do harm: Air bags (they can be hazardous to small children and the elderly); over-the-counter calcium supplements

(they contain dangerous levels of lead); exercising out-
doors (estimates are that each year, there are more than
60,000 premature deaths caused by air pollution).
These are the mixed signals that lead to confusion and
charge the air with even more AtmosFear.

And if that isn't enough, the situation is going to
get worse. As viruses and bacteria mutate and new disease resistant forms emerge, our food and water will
carry even greater risks. Should we just put a warning
label on the entire planet?

One Day, You'll Be Wearing Rubber Gloves While Reading This Book

Remember when people thought Howard Hughes was
crazy because of all his germ fears and fetishes? Today,
he'd just be thought of as prudently cautious. That's
because we are living in a sea of germs and an ocean of
disease.

Globally, the threat of tuberculosis is on the rise.
Still the top infectious killer of youth and adults worldwide, according to the World Health Organization, two
billion people are currently infected. Each year six to
eight million new cases of the disease kill about three
million people. Even more frightening? The stubborn
multidrug-resistant strains of TB.

Just as shocking, our blood supply can't be trusted anymore. Our white blood cells may be telling us little white lies. The New York Blood Center, the largest independent blood-supplier in the United States, is under investigation by the federal government for "allegations of improper screening for the AIDS virus, as well as tampering with the tests," reports the *New York Times*. No wonder so many concerned patients are banking their own blood before elective surgery.

Asthma is growing at an alarming rate. Take a deep breath before you read these statistics: Currently, 14.6 million Americans suffer from asthma (5 million of them are children). That's up by 61 percent from the early 1980s, reports the American Lung Association. No wonder so many parents are paranoid every time their kids catch a cold: Is that wheeze just a cough, or the beginning of asthma?

Then there are brand new threats like the hantavirus that heighten AtmosFear. Recently, it was shown that this deadly virus isn't just contracted from rodent droppings— it can be transmitted between humans. Scientists have also identified a new species of disease-carrying tick, even more common than the deer tick that spreads Lyme disease. The media is ablaze with stories about a fatal flesh-eating strep virus. Dengue, an often-deadly mosquito-born infection, is an epidemic on the march: Before 1970, only 9 countries had experienced the disease; by 1995, 41 had. And get this: 40 percent of the world's population is at risk, including the United States.

And, of course, deadly ebola, though temporarily halted, still lurks and runs the risk of breaking out of small clusters and becoming a global pandemic.

AtmosFear is so pervasive it's even finding its way into rap lyrics. In their song "Triumph," the popular group Wu-Tang Clan raps about "global pestilence" and how "the hard-headed never learn."

Our Threatened Immune Systems

Not only are the threats getting stronger, we're getting weaker—a combination that makes AtmosFear far more ominous. Exposure to toxins like pesticides and other chemicals found in our air, water, and food supply weaken our bodies' natural defenses. Leading experts believe that increases in the rates of many cancers is linked to the continual battering that our bodies take from the environment. That's certainly reason enough for AtmosFear.

One theory that's gaining more credence is that the use of endocrine-disrupting hormones in pesticides is linked to prostate cancer in men, breast cancer in women, and lower levels of fertility in both sexes.

The marketing implications? Walk into any health-food store, any supermarket, any drug store, and you'll find dozens and dozens of products that promise to boost our immune systems and destroy free-radicals. (Today, those are the radicals that strike fear into the heart of Americans.) These products weren't developed out of thin air—but out of AtmosFear.

AtmosFear is Everywhere

AtmosFear is on the job.

We are under siege from "closed-building syndrome." Large office buildings with dangerously recirculated air are corporate tombs that lead not just to Legionnaire's disease, but a host of respiratory, eye, and auto-immune problems. Even people who live down-wind from these buildings are vulnerable from air-borne bacteria.

AtmosFear is at home.

We live in a self-created zone of toxicity where we breathe formaldehyde and other fumes from glues, plastic resins, carpet pads, and plywood laminates. And of course, there's fiberglass insulation, found in millions of attics across the country. An innocent blanket of pink it's not. In fact, because of the size and sharpness of its particles, fiberglass can be inhaled, and is often labeled "the next asbestos."

AtmosFear is on planes.

Despite public outcry, airlines are still saving money by reducing the number of times air on a plane is circulated each hour. That means you're sharing bodily fluids with that sniffler in seat 4B, who's been coughing and sneezing the entire flight.

Even more frightening was a psychiatrist's terrifying trip on a Delta L1011 enroute to Atlanta that suddenly lurched to the right and began a rapid descent. Oxygen masks were released, yet a number, including hers, didn't drop. (A quick-acting passenger helped her yank down her mask.) No announcement whatsoever was made for reassurance. The next day she dialed a customer service number to inquire about the incident. Later a Delta customer service rep called back and explained, "The cargo door blew, depressurizing the plane, and some of the masks didn't come down. That's why we're retiring these older planes."

The fear of flying. Whether it's mechanical failure, human error, or acts of God—all the elements create ever upward AtmosFear.

AtmosFear is all around us.

- More people in Scotland die from air pollution than car accidents. Polluted air increases babies' risk of Sudden Infant Death Syndrome.

- Stuffed animals harbor zillions of dust-mite antigens that can directly damage young bronchial tubes.
- Douches and "feminine hygiene sprays" are now believed to possibly be a cause of ovarian cancer.
- Computer and laser printers emit allergenic VOCs (Volatile Organic Compounds). VOCs are the invisible gases emitted from everyday items like paints, adhesives, carpeting, new furniture and copy machines.
- Scientists are even investigating possible health effects caused by cell phones. The *EMF Health Report* states "at issue is whether exposure of the (cell phone) user to these microwaves damages brain cells and induces cancers, such as brain tumors, or other diseases." Guess E.T. better not phone home.

What Really Makes AtmosFear So Frightening: *Medisin*

The scariest part of AtmosFear? It's what happens when doctors, nurses, the clinics and hospitals who are supposed to make us healthy wind up making us sicker. Think about the implications of that cruel twist of fate. It destabilizes our trust and our fright level zooms.

A report in the *Journal of the American Medical Association* found that prescription drug errors made in hospitals nearly double patients' risks of dying. A recent study by Lori Andres, professor at the Chicago-Kent College of Law, found that misdiagnoses and lost test results risked the lives of nearly half the patients in surgery and in intensive-care units.

A staggering ten thousand people die each year because of hospital errors. Reacting to this, complainants in Iowa sued to find out what's really going on in their hospitals—but the Iowa Supreme Court ruled that these state-owned institutions are not required to release information on "nosocomial" infections—a fancy word for the infections that patients catch in hospitals. Public disclosure would reveal the severity of the problem. (And we're sure hospitals will have to come clean once alerted Vigilante Consumers get on the case.)

As hospitals plunge further down on the confidence scale, we foresee a new breed of "membership" hospitals in the near future. These super-clean, super-scrupulous institutions will offer a level of insulation and protection against the germ nightmares both inside of and outside their walls.

Many predict that HMOs and managed care organizations will fall down on the job even further. Driven by profit at all costs, they'll spend less time with patients, hire cheaper, less experienced doctors and nurses, and invest less in safety measures. You know what they say—the hospital is no place for a sick person. We're calling this descent into a Hades-like level of torture and indifference medisin.

When you fear one thing, you fear everything.

Fears feed on each other. We are so sensitized by Atmos-Fear that we are quick to react—and often overreact—to the slightest shred of news. Thanks to the velocity of word-of-mouth that comes from high-speed communication and the Internet, even the most questionable rumor gains the force of truth.

If raspberries from Guatemala are found to contain bacteria, we stop eating raspberries from everywhere. If one car seat is recalled because it can come loose in a crash, millions of us race to return whatever car seat we happen to own.

Small wonder that we obsess over best-selling books like *The Hot Zone* and *The Coming Plague* and turn them into popular movies. Bad news falls on receptive ears.

AtmosFear has put all of us on high alert. It even accounts for our fixation on threats from outside our own atmosphere—which range from raging debate over the famous Roswell UFO landings, to movies like *Independence Day, Contact,* and *Men in Black.* As if there aren't enough internal threats, we have to manufacture external ones, too.

Marketing to the AtmosFear-ful

AtmosFear is so pervasive that canny marketers are already seizing on the opportunities it presents. *Advertising Age* writes that, "Germ phobia is creating new consumer markets for anti-microbial products." Hasbro is testing "germ-fighting" toys to better protect infants and toddlers. Who will be the first to market specific products for that other high-risk group—the elderly?

A new product from Gojo Industries is Purell Instant Hand Sanitizer. Requiring no soap, water, or towels, it claims to be effective against 99.9 percent of all common germs. Or there's Proteque, a cream that forms a protective barrier to "keep irritants, allergens, and bacteria away from your skin."

Chesebrough-Pond's is introducing an Antibacterial version of Vaseline Intensive Care, and Keri lotion, from Bristol-Myers Squib, ran a campaign in New York City's subways warning straphangers of the nasty germs that are hanging around on the A-Train. Sales increased 13.2 percent.

And just the other day a "junk" e-mail arrived at the BrainReserve offices. It began, "Research indicates an alarming increase in the number of serious health hazards caused by germs, bacteria and viruses. Never before has it been more important to protect yourself and your family's personal environment."

The product it was selling is Saniguard, "the world's first, portable, dry-on-contact sanitizing surface spray." Seems like germ warfare is taking on a whole new meaning where you have to spray everything from steering wheels to restaurant chairs. Another such targeted product is Germ Guard, a round device with a disposable filter that can slip over the mouthpiece of any telephone. The company's ad asks, "Why are public pay phones only black and dark gray, not white?" Their answer, "because the darkest colors hide filth and germs that can make you sick." Scare tactics . . . or AtmosFear?

The opportunities are truly vast. For instance, those entrepreneurs who started the O2 Spa Bar chain are clicking with AtmosFear. In Toronto, New York, and soon Los Angeles, consumers spend up to $20 for the pleasure and privilege of breathing a hit of pure, untainted oxygen. As the outside air gets worse, we will witness light, portable oxygen machines emerging— perhaps Sony "Breatheman." Inside, we see home air purification as one of the new industries for the new century. All products —including building materials—

will have to be certified to guarantee that they don't release any hazardous fumes into the air.

At BrainReserve, we're telling our clients that "clean," "source-protected" foods will be the next wave. That means the entire growing and manufacturing chain will need to be scrutinized and documented for purity. Look for mass marketing of organic and toxin-free foods. And to reassure us before we take a bite or a sip, we predict that everyone will own one of the newly-reliable portable food testers.

Advertising, too, will move beyond snappy campaigns. If commercials or print ads are promoting a hamburger place, viewers will be interested to know how the beef was fed, processed, shipped, stored, and, finally, prepared. The same will hold for the bun, ketchup, and special sauce. "Look before you leap" will become "read before you eat." The cost of these upgrades? High.

Ten years ago, when we worked on a New Directions assignment for Burger King, BrainReserve suggested that they test-market a chain of Veggie Kings. Our reasoning: we felt that beef sourcing was going to be an increasingly "iffy" subject . . . and that Americans would become more conscious of how their food was handled. Just think how much more secure Burger King's market position would be if all their "eggs" are not put in the same meat grinder.

But remember: fear begets fear. On the horizon,

there will also be a new Vigilant Vegetarianism, as we even lose confidence in the way our veggies are grown and handled. Consumers will start to own or lease controlled, clean plots of land—like time-sharing, only farm-sharing. It's the only way to truly know and protect what we eat.

This kind of intense scrutiny of everything we eat and drink will lead to a rush of "clean-food" seals. And here's a new business opportunity: Start a Food Bureau of Investigation (FBI) to insure compliance. Or set up a web site offering complete "product biographies." And, one day, we expect to see restaurants post the health reports of kitchen workers the same way elevators display maintenance records.

Does all this sound far-fetched? We think it's nearly here. Just look at the lengths some island nations go to protect their populations. England won't even let in a bejeweled pet Yorkie without a six-month quarantine against rabies. And the Japanese already require that their cars are anti-bacterially treated (pre-purchase) and that their yen come out flattened and sterilized from ATM machines. Just you wait.

It's a scary world, and it's getting scarier. More and more, everything we taste and touch can be carrying the seeds of our destruction. A dark cloud is hovering above us and we're feeling its shadow. That cloud is called AtmosFear.

CLICKSCREEN

Every idea needs a reality check,
a future test—a ClickScreen.

At BrainReserve, we take no action—and make no recommendations—without the help of a tool we call ClickScreen. What is ClickScreen? It's a trend-based screening test that we use to make "go" or "no-go" decisions about an innovative product, a new service, a start-up business, a marketing plan, even a corporate acquisition. We have applied it to such diverse projects as the launch of the popular Bacardi Breezer, the design of more user-friendly computers, and the development of a new public persona for a mayoral candidate.

Originally a sit-around-the-conference-room brain-storming session we called Discontinuity Trend Analysis, the ClickScreen helps us evaluate an idea, product, or concept on three counts:

- Trend-worthiness: Does an idea, product, or concept click with the trends, or is it a fad?
- Longevity: Will an idea, product, or concept keep pace with changing consumer demands over the long run?
- Viability: Does an idea, product, or concept appeal to a large enough audience to make it worthwhile commercially?

Our experience has taught us that we ignore the results of a ClickScreen at our peril.

How to ClickScreen

Here's an anyone-can-do-it version of our ClickScreen. Start with a blank page. At the top, jot down a one-sentence description of your idea (remember, brevity forces clarity). In a column on the left side, list the 17 trends: Cocooning, Clanning, Fantasy Adventure, Pleasure Revenge, Small Indulgences, Anchoring, Egonomics, FemaleThink, Mancipation, 99 Lives, Cashing Out, Being

Alive, Down-Aging, Vigilante Consumer, Icon Toppling, S.O.S., and AtmosFear Then add four new columns across the top, titled "yes," "no," "maybe," and "possible change."

Now ClickScreening begins. Ask yourself how well your idea is supported by each trend. Is it a perfect fit, a just-miss, or a never-the-twain-shall-meet? If your idea is on-trend, look for ways to enhance the match. If it takes a stretch of logic to make the idea fit a trend, rethink it. If the idea is contrary to a trend, don't just move on to the next trend. Think about how to reshape your concept to get it on-trend.

Successful ideas usually click with at least four trends. In fact, at BrainReserve, we recommend only those ideas that pass the acid test of clicking with four or more trends.

Don't be dismayed if one or two trends seem completely contradictory to your idea. Societal trends, like people, can be inconsistent. Think about the person who jogs five miles, then gobbles down a pint of ice cream (fitness and fatness), or Cocoons for weeks before signing up for Outward Bound.

A ClickScreen in Point

The banking industry illustrates the power of Click-Screen to point out what's off- or on-trend. Although many local branches or even large regional banks have finally recognized that they have to do better in the ways they treat consumers, banking as a whole is one of those everyday, universal activities that could be much improved. With ClickScreen, we can pinpoint problems and highlight trend-based solutions. To wit:

> *Trend: Cocooning.*
> *Banks: Off-trend.*

Think about the image banking enjoyed in the 1930s, '40s, and '50s. The quintessential white-pillared, brick bank was the center of a town and was run by a grandfatherly banker who saved homes and businesses in times of trouble. Banks were essentially Cocoons.

But over the years, familiar tellers have become strangers, lines have grown long, and rules have become increasingly rigid. Instead of fixing their internal problems, banks have set up ATMs—in effect, booting customers out of the Cocoon.

When we are forced into the inner sanctum, as happened to me at the local branch of the Bank of New York the other day, the indifference is chilling. The ATM, in a separate building, was malfunctioning and someone had posted a sign: "Please go and see a teller for your transactions." After I waited in line for 15 minutes, the teller told me he couldn't give me money from my account simply with my ATM card. He said I had to have a check. Otherwise, I should go find another ATM. Venturing some logic, I said, "Then you shouldn't have that sign out there." He merely shrugged and said he didn't know the ATM was broken.

Inconvenience is one issue. Security is another. Headlines blare that safe-deposit boxes are no longer safe. In the bank across the street from BrainReserve the safe-deposit section was flooded when a water main broke. Every piece of paper was destroyed. So it pays to read the small print of your safe-deposit rental agreement: Most have clauses that absolve banks of any liability, unless extraordinary lapses of security occur. What do you think banks are doing now when they offer to sell insurance on the contents of your box?

Trend: Clanning.
Banks: Off-trend.

When was the last time you looked forward to seeing friends at the bank or meeting some new, like-minded folks there? When was the last time you felt like a depositor, not an account number, at your bank? When was the last time you felt that you had anything in common with your fellow depositors (other than bad service)? If you ever had such feelings, they are probably ancient history now.

Trend: Fantasy Adventure.
Banks: Off-trend.

There's nothing titillating, sensual, or magical about banks. That's strange, considering that a bank's role is to facilitate money—and money facilitates the possibilities of turning dreams into realities: a new car, an exotic trip, the longed-for kitchen renovation, a college education. Instead of offering dramatic excitement or aesthetic pleasure, most banks are somber monuments to monotony. It's hard to get excited about the plastic plants illuminated by fluorescent lights.

Banking hasn't a shred of adventure. It's hard (not to mention expensive) to do your banking while you are traveling in an airplane. If you go on a long vacation, your bills can pile up, unpaid. True, many creditors now ask for access to your account so that they can make automatic withdrawals on specified dates. Just send them one of your checks, properly voided. But as customers, we pay for the convenience by giving up our control over when and how our money is disbursed.

Trend: Pleasure Revenge.
Banks: Off-trend.

The somber, visit-to-the-principal's-office atmosphere of most banks makes us feel that we've been caught smoking and are about to be lectured to or punished. There's a lot of revenge in this experience and little pleasure.

And the next time you ask for a home equity or small business loan, take a pulse-reading of the reception your bank gives you. The sidelong glances, the winks, the snarls—all these are signs that you are getting the revenge treatment.

When it comes right down to it, what services do banks still provide? The latest insult to consumers is getting charged a fee to talk to a teller. Minute by minute, the average cost from the bank's point of view is about $2 to $3 for every vocal interchange. Some banks are giving you two free talks, by phone or face-to-face, before slapping on a fee. Or they're charging you if you use a teller for something that could have been done by machine. Check your statements to see if your bank has joined up with this new non-service-oriented kind of punishment. After all, extra service charges tacked on here and there are providing a $15-billion-plus income for banks today—and that's not small change.

Trend: Small Indulgences.
Banks: Off-trend.

Can you imagine saying, "Oh, I'm going to treat myself to a trip to my favorite bank. I really deserve it!"

Not very likely. Few banks have progressed beyond being a because-I-have-to experience, about as much fun as going to the laundromat.

Trend: Anchoring.
Banks: Off-trend.

Banks are definitely not a stop on the ride to inner peace. We don't expect a bank to be a spiritual haven or to help us find our meditative core.

Trend: Egonomics.
Banks: Off-trend.

Except for those tiny name-and-address lines on our checks and our personal, confidential ATM codes (98 percent of us use our birthdays or a similarly easy-to-remember and easy-for-others-to-figure-out date), there is little personalization or customization in banking—not in the monthly mailings, not in the telephone contacts, not in the teller service, and certainly not in the products. Having, on average, only three different kinds of checking options to choose from doesn't make us feel unique.

Few banks look closely at checks or scrutinize signatures anymore, unless the check falls into the category of five-figure amounts. One bank manager revealed that his bank examined only those written for $10,000 and up. The same bank scanned only one check in 350 of those written for less than $5,000. This is astonishing. Why fill out a signature card in the first place, you ask? Rarely do most of us write out checks for over $10,000.

Weren't you always sure that if you signed your check in a peculiar way, crossed something out, or made a sloppy numerical mistake, your bank would refuse the check? If you're curious, test your bank's sure-sightedness by varying your signature or leaving it off altogether. Banks blame the lack of scrutiny on a shortage of both time and labor—a standard excuse—and they allow bundled checks to pass through unchallenged. The result? Check fraud is rampant. The Bank Administration Institute reports that such fraud costs U.S. banks and their customers as much as $10 *billion* each year.

Trend: Vigilante Consumer.
Banks: Off-trend.

Banking customers become Vigilante Consumers for their own self-interest (no pun intended). It doesn't seem that anyone else is keeping track of whether a deposit is really credited or if the interest on your line of credit is calculated correctly. (Don't worry, it's immediately adjusted upward when it's in the bank's favor.) If the smallest thing goes wrong, you're handled like a criminal. It must be that the banks have taken a lesson from the IRS.

In general, the discrepancy between the bank ads in the papers or magazines and the reality of the banking experience is making customers mad as hell. When the copy announces that "your personal executive will expedite all your transactions" or "your financial partner will maximize your money's productivity" or "we work hard every day to earn our customer's trust," does this sound anything like what's happened to you, unless you're superrich? Security and such acts of random caring are illusions.

Trend: Being Alive.
Banks: Off-trend.

Being Alive is about living better and joyfully, focusing on the present, and minimizing stress. Even when banks become more interactive and introduce added electronic banking services, there's a problem: We get even more anxious about trusting high technology to keep our money secure. Do you feel your blood pressure rise when you read that Consumer Loan Advocates, a nonprofit investigative group in Lake Bluff, Illinois, recently found that 47.5 percent of adjustable rate mortgages (ARMs) have errors in calculation? Do you boil when you discover that you are paying a higher rate than your neighbor for nearly the same loan? Do you want to scream when the prime rate goes up, immediately followed by a rapid rise in your credit card interest payments, but the interest the bank pays you on your savings account remains stuck around 3 percent?

Trend: 99 Lives.
Banks: Off-trend.

The banking industry is not well structured to accommodate or support our multifunction, multirole lives. True, when they are working, ATMs can save us lots of time. But some banks limit their hours, and despite the surveillance, ATMs are unfriendly at night and in less public places. Our 99 Lives' needs go unmet. Banks are still paying much more attention to their own goals and ignoring ours. Now that banks are merging, laying off employees, and closing "nonperforming" branches, banking is getting *less,* not *more,* convenient.

Trend: Cashing Out.
Banks: Off-trend.

Instead of recognizing your personal achievements and greeting you with a Welcome Wagon, banks often treat cash-outers with an ominous air of suspicion. Without an established period of residency and a regular well-paying job, banks offer little more than opening basic checking and savings accounts.

Trend: Down-Aging.
Banks: Off-trend.

Banks have changed enormously. Alas, most of the warm, cuddly, nostalgic elements are gone: the sincere greeting using only first names; the passbooks we clutched proudly as our balances rose; the Christmas clubs; the hokey calendars; the sound, look, and feel of permanence and security. In fact, from having to deal with the tiniest of small-print brochures to the most unintelligible tellers behind a cage, the child in us quickly ages.

Trends: FemaleThink and Mancipation.
Banks: Off-trend.

Bankers, whether female or male, tend to think like, well, bankers. Most procedures, products, and promotions are designed only with the bank's direct goals of profitability and cost-cutting in mind. There is little thought given to developing a real relationship and much emphasis on the transaction. This is definitely risk-averse OldThink. Until bank boards and top management include FemaleThinkers and Mancipated males, until the specific service needs of every consumer group (parents, school kids, oldsters, travelers, entrepreneurs, and others) are met, banks will continue to disappoint consumers.

Trend: Icon Toppling.
Banks: Off-trend.

Bankruptcies (even the Queen of England's own investment bank, the venerable Barings PLC, toppled); disastrous real estate loans; the savings and loan debacle; mergers that leave thousands unemployed; never-to-be-repaid loans to repressive foreign regimes instead of financing for local, job-creating enterprises; employee fraud—the negative list is very long. Does that sound like a description of an admirable societal icon or more like an industry teetering on the edge of toppling?

We knew banks were in trouble, but until we put the industry through the ClickScreen, we didn't realize how completely off-trend the whole business is.

Trend: S.O.S.(Save Our Society).
Banks: Off-trend.

A few banks—both local and national—do try to play a significant role in their communities and encourage employees to contribute as well. Small banks, however, tend not to appear on the lists of nonprofit donors and sponsors of cultural and environmental projects. They don't often offer matching gift programs or provide low-interest loans for start-up businesses, renovation, capital equipment, or low-income housing.

With the merger frenzy going on, there's a valid question as to whether the larger consolidated banks will continue established society-friendly policies. When Chemical Bank, which had a liberal loan policy in poorer communities, merged with Chase Manhattan, reportedly more strict in its willingness to make loans to small businesses run by minorities, there were intense negotiations over what the new bank's attitude would be toward these loans. The Community Reinvestment Act (CRA) now requires banks that operate branches in various neighborhoods to make substantial efforts to provide loans and services to the people and businesses in those communities.

These types of loans represent greater risks for banks such as the merged Chase Manhattan and Chemical. In 1995, Chase lent $1 billion for programs to provide affordable housing primarily to the urban poor, many of whom (but by no means all) are minorities. NationsBank, headquartered in Charlotte, North Carolina, became the target of protest groups objecting to its proposed merger with Boatmen's Bankshares in St. Louis. To counter the protests, NationsBank pointed to its sterling record of making $13.4 billion worth of loans to low- and moderate-income areas between 1991 and 1996.

Can we see these actions as responses to the S.O.S. trend? Well, that depends on how skeptical you want to be about the banks' intentions and motivations. Banks are in the business of making money, pure and simple, not in making gratuitous public- service handouts. Those banking officials contemplating big mergers often make sweeping pledges not to forget the less fortunate in the community, and they do so to undercut their toughest critics. When Chemical and Chase Manhattan merged in September of 1996, we heard pledges of $18 billion over a five-year period. In 2001, we'll take out our calculators and tote up how the megabank has done in this regard.

And it's not just a matter of people and their neighborhood businesses. In the environmental area, banking requires tons and tons of paper, most of it not recycled. There are multiple copies made for loan applications, deposits, and monthly statements. The U.S. government alone processes over 450 million checks each year (despite the fact that it shuts down periodically when the political partisans cannot agree over the budget). In this country individual consumers write nearly *50 billion* checks each year.

Citibank, for example, now charges customers who keep a daily average balance of under $2,000 a monthly fee of $9.50 plus a surcharge of 50 cents for each check they write. When banking institutions look at such profits, it's no wonder they pay only lip service to S.O.S. issues.

The On-Trend Bank

What would it take to make commercial or retail banks responsive to current and future consumer needs?

Believe it or not, the prognosis for banks is not hopeless. Nor is the solution quick or simple. It rarely is. But in fact, every time you say or think, "I really wish my bank would do this or offer that," you are discovering opportunities for improvement and competitive advantages that need to be considered and evaluated with a ClickScreen.

One solution would be to study what "perks" the banks are offering their upscale customers, then copy or downscale them for the masses. Income levels may be different for the two groups, but the needs are similar. The prototypical bank of the future that has the best chance to survive and thrive needs to inspire confidence and loyalty. Those qualities will be evident in the clicking bank that designs its services in accordance with our 17 trends. As you'll see, it could be called a virtual bank or technobank, but those labels don't capture

the additional ingredients of user-friendliness, the insti-
tutional response to human needs, the when-I-want-and-
where-I-want bank.

Cocooning

Make the bank a refuge from the storm. Offer preferen-
tial treatment and personal service. A recent commercial for London-based National Westminster Bank
(NatWest) is on the right track when it shows a mother
with a newborn child and announces that a service representative will make a house call to open a savings
account in the baby's name.

Without ever leaving the Cocoon, every consumer
should have easy 24-hour access to account information
and to make deposits and withdrawals, exchange cur-
rency, buy and sell securities, pay bills, and receive hard
copies of all transactions, including updates for balances and budgets. All interaction will take place
through common home utilities such as the telephone
and television rather than the personal computer. Or we
could get a dedicated instrument like France's MiniTel,
a service that links telephones and home computer to
provide almost instantaneous information on bank
accounts, airline reservations, and the like. In a novel
experiment, the First Direct Bank in Leeds, Great
Britain, is a 24-hour telephone-only bank, the first of its
kind. It is also the fastest growing bank in Britain—half

a million customers, but not one branch. Still, First Direct opens over 10,000 new accounts each month. Even better, the bank turns a healthy profit: It is reported to realize profits from 60 percent of its customers, and that is 20 percent better than the average in Britain.

Banks themselves could become cozier and more comfortable places in which to do business. Why can't a bank provide easy chairs, couches, and desks instead of standing tables? If physicians' offices now come equipped with TVs to watch and scads of magazines to read (even if they are old), why should we expect less from our banks? Often mentioned as one of New York City's best banks, the Republic Bank for Savings has live piano music at many of its branches, plus lower fees than most. Now *that's* clicking.

Clanning and Egonomics

Banks responsive to Clanning are on the way to addressing Egonomics as well. (We often see that clicking on one trend is a surefire method to related trend solutions.) The on-trend bank would reflect its environment; it would capture the essence of a neighborhood and provide a sense of the traditional town square where people used to congregate, talk about the weather, and conduct business.

Bank managers can take a gigantic step by staffing

the bank with people who speak the same language as the customers and who are more or less in the same age groups. The bank can invite customers with similar needs to attend free seminars or information sessions: For example, first-time home buyers, women who are owners of small businesses, recent retirees, or people who are acting as executors of family estates could profit from the bank's expertise and conduct their business in ways that create fewer problems in the bank's processing.

The bank of the future might form a new-enterprise club for eager entrepreneurs, providing helpful instruction on constructing a business plan that will meet the bank's requirements. How much more congenial this effort would be than the banks' current position of acting as the stern, supercritical evaluator of new business plans. By being the catalyst for Clanning, the bank becomes a member of the Clan. Click.

Fantasy Adventure

A visit to a bank could be great fun or could lead to fun and learning. For example, the lounge or waiting area might be equipped with video monitors on which to "visit" proposed vacation destinations, select among hotel rooms, schedule boat excursions or scuba-diving adventures. The bank's travel agency will make all reservations and book your flight, change your money, sell you EuroChecks, have money waiting for you at your destination, provide a credit card to charge all purchases with an adequate, preapproved credit line (not to mention collecting more airline frequent-flyer miles into your account), and, of course, make the loan necessary to pay for it all. Art and photography shows, seminars or videos on home renovations, visits to the vault for schoolchildren, primers on investing in stocks and mutual funds—the list is limited only by space. Click.

Pleasure Revenge and Small Indulgences

For perfect Pleasure Revenge and Small Indulgences, there could be a free beverage and coffee bar with exotic brewed coffees, herbal teas, cookies or chocolates, and (dare we dream?) ice cream in summer.

Banks might borrow an idea from the you-never-know-when-you'll-win school of motivation, exemplified by slot machines and lotteries. Imagine the increase in happy customers if the bank randomly handed out $5 or $10 cash-redeemable vouchers. Frowns would melt into smiles if banks gave out small monetary awards to anyone who waits more than ten minutes for a teller or an ATM machine.

Does anyone remember being given an electric can opener, a toaster oven, or a small television to open a nice-sized savings account? How about something like a better rate (plus a little gift) now and again to encourage savings? Why should we get 3.25 percent on money in the bank when, with a little effort, we can get 10 percent or better elsewhere?

Best of all, the on-trend bank could be an enabler of small-sized dreams: If high interest rates have precluded a major renovation on your home, then an easy-to-get miniloan for a whirlpool spa or well-stocked workbench may bring enough satisfaction. Click.

Anchoring

No, Virginia, money doesn't buy happiness, but the stress of financial problems is antithetical to a feeling of security and spirituality. Even Abraham Maslow's hierarchy-of-needs model states that economic needs must be met before one can aspire to higher states of self-actualization. So what does this have to do with on-trend banking? Simply this: To the extent that a bank treats you with respect and understands your individual situation and needs, the closer you'll be to a firm Anchor. Your bank could help you in budget planning, check up on your projected Social Security payments, advise you on investment research (with appropriate warnings, of course), and alert you when lots of cash is lying idle in your accounts. Click.

99 Lives

Mobile bank vans could be the Good Humor trucks of tomorrow. A mobile bank van would pass by your home, office, plant, or shop to bring small bills, make change, deliver cash, accept deposits, and offer free sorting and rolling of coins. What a help for the small business owner alone in the store, for the single parent caring for children at home, or for the disabled customer who cannot make the trip to the bank. This bank-on-the-move could also drop off free overnight "rentals" for a line of video or CD-ROM seminars that explain how to create a home budget, plan for retirement, apply for a mortgage or home equity loan, and receive help on tax preparation.

Should our society become "cashless," a concept finally on its way, the clicking bank will make appropriate changes in its services. Many large banks are now testing cash cards with embedded computer chips, "electronic purses" that allow you to load money onto the cards at ATM machines or specially equipped telephones, much as library patrons add to their cards for copy machines. In Great Britain, a similar "stored value" card system called Mondex is already in use. Meanwhile, we're still getting used to the concept of debit cards, which come preloaded (and prepaid) with an exact amount to spend.

In the cashless future, the newly plumped up bank card will be used to pay bills, make calls at corner phones, ride the subway, and tip the waiter at dinner— all without the bother of ever handling "real" money. To help pay for this service, banks will no doubt have to charge small fees—both to the consumer who uses the card and to the merchant who accepts it—but the clicking bank will keep these service charges *small*, recognizing the added value in having satisfied, loyal customers.

Wouldn't it be helpful if the computer-driven banks could become more interactive by signaling our answering machines or computers if our balances are getting low? True, this feature would run counter to the banks' practice of imposing a hefty service charge for overdrawn accounts, but the clicking bank will know that customers would much prefer the warning to the penalty.

There could be one-stop financial shopping and continuity among different sectors of the bank: real estate, insurance, mutual funds, educational needs, trusts, travel. And to save travel time and cut back on lunch-hour lines, every large building or office complex could have its own minibranch.

And what about dual or triple tasks? Bank customers will appreciate the convenience of having the option to drop off videotape rentals, dry cleaning, or prescriptions. And what about 24-hour banking for a day or two each week? Click.

FemaleThink

Setting an example, there's the Grameen Bank that was started in Bangladesh by future-thinking Muhammad

Yunus. The name "Grameen" means "village," and the institution has created a village of goodwill by making small loans, averaging only $65, which have given hundreds of thousands of women enough start-up capital to begin their own businesses. It's a shareholders' bank, controlled primarily by poor, rural women working together to build a nation of entrepreneurs. When we interviewed Susan Davis, executive director of the Women's Environment and Development Organization (WEDO), which acts as an advocate at the United Nations for women's issues, she told us, "When you're denied the tools or means to create self-employment, you're denied a basic human right."

Grameen is smashing the OldThink banking idea that you can borrow large sums only if you have lots of collateral or can leverage your assets. The Grameen model is spreading around the world because women are good credit risks: The repayment rate for loans is a very high 98 percent. Click.

Cashing Out

Instead of showing all bankers as the most extreme of buttoned-up employees in their three-piece suits, why shouldn't the new "relaxed" dress codes invade banks too? Bank managers and tellers might wear clothes more in keeping with what their customers are wearing—within reason, of course. If the three-piece suit presents another barrier to cordial relations between bankers and their clients, think what the corduroy jacket will do for customer relations, or how cowboy shirts and Tony Lama boots will open doors for banking customers in the West. Click.

Egonomics

Imagine calling, being on-line with, or entering a bank where you always have an assigned individual who knows your name and your credit history. Chase Manhattan is trying a version of this, now providing client specialists (that is, human beings) on call 24 hours a day, who promise to update your personal history whenever you call, fax, or modem any interaction. But let's take that service one step further and imagine that, whenever necessary, your "private banker" (that's what the really rich have) would shepherd you to the right specialist to address your current concerns—and that person takes care of you at once.

On a larger scale, you should be able to customize your own loan. You would still pay the fees, but only specific ones based on your record. Whenever you wish, you could view your year-to-date revenues and expenses (posted by category) from the budget developed with the help of your bank liaison.

At appropriate times, your designated tax consultant at the bank will help you file your returns. As you get older, the font size of any document the bank sends you will automatically increase. Signature cards and the archaic procedures will be long gone, and you will be recognized at any bank or ATM anywhere in the world by means of voice print, a facial thermogram (no two people have the same amount of heat radiating from blood vessels in the face), or the eye retina—in a wink. Click.

S.O.S. (Save Our Society)

To help Save Our Society, banks should give used computer systems to schools in low-income areas; office equipment to senior citizen centers, thrift shops, or small business charities. Bank managers should make community service and social involvement part of every employee's job, for example, by sponsoring banking fairs at schools. Loan officers might require fewer points on a mortgage or reduce the loan percentage rate whenever customers donate to charities using their bank credit cards.

To protect the environment, banks will provide "green" accounts, not the color of money, but the color of environmentally friendly processes that require no paper or significantly reduce the amount of paper that is used. Here's a free slogan for any bank to use: "Don't Cut Down Trees, Push Buttons."

Bank stationers can print checks on recycled paper and offer an environmental affinity card through which small donations will go directly to the Nature Conservancy, Greenpeace, or the Cousteau Society. Click.

Case proven. Banks can do a lot of little things to regain their positive image and click with the trends. No industry can keep insulting its clients forever without a rebellion. We all feel we have an inalienable right to respect, especially when we are handing over our hard-earned money to the banks for growth and safekeeping. We want our friendly bank back. We want our on-trend bank of the future.

The ClickScreen will quickly reveal where the trouble spots are in an industry such as banking, and it will do the same for any product or service that you are planning to offer. If you try it on your business, your idea, even your life, you can see where anything—from an entire monolith of an industry to the smallest of business sketches—can head. Use it as a tool to help make planning smarter, more focused, more future-directed. If you relate it to your problems and challenges, as we just did, you'll be pointed in a trend-true direction that will instinctively feel right. And wherever you go, you'll click.

BRAINJAMS

Get clicking!

You don't have to sit on a rock like Rodin's *Thinker* (elbow to knee, fist to forehead) and ponder how to click by yourself. Get the best minds you know to help create your future . . . and theirs.

First step: Make up lists of the most diverse people you know (or want to know), call and ask for a few hours of their valuable time. There is no such thing as failure here; all can contribute, all can benefit. Even though you're technically the focus of the gathering, each person will walk away with a gulfstream of ideas. When you tap into stimulating brain molecules, everyone becomes instantly energized. What's surprising is that often the glibbest talker is not the major contributor. Many times, it's the shy stranger who turns into the most imaginative, intuitive, original participant.

The process is fascinating and strange, since brainpower doesn't intensify by any known mathematical equation. Ten thinkers concentrating on one subject can race (much as the velociraptors in *Jurassic Park*) to a better, sharper, more intense conclusion in one hour than one thinker in one hundred hours. Answers get even more interesting and more varied if the people-mix is mixed up enough.

The secret of success is having an impartial leader who stands (*not sits*) preferably near an easel pad and jots down *all* the mumbo-jumbo (a brilliant idea may be buried for later retrieval). This moderator stays impartial and calm and reminds the group to headline answers, to stop telling rambling tales, to filter out any negativity, to push and probe in the quest to find the kernel of the solution.

Here are some exercises we use to start our brains jamming at BrainReserve. Look them over, then sit down and devise your own.

EXERCISE #1

Suppose Sony has just introduced a new product called FutureCam 6, which allows users to look at the world in the year 2010 and take a picture of anything there:

- What scene or place would you take a picture of?
- Who would be in it?
- Take a picture of the first "page" of the national newspaper (or whatever has replaced it) on New Year's Day, 2010.
- What are the five biggest headlines?

EXERCISE #2

Close your eyes, breathe deeply, and relax. Imagine that you are walking down a long, quiet hallway. On your left is a door marked "My Office, 2010." Open the door and walk inside.

- Tell about the sights and sounds, the smells, if you like.
- What does the furniture and equipment look like? What is it used for?
- Are any other people there? Who?

Now walk out of your office and go farther down the hall. On your right is a door marked "Home, 2010." Walk inside and describe everything you see.

EXERCISE #3
Think back to when you were 20 years old.

- What was your fondest dream for the future?
- What is your fondest dream now for the year 2010?

EXERCISE #4

- Describe yourself in the year 2010.
- Describe your product or service.
- Describe your company.
- Describe your competitors.
- Describe your friends.
- Describe your enemies.
- What will be your greatest success?
- What will be your greatest failure?

EXERCISE #5
Think of your different "personas" and describe each briefly.

- Who are you today (include personal description)?
- Who are you on the telephone?
- Who are you/would you be on a video-conference?

- Who are you/would you be on a computer bulletin board?
- Who are you/would you be on a virtual reality screen?

EXERCISE #6

Identifications: What's the first single image (we call this a "badge") that comes to your mind when you hear the following names?

- McDonald's Happy Meals
- Jell-O
- GapKids
- Fisher-Price Toys
- Levi 501s
- Nike
- Marlboro
- Mustang
- Huggies
- Your idea

EXERCISE #7

How can your idea become a "badge"? Describe what it would look like.

Think:

- Packaging
- Public relations
- Human relations
- Marketing
- Personnel
- Equipment
- Education
- Good works

EXERCISE #8

Here's a technoJam.

- Take a moment to think about what life was like in the 1960s (or the '50s or '70s), and then list words and phrases that describe women and men at that time (list separately).
- Now do the same thing, but for women and men in the late '90s.
- You are a computer whose name is Melanie or Max. Describe yourself.

- The term is "Scary Technology." What would be the description (i.e., what frightens you about technology, what bad things could happen)?
- You are making an extensive list of considerations before you even begin shopping for your computer. What's on the list? (Cues: where/why/how/what.)
- What services/products come to mind when you see/hear the words: empowerment, control, luxury, freedom, safety, and pleasure?
- You are the owner/founder of a small "kitchen table" business, and you are writing a letter to be broadcast to your client list. What is your communiqué headlined?
- You are: (1) a college student majoring in fine arts, (2) a sole proprietor dealing in marketing to consumer goods companies, and (3) a small business owner dealing in landscaping services. How do you use your computer in ways that distinguish you from all other users?
- Finish the sentence: "Going on-line is like . . . "
- Immediate top of mind: As a consumer, what words come to mind when you hear: LAN (local area network), integrated solutions, channels, and mobile.

EXERCISE #9

Play the old word game of mix and match. In this exercise, be as wild and creative as you can possibly be. Consider the areas that are represented here, match them with three of the trends, and finish the sentence: "My idea is in tune with [trend] because . . . " (Example: "My E-mail watch is in tune with Fantasy Adventure/Wildering because it's portable enough to let me work in my tent, on my boat, or in my log cabin.")

EXERCISE #10

Here's a fast-food chicken BrainJam, but you can apply it to most any idea.

- What was your favorite main-meal food when you were a child? Why did you love it?
- What was your least favorite main-meal food? Why did you hate it?
- Think of a food preparation that you have completed from start to finish within the last week, in all of its details (or your favorite recipe). What was pleasant/unpleasant about it?
- Name your favorite food texture. What does it remind you of?
- Name your favorite food smell. What does it remind you of?

- List your favorite food for each time of the day: breakfast, lunch, snack, dinner. What characteristics make that food right for that part of the day?
- A famous tag line for a food product was "Shake and Bake." Think of other things that you might do to food in the preparation process, and come up with new tag lines.
- Make a list of favorite flavor combinations.
- Imagine you are the Minister of Meals on Calumer, a distant planet whose people share all of the best characteristics of what we imagine for midwesterners on Earth: basic values, hardworking, family-oriented. An interesting fact about Calumer is that its inhabitants have, for as long as they can remember, eaten only one food: the Calumerian wog. They have eaten it at all ten meals of the day, all nine days of the week. Within the last decade, a terrible ecological disaster has befallen Calumer, and the wog population has died off. You have been sent to Earth to find a wog substitute, and your official contact, Julia Child, has suggested chicken. She presents you with a freshly plucked specimen. Your first reaction is amazement. You've never seen anything quite like it. What do you think of next?

Look at the chicken. Describe it in the most flattering terms possible. If you could reinvent that chicken, what would you do (i.e., change its shape, color, texture, even rename it)?

- Think of foods that you have served with chicken. Now incorporate them so that they are included in the actual recipe.
- Create new chicken preparations (cues: dips, sauces, coatings, stuffings).
- Hand out lists of the Trends. Describe a chicken recipe or meal that goes with at least four of the trends.

BrainJams will help you fine-tune your dreams and redefine your desires. They can be used as a starting point or as a constant checklist along the way. Think of them as a tool to get you unblocked, unlocked, unfrozen, and un-shut down.

While it's possible to live without air for seconds, without water for days, without food for weeks, it's *not* possible to click without a constant flow of ideas. Keep BrainJamming!

CLICKCAREERS

Change your work.
Change your world.

I t's 1958. You ask any group of six-year-olds what they want to be when they grow up. The answers come fast: an astronaut, a doctor, a fireman, a cowboy.

It's 1998. What's happened to them?

The astronaut-wanna-be didn't go into orbit because NASA downsized. He now works as a ticket-taker at Disney's Space Mountain.

The doctor is paying off her student loans. She can't afford to go into private practice because of the high costs of setting up an office, buying the diagnostic equipment, paying for insurance. So she has taken an HMO job at a salary of $65,000 (making less than her autoworker father who never graduated from college). As for her dream of becoming a caring, sensitive physician, she is encouraged to see as many patients as she can in as little time as possible. In fact, she is actually penalized if the same patients see her too often.

The fireman is about to be laid off because the city where he works is privatizing the fire department. The new company is hiring people at less than half his current salary.

The cowboy is doing just fine, thank you. He settled in Montana, worked on a ranch, saved his paychecks, and plunked down $100 an acre for land as far as he could see. Lately, land values in Montana have skyrocketed, driven up by West Coast refugees fleeing smog, fire, floods, earthquakes, and a general toxic lifestyle. Now the land is worth $2,500 an acre, and our cowboy is galloping on "don't-fence-me-in" land worth $5 million. Falling in love with cowboy movies as a kid certainly paid off.

The message: Traditional career planning is out. Trend-based career planning is in. Identify the most on-trend activity at your company. That's where your future will be. Find out everything about the job that interests you most. Use your connections to gather information. Present yourself as a candidate to Human Resources or go directly to the division's management. Tell them you would even be willing to take a pay cut for the opportunity.

Remember, the future doesn't arrive unexpectedly one day. It comes announced. What-will-be-will-be enters our world slowly and gradually, calling attention to itself with dozens of blips on our radar screen. We just have to be alert for them and know how to make use of what we see. That's the essence of learning to create career opportunities that spring from the trends.

Another thought: It seems as if every week a different magazine or newspaper or TV show reports on the "Best Jobs of the Future." Our advice—ignore them. Or take them with a very substantial grain of salt. These so-called predictions look at the forecasts of the Federal Bureau of Labor's computer, based on the Federal Reserve and military spending, and simply report those findings. They're calculated on what's available today—not on the trends. If you go by the trends, the jobs will be obvious. America will need more child-care workers as more mothers go to work; more dry cleaners, more takeout-food establishments, more beauty clinics, and more manicurists, for the same reason. And a given: We will need more computer repairers. More home-care aides and physical therapists, as the population ages. Additional environmental experts, as natural crises become commonplace. Fewer receptionists and switchboard operators, as voice mail takes over. Less unskilled labor, as automated machinery replaces humans.

Some of the most exciting jobs of the future are the ones that haven't been created yet. As the *Economist* wisely pointed out, "Many jobs listed in the vacancy columns of today's newspapers—such as aerobics teachers, software engineers, and derivatives specialists—did not exist in 1970." Want to click into a career as a personal information consultant—someone who helps individuals cope with and manage the information overload in their lives?

One way to see what emerging needs are not being answered is to use trends as your telescope. When the trends intersect, the results can be astonishing. Here's an example of what we mean. In the field of travel, if you combine Cocooning, Egonomics, and 99 Lives, you could discover a new category of vacation planner who comes to your living room at your convenience and brings brochures, videos, information on the best means of transportation and hotels. Everything you will need to plan a vacation. Think what an improvement this is over the usual haphazard way of planning a trip. Normally you need to call back and forth, do hasty research, and often face disappointment when you get to your destination.

We don't know if anyone is pioneering this concept, but with so many travel agents across America, it seems a perfect way to click into better service to your customers. Now that travel agents are facing a policy of reduced fees by many airlines as well as the threat of on-line delivery replacing the core function of a travel agency, this beleaguered group had better get innovative.

As we scan the careers of the future and consider the information superhighway, we foresee a giant click. Techno-America is creating enormous opportunities. There are openings for developing "content" for the vast reaches of cyberspace. For becoming an Internet guide to help struggling "Tech-Nots" get on board.

Another huge opportunity comes from the chance to sell products on the Internet. Bypassing traditional distribution methods, millions have the opportunity to Click with less investment than ever before. Other sources of career guidance are the on-line services themselves. America Online has a career center that gives you access to a counselor on-line, as well as the ability to search out data on potential employers. It's also smart to list your skills in the center's talent database.

But why not go one step further, and open a business with an original idea that may be the base of a brand-new franchising opportunity? Remember, today's household-name franchises started off as a local-something-or-other. Again, let the trends be your North

Star. Here are some start-up opportunities we've brain-stormed:

Play centers like Discovery Zone and Gymboree are popping up across the country. These safe, Cocoon-like environments appeal to parents as neighborhoods grow more dangerous. How about adding Fantasy Adventure to the play center concept and opening one with a theme such as the Wild West, space travel, Peter Pan, or Alice in Wonderland?

Or take the Click one step further. Why not open entertainment centers for senior citizens? You could provide seniors with virtual-reality rooms where they can meet their favorite old-time screen or TV stars. Media rooms can large-screen the great classics. An exercise space can offer low-impact swings, trampolines, and climbing paths.

Although heading out to a restaurant can be fun, many families still prefer the warmth of a home-cooked meal—especially if somebody else does the cooking. Why not create a business that comes into the home and prepares a delicious, home-cooked meal (the ultimate Cocooning fantasy)? This new service will give families a choice of meals (including low-fat and vegetarian), buy the necessary ingredients, prepare and serve the meal, and clean up afterward. Here's a possibility for the first no-hassle holidays. To make this a click, the service needs to be priced moderately—somewhere between the cost of Mom doing it herself and that of going out to a restaurant.

The Vigilante Consumer—ever skeptical, ever doubting—provides the basis for a new business opportunity that we call document review. This business supplies experts who can come to your house and complete a review of all your personal and business documents. The service will have many purposes: to make sure you're not getting ripped off in any way, to see that you're getting the most for your money, and to verify that everything is current and in order. Moreover, it will cover car leases, insurance policies, phone services (so many people haven't signed up for their carrier's discount packages), mortgages, real estate taxes, credit cards . . . you name it. The payment structure is what makes this business so attractive to the consumer—no costs up front, but the business gets to keep 50 percent of the initial savings.

These three businesses have potential as freestanding operations. Even better, once you get them off the ground, they might be acquisition candidates for companies willing to pay big bucks to entrepreneurs who've clicked with breakthrough businesses.

It doesn't exist yet—but it will—because new fields are created when new technology creates new needs. Take the cellular phone industry or the computer-driven credit card industry, in which theft and fraud are literally costing about a *million dollars a day* because the thieves are consistently two jumps ahead of the technicians. It's hoped that the shortsighted solution for car and cell phones of punching in a longer string of numbers and PIN codes will be short-lived. What an opportunity for some techno-wizards to come up with brilliant yet marketable solutions to both stymie and catch the high-tech crooks.

The whole point of doing something different is to challenge the excuse of not Clicking, to stop saying, "I can't change careers or do something I want because I don't have any experience or the right qualifications." We believe that "hurdles are put there to jump over." Seek and ye shall find a mentor to help you maneuver some of life's trickier paths. Leaning on a mentor can never be viewed as a weakness. It's very comforting to have someone to bounce even your wackiest ideas off (sometimes the most way-out ones are the best, but too far in the future). If you interview very successful people (as we did), you will hear deep praise, intense loyalty, and generous credit for the mentors who've assisted them along the way.

It all ties back to our Click equation:

C for **C**ourage—*the courage to embrace a changing world and find your place in it.*

L for **L**etting Go—*the act of leaving your fears and anxieties behind.*

I for **I**nsight—*the ability to look at the same landscape as someone else, and see something original.*

C for **C**ommitment—*the internal reservoir that keeps you headed toward your personal promised land.*

K for **K**now-how—*your well-tuned skills and genuine depth of understanding that let you compete in a marketplace that doesn't tolerate mediocrity.*

In this time when ideas and careers are moving at the speed of light, if you Click on the right switch, you can change your life forever.

CLICK MESSAGES

Words from (and for) the heart.

Time-travel back to the ancient past. Your dad was the blacksmith in the village. You were his worthy apprentice. You were called William the Smith, son of Richard the Smith (or Molly the Baker or Cecilia the Candlestickmaker) and all those in the hectarehood knew you as the Smithies.

Today, no one in the last generation has been a computer morphing expert or interactive television repairman. How do you apprentice for the future? From whom do you learn? You either need to make a friend of the inventor or fervently hope that your direct supervisor is well-versed in the new technology. Ditto if you're the first female Catholic priest (not likely now) or female test pilot, or the first Mexican American employed at a certain level at a company or . . . or . . . or the first in any position.

In Homer's heroic *Odyssey,* the best friend of Ulysses went by the name of Mentor. When the adventurer set out on his famous wanderings, Ulysses asked the trustworthy Mentor to take charge of his household and be the sole teacher of his only son, Telemachus. Thenceforth, anyone called upon to teach life's lessons has been known as a mentor. In today's world, the base definition has been expanded to encompass any form of senior adviser as well as any role model. Now more than ever, everyone wants and needs a mentor.

I remember my first mentor, my grandfather, Isaac Storper, telling me and my sister, Mechele, "Everything you do is right." He was wrong, of course, but it made us feel loved. Clara Cecil Storper, my mother, used to say, "Don't let the bastards get you down." This echoed over and over in my brain whenever I had to defend an idea that seemed too innovative, too novel, or too wild—and in my case, this always proved to mean simply "too future."

Lys's mentor and dad, Allen Montague Margold, always offered total support, telling her, "Keep your chin up, very, very high." He ended all his letters to her with mottolike bits of advice: "Attempt to look for the good in a stressful experience," or "to adjust is the badge of intelligence." Over the years, Lys's mother, Virginia Ackerman, has been an inspiration to us both. We often invoke her name, her energy, and her age-doesn't-matter attitude. Her philosophy: "Tomorrow's another party."

In the business world, John Greeniaus, president and CEO of Nabisco Inc., is a mentor to many. He offers co-workers and friends (including BrainReserve) support in the form of carefully timed little notes, cards, and cut-out articles. He always seems to know—and, more importantly, understand—exactly what's happening. In the spirit of John's generous mentoring, we offer the words that have inspired many of our favorite people to click.

Jessye Norman—opera star

Blessed with one of the world's most magnificent voices, this artist feels that the cornerstone of her success came from a phrase that her mother told her when she was only 12 years old (she was trying to practice a scene from *Macbeth* while her brothers teased her). "Just keep on going, Jessye."

Diane Sawyer—TV anchor

Most people are surprised after meeting Diane Sawyer that she's not caught up with "power" and "being a celebrity." This naturalness probably comes from her father's three rules for life: "Be kind, be kind, be kind." To be on the receiving end of one of her warm and formidable hugs is to understand how she translates belief into action.

Gloria Steinem—author, feminist

Steinem has always found satisfaction in the feminist cause, guided in part from a life-lesson learned from her mother: "Don't let your possessions possess you." This one insight helped free her up for the more important things: a larger vision, a generosity of spirit.

Leslie Wexner—CEO, The Limited

Stressing the value of making each one of the life stages rich and fulfilling, Wexner's father once gave him this nugget of advice: "You don't retire *from,* you retire *to.*"

Wolf Schmitt—CEO, Rubbermaid

Wolf's father was an early-on believer in a concept that has only now become acceptable: the power of visualization. The words that have guided Wolf since he was a very young boy: "Try to *see yourself* doing what you want to do, and you'll be able to do it."

Laurie Kahn—executive vice president, director of television production, Young and Rubicam
It's especially important for a young girl to be boosted by words of encouragement from a father. Laurie's dad, Howard, prepared her for the competitive world of advertising (and the rest of life's trials) by instructing, "You can do anything you want to do."

Nora Ephron—author
Ephron got her overall viewpoint about the way to look at things from her mother, who said simply, editorially, "Everything is copy."

Cher—actress, singer, entrepreneur
Cher has clicked so many different times and in so many different ways in her career, so it makes sense that Cher's mother taught her to take a long-range view. She said, "If it's not going to matter in five years, it doesn't matter now."

Ayse Manyas Kenmore—BrainReserve board member, real estate magnate
A part of our extended family (we dedicated *The Popcorn Report* to her and her husband, Bob) and former BrainReserver, the well-loved

Ayse is Turkish and heard this old proverb first from her grandmother in Istanbul, Safvet-Hanim, and later from her mother, Fazilet. Simply worded and very much to the point of her richly charitable life: "A thousand friends are too few, one enemy is too many."

Jim Morgan—president, Philip Morris

In a reversal of what would be expected 40 years ago, his father spoke to his inner values ("It's not what you are, but who you are"), while his mother infused him with business advice. She explained about competitiveness: "In spite of the fact that everyone knows that there's enough to go around in the world, in reality, it's a competitive world and only people who are smart, work hard, and stay focused will ultimately win."

Kate Newlin—President, BrainReserve Consulting

Kate learned her incredible 24-hour, 7-day work ethic from her father, Dale A. Newlin Sr., a retired Army colonel who fought in both World War I and World War II. He used to say to her: "If you work hard in America, you have to get ahead."

410

Adam Hanft, president, Hanft, Byrne, Rayboy, Abrams & Partners

One of our oldest friends in the business, Adam well remembers what he was taught by his college philosophy professor, "Never take 'no' for an answer, and most of the time, don't take 'yes' either."

Sander A. Flaum—president and CEO, Robert A. Becker, Inc.

Sander, my brother-in-law, recalls his mother Rose saying, "Do a good deed daily." And every single day, Sander tries his best to follow this beneficent rule.

David Fink—corporate real estate lawyer

David's grandmother, Bryna Poliacoff, a survivor of the Russian Revolution who fled to Turkey then emigrated to America and opened a famous Jewish restaurant in New York City's theater district, advised David that, "Life is short and changeable. Experience happiness in the everyday."

Ray Smith—CEO, Bell Atlantic

The clearest piece of advice that Ray Smith got from his mother was, "Get educated." Because neither of his parents went through high school (having to work instead), getting an education was the most important priority in his family. It was the path to being stimulated culturally and intellectually.

Jacqueline Simon—professor of politics

Closest confidant, dear Jackie told us about a phrase she learned from her mother, Rose "Lulu" Albert, specifically in reference to how to handle the ending of a love affair: "One nail drives out another." In other words, a new focus will help make you forget the past. This sound advice can also be applied to everyday disappointments, by reminding you that a new and better experience can replace every bad one.

Ash DeLorenzo—BrainReserve trend director

Ash's Taurean father, Big Al Feinstein, behaved in the least expected manner when things got tough. If he had a disastrous day in the stock market, he would take the family out to dinner, saying, "Anyone can celebrate when something good happens. It's when things go bad that we *need* to celebrate."

Gerti Bierenbroodspot—artist

Her mystic (and also Taurus-sign) father, Charles Theodoor, and her Bauhaus school mentor, Arthur Goldsteen, each taught her about spirituality, integrity, and art. But at one time when she was in her 20s, they sat together, facing her, and both instructed, "Continue what we've started." A directive, an inspiration perhaps, to the beautiful paintings she's creating now.

Olive Watson—real-estate salesperson, philanthropist

Besides teaching the fearless (little) Olive how to fly a jet and ski the highest mountain, her late father and IBM's great leader, Tom Watson, used to give her sound advice. One of the wisest and most helpful for the challenges of life: "Stand up for what you *believe* in and be *prepared* to defend your position."

Jonathan Canno—president and CEO, Equitable Bag Co.

Canno's savvy, industrialist grandfather, Maurice Rosenfeld, the founder, in 1919, of the paper bag company that still provides the finest of shopping bags for every major store in New York, welcomed him to the firm with this tough advice: "Some people get heart attacks and some people give them. Make sure that you're one of the latter." Jonathan listened carefully, but, not wanting to cause any harm, he tempered the words to mean "Stay sharp and don't let anyone get the better of you."

Mary Kay Adams Moment—BrainReserve partner

Mary Kay's parents, Mary and Frank, soothed her young ruffled feathers when her older brothers teased her, saying, "Ignore them, they're probably just jealous." This advice has given her an excellent perspective. Although she understands not everyone is consumed by jealousy, Mary Kay realizes that most of the time it really is the other person's problem. And then she calmly, sweetly tries to help the culprit through it.

Joycelyn Elders—former Surgeon General

Elders tells a tale, called "Dancing with a Bear," not only to her children, but to the many young audiences she has addressed over the years. "When you're dancing with a bear, you can't get tired and sit down. You have to get the bear tired, so he'll sit down. Reach out and find other dance partners to help you wear out the bear." Good advice about the importance of cooperation—for all.

AFTER-FUTURE THOUGHTS

Coming soon to a future near you!

The future moves fast. What seems like a crazy hypothetical idea one moment can turn into a reality the next. You have to be ready to buckle up and take the wild ride toward tomorrow.

Information is flying around our heads with macro-speed. The pandemic power of the World Wide Web has created a new sense of urgency into the worldwide marketplace. Coasting in cyberspace, gene swapping, even selecting whether to create a female or male baby—all are possible or on the brink of being so.

One thing for sure, the F-U-T-U-R-E doesn't hold itself back and wait patiently for us to wake up and act. Clicking with the trends can save precious time by directing you away from something that's nothing and toward something that's really something. We firmly believe that the best measurement for a sound idea is not good versus bad, not new versus old, but on-trend versus soon-to-be-obsolete.

Now, right up to these last pages, we're still having future thoughts and more will pop up after the close of the book. Here are some of them. Click away!

Age Countdown

If the secrets of your genetic blueprint can be deciphered and your expected longevity predicted, more or less, what will happen to fitness programs, the whole homeopathic market of vitamins and herbs? A bottoming out? Or will hope spring eternal?

Invisible Helmets

As pollution worsens in major cities, from Los Angeles to Mexico City to Beijing, we could be donning individual breathing bubbles—not necessarily the hard fishbowl helmets astronauts wear in outer space, but more flexible and form-fitting. A kind of Saran Wrap protection against free-floating toxins. The helmets will have all the advanced communication technology built in. Or, in less polluted areas, we'll wear designer CitiMasks to filter our air. When pure air and clean water become precious commodities, there will be lotteries with specified-term supplies for the top winners.

Life Companions

Instead of engineering a "perfect" tomato, why not concentrate on a strain of dog and/or cat breed that can last up to a human lifetime. More wet kisses, fewer tears.

Orphans On-line

What about starting a central, global computerized adoption register to keep track of all the babies and small children waiting for homes. No politics, just a helping hand for innocent kids. An on-target charitable opportunity for Bill Gates (he has the resources, the money, the reach) to give back earlier than he's planned. This idea could work for abandoned pets, as well.

Center-City Living

As more people open their own small, entrepreneurial businesses at home (as more than 2 million did last year), emptied-out office buildings should turn residential. Or empty commercial space could provide shelter for the urban poor and homeless, or could be a space for elder/child care. Now, if only there were a way to open those sealed office windows.

Superstore for the Disabled

With an estimated 20-million-plus Americans disabled to some extent and an aging population, isn't it time for a Home Depot/Toys "R" Us-type of megastore where you can find everything in one place: amplified telephones, voice translators, etc.

Knowledge Chips

Someday, soon, there will be tiny computer chips that you can buy—or rent—to insert/implant into your brain. Think of all the applications. You'll be able to speak fluent French or Chinese for a business meeting, a vacation, or forever. Or you can recite love poems when you go a-wooing. Or you'll be able to comprehend a television repair manual when your set goes on the fritz. Or you'll jump in and instantly know how to play golf/tennis/croquet—although you'll only excel as much as your muscle tone allows.

DNA Matchmaking

Using genetic research on health and personality traits, you can be matched with a potential spouse, fine friend, or business partner who fits with your gene pool. The Japanese are already doing it with blood types.

Catavans

A melding of the catalog and the van—large vehicles will roam neighborhoods and demonstrate/sell a range of goods, to purchase on the spot or order for next-day delivery. This fills a need-niche between the mall (time-consuming, hectic) and the mail-order catalog (can't try/touch, impersonal).

Show 'n' Tell

Schools will be hooked up with closed-circuit TV live inside prison walls to show and tell kids exactly what it's like "on the other side." No romance. It will serve as a strong deterrent and encourage youngsters to stay straight.

Cheating Crisis

Since the Internet will give students an unprecedented opportunity to "borrow" homework from other kids ("Quick, E-mail me a book report on *The Great Gatsby*"), new educational cops will have to patrol on-line.

Spiritual Opportunities

We'll see a noteworthy rise in employment in the "spiritual" industry. If the CIA can turn to psychics, why couldn't mayors, judges, CEOs work through mediums and channelers to help figure out which people/products/companies to hire/acquire, who is good or bad?

More Steps

Anticipate more 12-step programs, as a way of connecting. MOA (Mail Order Anonymous) for catalog junkies; IA (Internet Anonymous) for people who can't get off-line; even more general CA (Communications Anonymous) for those who are overly attached to cellular phones, car phones, beepers, faxes, E-mail, multiple lines, Call Return, voice mail . . . or, even worse, just plain call to listen to someone's message machine who isn't home or invade another's voice mail.

Penmanship

As a reaction to the domination of computers, flowing, show-offy handwriting with swirls and twirls will be the new status symbol. With the effect of different aromas down to a science, our pens will emit scents to make us more creative or boost our memory.

Pfff—Safe

There will be a portable spray for flash sanitation—to provide peace of mind by sterilizing dishes, cutlery, toilet seats, needles, etc. Especially good for on the road.

Sleep Breaks

Naps will be a necessary part of the workday, as the rest/relaxation quotient is proven to help us live longer. There will be Cocooning pods with filtered aromatherapy in every home and office, plus you'll be able to rent them for quickie snoozes when you travel.

No More Nightmares

New laser therapy, under the guidance of a knowledgeable psychotherapist, will be able to erase hideous memories or trauma. Victims will no longer have to spend tortured years reliving child abuse, rape, or horrible accidents. Conversely, the inflamed area of the brain that produces the impulse to rape or commit child abuse could be blasted away by laser pinpointing.

Population Control

In densely populated countries, boys and girls will be "contracepted" at birth, then activated after being granted approval (for good conduct, strong familial instincts) later in life. This same method of activation can even be used to restart an older woman's hormones, postmenopause, if she so desires to wait for motherhood until postcareer.

Compu-Plates

New microprocessor technology allows for instant calorie and nutritional computation at each meal, even in restaurants. Sensors and scans will weigh and calculate the calorie/fat/vitamin count of breakfast, lunch, or dinner.

Communication Booths

The phone booth of the Year 2010 will still be located at convenient street corners but will have a port for plugging in your computer as well as quick connections for picking up and sending E-mail or faxes.

Presto, Chango

Breakthroughs in hologram technology will create an instantly changeable world of home decorating. You'll be able to "faux decorate" and dwell in completely different looks—say, country French or stylized Art Deco—by simply pressing a button.

Do-It-Yourself Plastic Surgery

Aging baby boomers will be able to purchase a new handheld appliance that can erase fine lines and wrinkles right in the privacy of home.

Goggles-to-Go

Special computer goggles can pick up your video game of choice, using wireless technology and a portable joystick. At your whim, you can play anytime, anywhere, any game you want.

Home Generators

Small, low-cost generators will become as popular as microwave ovens and air conditioners, cutting our dependence on big utility companies.

MicroChurches

Following the marketing precept of "fish where the fish are," churches, mosques, synagogues, and New-Age services will open minibranches in corners where people congregate—at malls, sports arenas, beach parking lots, Price Clubs, Costcos.

Mass Security

As crime worsens, the need for house watchers, car watchers, and bodyguards (today's escorts of choice) will grow. An opportunity for large insurance companies to expand and offer such services. Or maybe trained local neighborhood-watch groups will carry tranquilizer guns.

On-Your-Block TV

The growth of fiber optics and the Internet will let ordinary American households create their own television shows. You'll be able to tune into neighborhood talk shows, real situation comedies, and maybe (we hope), live and sparkling BrainJamming sessions.

Fodder for thought. In the future, all these ideas will be in the present. If you'd like to share some of your ClickThinks, become interactive by writing us (c/o HarperCollins, 10 East 53 Street, New York, NY 10022), visiting us at faithpopcorn.com . . . or just beam us up.

READING LIST

This is the BrainReserve reading list. Unless you're a professional trend forecaster, you probably don't need to read or scan everything we do. A good plan would be to rotate your reading. Alternate *Newsweek* with *Vibe, Elle* with *Consumer Reports, People* with *The New Yorker.* If you're a baby boomer, take an occasional look at a Generation X publication, and, conversely, try reading *Longevity* even if you feel you're going to live forever. Cover all the bases, not every day, necessarily, but at least to try to keep up with what's going on. It helps you to visualize and be prepared for tomorrow.

Here's what we've been reading:

General Interest/Information

The Economist
Modern Maturity
New York
Newsweek

Psychology Today
Time
U.S. News & World Report
Vanidades

Women's Publications

Allure
Elle
Essence
Family Circle
Good Housekeeping
Harper's Bazaar
Ladies' Home Journal
Mademoiselle
Mirabella
Victoria
Vogue
W
Women's Wear Daily
Working Woman

Men

Details
Esquire
Gentlemen's Quarterly
Maxim
Men's Journal

News

Daily News
Financial Times

International Herald Tribune
Le Monde
New York Observer
New York Times
USA Today
Village Voice
Wall Street Journal
Washington Post

Science

Discover
Omni
Popular Science
Science
Science Digest
Scientific American

Health

American Health
Fitness
Health
Longevity
Men's Health
Prevention
Self
Shape

Food/Liquor

Bon Appetit
Cook's Illustrated
Eating Well
Food & Wine
Food Arts
Gourmet
Saveur
Vegetarian Times

Home

Architectural Digest
Country Living
Elle Decor
House Beautiful
Martha Stewart Living
Metropolitan Home
This Old House

Travel/ International

Arena
Condé Nast Traveler
Elegance (Netherlands)
Harper's & Queen
Marie Claire

Soviet Life
Tokyo Journal
TransPacific
Travel & Leisure

Entertainment/Gossip

Barks
Billboard
Buzz: The Talk of LA
Entertainment Weekly
Hola
In Style
Interview
National Enquirer
People
Premiere
RayGun
Rolling Stone
Source
Spin
TV Guide
Time Out
Us
Vanity Fair
Variety
Vibe

Literary/Art

Art & Antiques
Atlantic Monthly
Grand Street
Granta
Harper's
I-D
Journal of Popular Culture
New York Review of Books
New Yorker
Paris Review
Publishers Weekly
Quarterly: New American
    Writing

Business

Business Week
Delaney Report
Entrepreneur
Entrepreneur's Home Office
Far Eastern Economic Review
Forbes
Fortune
Inc.
Japan Economic Journal
Nikkei Weekly

Smart Money
Worth

Politics

American Spectator
George
Manchester Guardian
Mother Jones
Ms.
Nation
New Republic
Politique Internationale
Reason
Washington Spectator

Environment

E: The Environmental
    Magazine
Earthwatch
Mother Earth News
World Watch

Newsletters and Trade Publications

Advertising Age
Adweek

American Demographics
Boycott Quarterly
Brandweek
Chain Drug Review
Consumer Confidence
  Survey
Consumer Reports
Crain's New York
  Business
Food & Beverage
  Marketing
Food Marketing Briefs
Harvard Women's Health
  Watch
Iconoculture
John Naisbitt's
  Trend Letter
Market Watch:
  The Wines, Spirits,
  & Beer Business
Marketing News
Mayo Clinic Health Letter
National Home Center News
New Product News
Supermarket News
Tufts Nutrition Letter

Gay/Lesbian

Advocate
Curve
Diva
Genre
Out

New Age

East West
Family Therapy
  Networker
New Age
Tricycle: The Buddhist
  Review
Whole Earth Review
Yoga Journal

New Tech

Home PC
MacWorld
PC World
Wired

Offbeat

American Benefactor
Coffee Journal

READING LIST

High Times
L Report
Libido: The Journal of
   Sex and Sensibility
New York Press
Paper
Utne Reader

Youth Market

Dirt
Sassy

Seventeen
YM (Young Miss)
YSB (Young Sisters
   & Brothers)

Online

scan.scan.scan
www.amazon.com
www.hotwired.com
www.suck.com
msnbc.com

In addition to reading, we see just about every interesting new movie (plus quite a few duds) and Broadway, off-Broadway, and off-off-Broadway plays. We braille the culture closely, going to lectures, business forums, art shows, museums, concerts, and cabarets. And, of course, we spend a lot of time in front of the tube, watching, taping, and digging for trends.

INDEX

INDEX

Mass Security, 425

Matthews, Kathleen, 276

Matzo Balls, 51

May 5th Coalition, 84

Mayan Mindbender, 73

Mayflower Inn, 234

McDonald's, 62–63, 80, 82, 203, 319

Me and Mom restaurant, 225

Meditation, 108–9, 111, 215

Meditations for Women Who Do Too Much (book), 121

Megami Tensei, 70

Melrose Place (television show), 48

Men Are from Mars, Women Are from Venus (Gray), 150

Men in Black (movie), 68, 352

Men's Fitness magazine, 185

Men's Health magazine, 185

Mercedes Benz, 162

Merrill Lynch, 232

Meskis, Joyce, 53

Messinger, Ruth, 147

MetLife, 174–77

Met-Rx, 187–88

MicroChurches, 424–25

Microsoft, 39, 168, 222, 331

Midler, Bette, 320

Millenium, 107–8

Milliken & Company, 325

MiniTel, 373

Minuchin, Robert, 232, 234

Mirabella magazine, 194

Mitsubishi, 303

Moir, Anne, 140

Moles, 46

Moment, Mary Kay Adams, 414

Mondex, 378

Monet, Claude, 100

Monkey Bar, 86

Monroe, Marilyn, 70

Monte-Bianco, 319

Moore, Demi, 86

Moore, Mary Tyler, 269

Moore, Michael, 286–87

Morgan, Jim, 410

Morgan, Marlo, 121

Morgans Hotel, 99

Morris, Robert Lee, 106

Moss, Kate, 290, 292

Moving Beyond Words (Steinmen), 268

MTV, 64, 113, 270

Multiple User Dimensions (MUDs), 212

Muscle and Fitness magazine, 185

Museum of Modern Art, 331–32

Music

  Anchoring and, 113–15

  Clanning and, 47–48

  Down Aging and, 270–71, 274–75

  Fantasy Adventure and, 64

  Vigilante Consumer and, 287

Mutant Message Down Under (Morgan), 121

My Point, And I Do Have One (DeGeneres), 267

Myst, 70

Mystical Tribe, 106

Mysticism, 106–7

Nabateans, 3

Nabisco Inc., 407

Nader, Ralph, 285–87

445

INDEX